McFly were formed in 2003 and their debut album, *Room on the 3rd Floor*, went straight to No. 1 in the UK charts, breaking the Guinness record for the youngest band ever to have a debut No. 1 album. In total, McFly have had an astonishing seven No. 1 singles, five platinum and gold albums and won a BRIT Award for Best International Pop Act. They tour all over the world and are currently recording their sixth album.

www.**transworldbooks**.co.uk

McFLY

UNSAID THINGS...OUR STORY

By
Tom Fletcher
Danny Jones
Harry Judd
Dougie Poynter

CORGI BOOKS

TRANSWORLD PUBLISHERS
61–63 Uxbridge Road, London W5 5SA
A Random House Group Company
www.transworldbooks.co.uk

UNSAID THINGS...OUR STORY
A CORGI BOOK: 9780552168540

First published in Great Britain
in 2012 by Bantam Press
an imprint of Transworld Publishers
Corgi edition published 2013

This book is a work of non-fiction based on the life, experiences and
recollections of the authors. In some limited cases names of people have
been changed solely to protect the privacy of others. The authors have
stated to the publishers that, except in such minor respects not affecting the
substantial accuracy of the work, the contents of this book are true.

A CIP catalogue record for this book
is available from the British Library.

Addresses for Random House Group Ltd companies outside the UK
can be found at: www.randomhouse.co.uk
The Random House Group Ltd Reg. No. 954009

The Random House Group Limited supports the Forest Stewardship
Council® (FSC®), the leading international forest-certification
organisation. Our books carrying the FSC label are printed on
FSC®-certified paper. FSC is the only forest-certification scheme supported
by the leading environmental organisations, including Greenpeace.
Our paper procurement policy can be found at
www.randomhouse.co.uk/environment

Typeset in 11/14pt Sabon by Falcon Oast Graphic Art Ltd.
Printed and bound by CPI Group (UK) Ltd, Croydon, CR0 4YY.

2 4 6 8 10 9 7 5 3 1

McFly would like to thank Adam Parfitt.

For the fans

Contents

Acknowledgements

There are so many people we'd like to thank; people who have been huge parts of our lives and careers and who have become members of the extended McFly family over the past nine years. It would be impossible to thank you all by name, but we're sure you all know who you are and hope you know how much you mean to us. We've had so much help and guidance throughout our career and we're blessed to work with people that we genuinely care about and who care about us too. Thank you a million times plus one for helping us get this far.

McFly

Prologue

Special Massage

Indonesia, 2011

Picture this.

Four nice young men have just arrived at their hotel. It's been a long journey. Crowds of fans were waiting at the airport – a relief, because none of them quite knew how well known they were in Indonesia, but which meant the guys had to be chaperoned through the airport by security. Now they're in the quiet of their own rooms. A moment of peace before they step back into the whirlwind.

Ordinarily on tour they would have their own physio travelling with them. Performing can put a strain on your body. Muscles need to be rubbed. Backs need to be cracked. But this is a flying visit and the physio has been left at home.

One of the guys glances through the hotel literature. Massages are on offer. Just the thing after a long flight. He calls reception and asks for a masseuse. 'Certainly, sir. Right away, sir. Your room number again?'

Ten minutes later, there's a knock on the door. A woman enters and looks the young man up and down.

'You take clothes off, please,' she says. Her English isn't good.

The young man strips down to his boxer shorts.

'And those, please.'

'These?'

'Take off, please . . .'

'Really?'

The young man feels a bit uncomfortable. This is not what he's used to. But when in Rome . . . He divests himself of his underwear.

At the masseuse's instruction, he lies face down on the bed, his modesty protected by a small, white towel. Nothing else. The masseuse starts rubbing his back. Shoulders first, then down the spine. She goes a little lower than he would normally expect, but that's fine, because now she's moved on to his legs, starting at the feet and moving upwards.

Calves.

Thighs.

Upper thighs.

Upper *upper* thighs.

This is higher than normal, he thinks to himself. But maybe that's just the Indonesian way.

He catches his breath. Did her hand just lightly brush his balls? Did she do it on purpose, or was it a mistake?

A mistake, he decides.

But then . . . nope . . . *definitely* his balls.

The masseuse lifts his towel so that his bum is open to the air. It's clear that something unexpected is happening, but he feels entirely too British to say anything. She is sitting on his legs now, massaging every square inch of his bare, naked arse. He'd really prefer it if she stopped, but he's let it go too far. How can he possibly start objecting now?

What should he do?

He's in a hot sweat. Fifteen minutes of intense bum-massage pass. The masseuse climbs off. 'You roll over now,' she instructs.

Roll over. Right.

He turns, awkwardly grabbing at the towel to cover himself. The masseuse starts on his torso, but it's no longer a massage. By anybody's standards, this is sensuous rubbing. He concentrates hard on keeping himself calm. Any sign of arousal from beneath the towel will give off a message he does not wish to send.

Suddenly she whips off the towel. And now there can be no doubt about her intentions. She's cupping his balls as she taps on his shoulder.

'You want special massage?' she asks.

'Er . . .'

'*Special* massage?' she presses.

'It's, er . . . it's special enough . . . thank you very much,' he squeaks.

A pause.

'You sure?'

He nods. A bit too vigorously. 'Quite sure,' he says.

In the adjoining room, another of the four young men has had the same idea. A knock on the door. In walks a different masseuse. 'You take clothes off, please,' she says.

The young man strips. As he does, the masseuse wanders around his room, trying on his sunglasses, rooting around in his wash bag.

'Can I keep my boxers on?' he asks.

The masseuse laughs and wags a finger at him. 'Take off, please,' she says.

This masseuse does not bother with a towel. She lays him face down on the bed and gets to work. This young man's girlfriend was once a masseuse, and he knows there are certain regions above and below which their hands are not allowed to wander, to avoid embarrassment to their male clients. These boundaries are soon crossed. Before long she's pummelling his bare arse. When her hand lightly brushes his balls, he tries to stop himself from laughing.

But now he's being turned on to his back. He's been less successful at hiding his unwanted state of arousal. His mind is desperately trying to work out what to say to get him out of this situation.

The masseuse starts at his feet, but it doesn't take long for her to move further up his legs. Closer and closer. Weirder and weirder. He's excruciatingly aware that a certain part of his anatomy is giving off the wrong signals.

'You like?' she says.

No reply.

'You want *special* massage?'

That's his cue to jump up and pull on his boxer shorts. 'I'm fine,' he says, uncharacteristically flustered and tripping over his words. 'Really, I'm fine.'

The masseuse is on her feet, and now she's rummaging through his things again. She picks up sunglasses, clothes, sunscreen. 'Can I have this?' she asks. 'Can I have this? You give me this?'

He says no. He tells her she has to go, but she won't leave. In the end, he presses a couple of T-shirts – gifts from Indonesian fans – into her hands. She checks them carefully, clearly unwilling to accept any old rubbish, before reluctantly leaving the young man in peace.

They say that great minds think alike. The third young man welcomes a hotel masseuse into his room. As he strips, she points encouragingly at his boxer shorts.

He looks down. 'These?'

She nods.

'Er, OK!' he says politely.

The masseuse starts to stroke his muscles. This is not what he expected. When her attention turns to those parts of his body that do not need attending to, he berates himself for not speaking out. For not telling her that he feels uncomfortable, that he would like her to stop and to leave the room. For just lying there, quietly pretending that everything is normal.

And then the question. 'You want special massage?'

He gives her a falsely apologetic look. 'No money,' he laments.

'No money?'

'No money.'

'Ah . . .'

She continues with the massage. It's as chaste and uninteresting as a massage can be. Fifteen minutes of awkward, unpleasurable silence before she quietly leaves the room and closes the door behind her.

The first young man calls the second.

The second calls the third.

'*Did you . . . ?*'

'*Did she . . . ?*'

'*What the . . . ?*'

They relive their embarrassment at what has happened, and share their relief that it's over. And then one of them has an idea.

The fourth young man doesn't like massages. They're boring. His friend calls his room. 'Mate,' he says, 'you want to book yourself a massage.'

There's a slightly confused silence.

'What for? I don't like massages.'

'Trust me, mate, you'll like *these* massages.' He's single, after all, and it seems only right that one of them should indulge in what is clearly a very common Indonesian custom.

His friend doesn't elaborate any further, but the fourth young man isn't stupid. He has a pretty good idea what's being hinted at. He thinks for a moment. Then he picks up the phone by his bed and calls down to reception.

'Hello,' he says. 'I'd like to book myself a massage.'

After all, they're a band on tour. And *someone* has to act like a rock star, right?

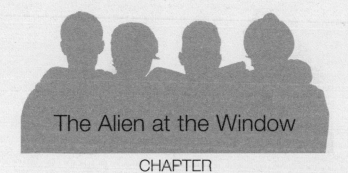

The Alien at the Window

CHAPTER

1

Tom: One of the first things I remember is the aliens that have haunted me all my life.

It was my dad who first introduced us. He used to tell me stories about them. I loved those stories, and would beg him to tell me more. One story in particular sticks in my mind, about travellers camping in a log cabin overnight, only realizing that an alien had been watching them for hours once its face had disappeared from the moonlit window. That story put an alien in my head that would never leave. Even when I was fully grown and touring the world, I'd always go back to my hotel room, or my bedroom, or wherever I was sleeping, and lie there terrified of the alien at the window. Even after playing in front of hundreds of thousands of fans, I'd have to sleep with the TV on, the sound down and the bathroom door open. I've never been scared of burglars. I've never been scared of ghosts. I'm just scared of aliens, and often I've been so scared of them I couldn't move. I know exactly what the phrase 'paralysed with fear' means, because I've experienced it nearly every single night. And even though these night terrors have been with me most of my life, I absolutely adore science fiction, especially alien and UFO stories.

Does that make me a total mentalist? I guess it must do.

But Dad introduced me to something else, too. Something far more important and which would have a far greater effect on my life. He introduced me to music. Our house was full of it. I've been lucky, and one of the luckiest things about my childhood was that music was everywhere. And when I stop to think about it, I realize that my good luck started long before I can even remember. Before the music. Before the aliens. It started with my parents.

My mum and dad – Debbie and Bob – weren't rich. Far from it. Money was always tight, not that I'd ever have known it when I was a kid because my sister Carrie and I had an amazing childhood. It's only now I look back that I realize how much my mum and dad sacrificed for us. We weren't spoiled – at least I don't think we were – but they did everything they could to make sure we had chances in life.

When I was very young my mum worked at a local video shop. I thought it was the coolest thing in the world because it meant free movies. I'll never forget the day she brought home a copy of *Teenage Mutant Ninja Turtles* long before anybody else had got their hands on it. That was when you had to wait ages for films to be released on video, so to have a copy before everybody else was awesome.

At the age of four, I started at my first school, Roxeth Manor. Not long after that, Mum did some voluntary work there, looking after the kids at break time and handing out their little packed lunches. She started working there full time a bit later, working her way up to where she is now – a senior teaching assistant. That's still her job: helping kids with learning difficulties bring out the best in themselves. Dad worked for Kodak. He was in the business of 'silver recovery', which is a lot less glamorous than it sounds. Back in the day, camera film contained traces of silver, and it was Dad's job to recover that silver from used rolls of film. It was properly hard work – twelve-hour shifts, which meant working several nights in a row in a massive, noisy, grinding factory in north-west London, near to where we were brought up. He worked there for twenty years but then, just after I left school, he was made redundant. I wasn't aware of it then, but looking back I can see how incredibly tough and stressful that time must have been for my parents.

But silver recovery wasn't his passion. Music was. Ever since I can remember, Dad played guitar and sang in a covers band, playing at the British Legion and local pubs and bars. Even when I was very small, before my sister was born, I'd go with Mum to hear him play, and Dad would get me up on stage to sing a song with him every time he played. Years later, I was able to return the favour and get him to play with me, only this time the stage in question was Wembley Arena – a very special moment for both of us.

Our house was always full of people playing guitar and singing. I was practically weaned on the Rolling Stones, The Eagles and Eric Clapton, maybe a bit of The Beatles and some country music – all the stuff he used to play in his band. My mum was the world's biggest Bryan Adams fan. She was in love with him, I think.

(Sorry, Dad.) No matter what happens in my life, I think that in her eyes the coolest thing I've ever done is exchange a few emails with Bryan, and speak to him on the phone a couple of times. In my mum's eyes, that's how you know you've made it. I'd love to arrange for her to meet him one of these days, although on second thoughts I'm not sure she could cope with the excitement . . .

For me, though, it was all about Michael Jackson. I absolutely *loved* Michael Jackson. Mum and Dad saw how keen I was on him and saved up so they could afford to take me to see him live in concert a couple of times, once on the *Dangerous* tour and once on the *HIStory* tour (where he flew off the stage and out of the stadium at the end of the show with a jet pack – maybe we should try that one day). I was even one of those kids who waited outside his hotel, hoping to get a glimpse of him or even meet him. I got so close. He came out of the hotel one day to talk to some of his fans and was only about a metre away from me when a girl jumped over the barrier to get at him. His security bundled him into a car, drove him away, and that was that. Now, whenever I walk off the tour bus to be greeted by lines of screaming fans, I try to remember that *I* was a fan back then. I still am.

With music being so big in my house, I guess it was hardly a surprise that I wanted to play guitar from the age of five. Dad sold one of his guitars so that I could have my own, and he and Mum paid for me to have classical guitar lessons. That was my mum and dad through and through. If Carrie or I really showed an interest in something, they did what they could to give us the opportunity to do it. I'm sure they went without a lot as a result. I learned all the basics about playing guitar in those lessons, but the real stuff – the stuff I use now – I learned from my dad and all the other musicians who were constantly round our house. Whenever there was a birthday, or a barbecue, or it was Christmas, the house was littered with guitars and full of people playing music. It's still like that now. And as Dad was also a singer, I was always singing around the house with him from a very young age.

Carrie and I were a bit different to most of the kids in our neighbourhood. Nobody else we knew wanted to play guitar, or sing, or dance. It wasn't cool. The other children didn't take it seriously. The only thing they took was the piss. We were the outsiders. In our own, peculiar, way we were the aliens at the window. I had a couple of close friends when I was much younger, but nobody I've really kept in touch with, and I'm sure that's partly because I always had different interests to kids my age, at least until the local high school started hosting Stagecoach classes on a Saturday morning. Stagecoach is a part-time performing arts school for kids, and my parents, always eager to give me every opportunity, let me go. I loved it – three hours a week of singing, dancing and acting in a place where nobody thinks you're weird for doing it.

One of the Stagecoach teachers also taught at Ravenscourt Theatre School in Hammersmith. She saw how into drama I was, and suggested I go to one of their summer workshops. It was a two-week course, at the end of which we put on a little show. The headmaster of the school came along to watch the show, and offered me a scholarship. I was nine years old.

That was that. I never went back to my normal school.

Ravenscourt wasn't just a theatre school. It was also an agency. All of a sudden I found myself constantly going out for auditions and even getting a bit of work. Sounds great, right? Well, truth to tell, and for reasons I can't quite put my finger on, I wasn't that happy at Ravenscourt. It might have been a world apart from my previous school, but I still didn't quite fit in.

During my first few weeks at Ravenscourt, I'd always be bumping into pupils from another theatre school, Sylvia Young, when I was out working. I remember thinking how well behaved they all were compared to the kids from Ravenscourt, who were always a bit rowdier. They also seemed a bit more professional, and took their performing rather more seriously than my fellow Ravenscourt pupils. I don't know who first made the suggestion that I should apply, but halfway through my first term at Ravenscourt, I found myself with my mum and dad, sitting in the office of Sylvia Young herself. She asked me to sing for her – I think I sang something from *Oliver!* – and the next thing I knew, she'd offered me a place. I started there the following Monday.

The Sylvia Young Theatre School was in Marylebone. Dad was still working shifts at Kodak. Mum was at school. My nan and granddad took me in every day – without them, I'd never have been able to go. It was impossible for my mum and dad to get me there and back each day while they were working full time. Nan and Granddad would drive me into London, and later on take me to Sylvia's by train. I owe them such a lot, and I hope I made the most of the opportunity they and my parents gave me. Certainly I'd finally found somewhere I felt like I belonged. Sylvia's was full-on. Monday, Tuesday and Wednesday were dedicated to academic work – they taught us all the maths and English and science that everybody else had to learn, and I was good enough when it came to my regular studies. I'd always been fascinated by science, space and aviation, and I loved art and creative writing. Thursday and Friday were purely vocational. We were immersed in the disciplines of singing, dancing and acting, and these were my passion – especially singing. I was also lucky enough to be one of the pupils who found themselves working a lot. It was all the standard stuff that kids get put up for – extras work on *EastEnders* and *Grange Hill*, adverts, voice-overs . . . I found I had a knack for dubbing my voice in time to foreign adverts that needed to be translated into English, so once or twice a week I'd be out working on little jobs like that.

I was ten years old when I went up for a general audition for *Oliver!* in the West End. It had been running for about a year, and my parents had already taken me to see it. I'd fallen in love with the show. Did I mention that I was lucky? It's true. The things I really want in life normally seem to come my way. I remember watching *Oliver!* and somehow knowing that one day I would be in it. I don't think I was being arrogant. It was just something I'd set my heart on, like kids sometimes do. I was *going* to be in *Oliver!* So when word got out around Sylvia's that they were auditioning for the show, I was the first in line.

I was used to the auditioning process by now, but that didn't mean it wasn't brutal. At least on the audition stages of *The X Factor* they let you perform before they send you packing. On the first round of one of these auditions they might well take one look at you and tell you to go home before you'd even opened your mouth. If you'd got brown hair and they were looking for somebody blond, there was no point wasting your time or theirs. If you weren't properly prepared, being rejected like that might mess you up, but we were taught early on at Sylvia's how to be professional about auditions, and to remember that if you didn't fit the bill it was never personal. I suppose a lot of people found the whole process daunting. It never really bothered me. I loved performing, and I'd been doing it from a young age. And remember: this was something I really wanted to do.

I got the part of Kipper, one of the kids in Fagin's gang. The child licensing laws meant that children could only work for a certain number of days in the year, so there were two teams on the show. That meant I'd do one week on, one week off during our team's three-month run, and I lived for those nights I spent on the stage.

I was very professional as a kid. I always knew my lines and, more often than not, I knew everyone else's too. One night, the kid playing the Artful Dodger completely lost his voice halfway through the show. He wasn't just a bit hoarse – his voice was completely gone and he could barely speak, let alone sing loud enough to be heard in the gods. There were ten of us kids on stage, and once you're on in the first half, you're on till the interval, two thousand pairs of eyes staring at you. Dodger was bricking himself as he passed the word round that there was no way he could sing another note, begging one of us to fill in for him. Of course, I was the only one sad enough to know all the lyrics to all the songs, so I found myself belting out 'I'd Do Anything' and 'Be Back Soon', while he did all the acting. Come the interval, the director hunted me out to say thanks, and I think that was the first time I'd properly caught his eye. When the three-month run came to an end, I was miserable. I hated the idea of leaving – I'd have quite happily carried on singing in Fagin's gang, performing in front of packed-out crowds, for ever. So I was made up when the choreographer asked me if I'd come back to audition for the part of Oliver.

I was still just ten years old when I got the part. It was around Christmas time, so come January I was allowed to start working again, this time in the lead role. I still had to go to school in the daytime, so it was full-on, and even though I was allowed to come in at first break, I went through a time during my stint on the show when I didn't want to go to school at all. I'd invent illnesses, or hide in the toilets and cry. It was a weird little period in my life, something I didn't understand. Over the years that followed I would have these episodes, but it would be a long time before I realized what was really going on in my head. But even though I was unhappy at school, I loved everything about being in *Oliver!* The cast were fantastic – Jim Dale was Fagin, and he was absolutely brilliant with kids. They were, all in all, three special months that I didn't want to end.

They did end, of course, and life went back to normal at Sylvia's. Or as normal as life can be at a theatre school. Sylvia's was a tiny, intimate place with never more than about a hundred and twenty pupils, which meant I knew almost everyone by name and everyone knew each other's business. Amy Winehouse was a few years above me, and I knew her about as well as I knew everybody else there. Even as a young teenager she was pretty much what you'd expect – rebellious, to say the least, but always very friendly. I don't know if she was asked to leave Sylvia's before her course came to an end, but I certainly remember that she left early. She released her first album at the same time as we released ours. Amy's went kind of unnoticed back then, but we found ourselves doing the rounds of the same TV programmes, and she'd always make an effort to say hello. That's the thing with Sylvia's kids. You're part of a group even when you've left. Even now, if I see someone wearing a Sylvia's uniform, I'll go and chat.

There was a guy in the same year as Amy. His name was Matt Willis. I could never have guessed at the time how profoundly the paths of our lives and careers would cross. I'm honoured now to call him a friend, but I doubt I was even on Matt's radar when we were at school. I must have just been one of the annoying younger kids to him. I was a bit of a teacher's pet, whereas he had a reputation for being a bad boy – not that it's difficult to get a reputation like that at a school where all the boys wear unitards and do ballet. Truth is, though, that I wished I was a bit more like him . . .

A year went by. One afternoon I'd gone back to my nan's house after school. We were sitting around eating curry – it was buy one, get one free, and Nan always used to joke that I could have the free one – when the phone rang. It was my agent, asking if I could get to the London Palladium by seven o'clock. The boy playing Oliver was ill, and his opposite number (two kids for each part, remember) lived in Wales and couldn't get there in time. Could I come in and play the part for one night?

I hadn't done it for a year, and there was an entirely new adult cast on board. But what the hell?

They delayed the show by fifteen minutes while I rushed into town and had half an hour with Robert Lindsay, who was the new Fagin; I didn't exchange more than a couple of words with the Artful Dodger before going on stage. Standing in the wings, eleven years old, not having sung any of these songs for a year, I was absolutely bricking myself. But the moment I set foot on stage it all came back to me. It went well and I had an amazing night, doing what I loved.

A week later, the same thing happened, only this time it was the Oliver from Wales who got stuck on the train coming in, while his opposite number was still ill. Action replay: I stepped in again.

The following day I was asked if I would do another three-month stint, and I jumped at the chance. Second time round, though, it just wasn't the same. I didn't quite gel with the cast the way I had done the year before – Robert Lindsay was replaced by Barry Humphries, and I'm afraid Dame Edna didn't have the same rapport with the kids that Jim or Robert had done. The show was coming to the end of its run and nobody seemed quite as enthusiastic as they had been first time round. I learned a lot, then, about the importance of surrounding yourself with people you have a bond with, and who are as committed to what you're doing as you are. Mostly, though, I learned that when you try to recapture a magical period in your life, it's all too common to find the magic has gone.

I think I still approached it professionally, though. Too professionally, perhaps. When you play Oliver, you're on stage constantly from the beginning of Act 1 until the interval. I must have been in a rush one night because I forgot to go to the toilet before stepping out on stage. I realized I needed the loo before the first song had even finished, but by that time it was way too late.

I held it in, and held it in. But that first act is long. I considered quickly relieving myself on stage while I was slightly hidden – maybe I could do the necessary while I was shut inside one of Mr Sowerberry's coffins for a couple of minutes. But I'm incredibly indecisive, and before I knew it the chance had passed me by. It was agony. AGONY! How I managed to sing 'Where is Love?' and dance around the stage during 'Consider Yourself' is beyond me. We were easily an hour into the show by the time Nancy arrived in Fagin's den to sing 'I'd Do Anything'. I'd reached the point where I *would* do anything. There was a moment in that song where I had to stand on the side of the stage just watching the action, and I simply couldn't hold it any longer. Everyone's attention was on Dodger and Nancy, so now was the time to do it . . .

Reader, I pissed myself. On stage at the London Palladium. With more than two thousand people watching. Fortunately I was wearing my grimy workhouse costume, so I don't think the audience would have noticed anything, unless they were watching the expression of sheer, joyous relief pass over Oliver's face. I whispered on stage to Dodger: 'Dude, I've pissed myself!' I'll certainly never forget the look on *his* face. Massively embarrassing, but I still don't think I had any other option. The show had to go on. Told you I was a professional kid.

My own enthusiasm for *Oliver!* had run its course, but not my enthusiasm for the stage. I carried on working alongside my studies. One of my coolest ever jobs was singing in the choir for the reissue of *Return of the Jedi*. If you were to come round to my house and see all the *Star Wars* memorabilia, you'd get an idea of how much I dug doing that. I even went along to some open auditions for various boy bands that were advertised in the *Stage* magazine, and generally got quite a long way through the audition process, but I was always too young – the minimum age for these bands was invariably sixteen, and I'd only have been fourteen or fifteen at the time and would never have had the guts to lie about my age. (Here's looking at you, Dougie Poynter.) In retrospect, that was a good thing. Those auditions were for very typical boy bands, and I really don't think I'd have been happy in them even if they'd gone on to have any success, which they didn't.

I left Sylvia's at the age of sixteen, and I still look back on those years as some of the best of my life, and some of the most significant, not least because it was there that I met the girl who would later become my wife. Giovanna and I met when we were thirteen – I'd been at Sylvia's for a few years and she had just started halfway up the school. I remember sitting in our tiny assembly room with my friend Jason, checking out all the new kids and wondering if we'd get any of them in our class. This gorgeous girl walked in – I immediately turned to Jason and commented on how fit she was – and one of the teachers told her to come and sit next to me as her surname was alphabetically next to mine. She smiled at me. 'Hi,' she said. 'I'm Giovanna, but you can call me G.'

'Hi.' I smiled back. 'I'm Tom, but you can call me T.'

Hmm . . . very smooth (not).

Despite my cringeworthy chat-up line, by the end of that day, Giovanna was my girlfriend. It didn't last long. Two days later I dumped her for a girl called Gemma Gould. Harsh but true. I instantly regretted it, and spent the next two years of my life completely obsessed with her. All I thought about was Gi, and I drove my class-mates absolutely insane going on about her. I'd totally messed things up by being the bastard who dumped her in the first week of her new school, and she quite rightly did her very best to make life as difficult for me as possible. I spent two years trying to persuade her to go out with me again. In the end I wore her down. She finally caved in and we started seeing each other properly in our final year at Sylvia's.

When school finished, we broke up again. Gi was from Essex, I was from Harrow, and they seemed a million miles apart. Splitting up felt like the sensible, adult thing to do . . . right up until the moment that we actually did it. Yet again, I spent the next two years trying to win her back, and although I had a few other relationships in that time, I always knew it was Gi that I wanted.

I loved being at Sylvia's, but when I finished there I felt like it was time for a change. I'd devoted nearly half of my childhood to acting and singing, had been working almost constantly, and felt a bit like I'd missed out on being a kid. I wanted something different, more normal. I had a good friend outside of school – my only friend, really, outside my little group at Sylvia's – called Neil. Neil's brother was in the Air Cadets and had encouraged us to go along with him. I was desperate to do so. My love of aviation was another thing passed down to me by my parents, who used to take me to air shows as a kid. We'd even drive down to Heathrow and park near the runway to watch Concorde land – sounds geeky, but it was an amazing experience. I signed up to 1454 Squadron in Northolt and thought it was awesome. We had uniforms and used to learn drill practice, and once a month you could go gliding or flying. I became obsessed with planes, and as a result I gave serious thought to joining the RAF (I later fulfilled that lifelong dream by getting my pilot's licence), but in the end I decided on something more humdrum. In September 2001 I enrolled at Stanmore College to study art, English literature, media studies and drama. It was one of the biggest mistakes I've ever made.

I'm very shy, not keen on socializing. Even now, when we have parties at home, I'll lock myself in the toilet for ten minutes, just so I can have a bit of time out where I don't have to talk to anybody. It's not that I don't like other people, it's just that I don't crave company. I'm fine being on my own. I like it, and I always have, ever since I was a young kid. So, I was the sort of person for whom the first day at school is a complete nightmare. I turned up at college on that first day of term as nervous as hell, and it was totally, completely, one hundred per cent as bad as I expected. Almost all the other kids already knew each other from their previous local schools, and none of them paid any attention to the shy new boy. I hated every moment I spent there. I had no real friends. I'd gone from studying at one of the best theatre schools in the world to something really amateur at the local college. I felt like I'd properly messed up.

A depressing month passed, the prospect of two years of unwanted time at Stanmore hanging over me like a shadow. I arrived home from college one day and my mum pointed out an advert in the *Stage* for an audition the following day at 10.30 a.m. It was for a boy band, but it wasn't just asking for guys who could look good, sing a bit and dance a lot. They wanted musicians, instrumentalists. This was an audition for a boy band with a difference. A boy band that could actually play. 'Why don't you go along?' my mum suggested.

I shook my head. Even though I hated being at college, I was still trying to persuade myself that I wanted to do normal stuff, to give it a proper go at Stanmore. I was being my usual incredibly indecisive self, though. I woke up the next morning thinking perhaps I *should* audition, before just as quickly rejecting the idea again. Mum and Dad left to take the dog out for a walk. The moment I heard the door shut, my decision flipped again. I *did* want to go and do it. I called them back from their walk, grabbed my dad's guitar and worked out a song to play – 'The Dance' by Garth Brooks – and we rushed into town.

The audition was at Pineapple Dance Studios in Covent Garden, a place I knew well because loads of auditions were held there. It was full of maybe two hundred kids with guitars, obviously all there for the audition, but as I walked up the stairs to the place where we were supposed to congregate, I saw a face I knew. It was Matt Willis and, to be honest, my heart sank a little.

We said hi. 'You here for the audition?' I asked him.

Matt shook his head. 'No,' he told me. 'I'm already in the band.'

Great. I might as well go straight home. Matt was much cooler than me, and I was certain he wouldn't want me in his band. I should have just gone to college. I said all this to my mum, but she persuaded me to stick around and do the audition anyway. Thank God she did.

We were divided into groups and the time came for mine to step into the audition room. There was a long table, with four people sitting behind it. Matthew 'Fletch' Fletcher – young, enthusiastic, *always* talking – and Richard Rashman – older, American and with a slower, lazier drawl – were the management. It was they who were putting the band together, the brains behind the operation. I didn't know it then, but they would become two of the most important people in my career. The third person was a kid called James Bourne – already in the band. Matt was the fourth. There were about ten people in my group. One of them was called Charlie Simpson.

It was one of those rare auditions that goes brilliantly. As each of the others got up to sing and play, I knew I had the edge on them, and when, at the end, the panel announced which three of us they wanted to see again later on that afternoon, Charlie and I were among their number.

The afternoon audition was more in-depth. I was properly introduced to Matt and James, and asked to sing some songs with them. Fletch and Richard put me on the spot, but it still went well. By the end of the day, the couple of hundred hopefuls had been whittled down to me, Charlie and two other guys.

I was called back to a second audition a couple of days later. This time we rocked up at the InterContinental Hotel in Hyde Park. This, I later found out, was where Richard Rashman stayed when he was in London, and I had no idea how important that place would later become in my life. It wasn't until I arrived at the

InterContinental, that I found out what the band I was auditioning for was going to be called. Busted.

Matt and James were there, and they played us a song they'd written called 'What I Go To School For'. I loved it. Everything about that song sounded perfect to me. I liked that it was very pop, but with proper musicianship. What struck me most, though, were the lyrics. It was a cheeky song about wanting to shag your teacher. No clean-cut boy-band clichés. It was what pop music is supposed to be: a laugh. To my ears it was light years ahead of your average boy-band fodder. When I heard it, I felt brave enough to play them one of my own songs that had similarly tongue-in-cheek lyrics. It was called 'I'm In Love With A Whore'. They all cracked up laughing when they heard it, and although it was a truly terrible song, I think it at least showed that I was in tune with the kind of music they wanted to make. They got us to sing 'What I Go To School For' with them, and it was then that I knew that I really – *really* – wanted to be in the group. With Fletch and Richard's 'We'll let you know' ringing in my ears, I went home, keeping everything crossed that I'd done enough, and trying to ignore the little voice in my head that kept telling me there was no way Matt would want me to be in his band, given that we were hardly best mates. I focused instead on the fact that James Bourne and I seemed to have a lot in common. He'd also played Kipper in *Oliver!* before going on to play the title role; and as we'd chatted, we'd realized that we'd worked together on some other projects when we were much younger.

The call came through that night. It was Richard

Rashman. 'Congratulations, Tom,' he said in his under-stated American drawl. 'We really liked you. We'd love you to be in the band.' He explained that Charlie was to be the fourth member, and asked if I could come down to the studio the following week.

I was on a total high. It wasn't just that I'd been accepted into a pop band that I was totally into. Getting into Busted was my escape route from college. I'd made such a huge mistake going there, and now I had another option. I could carry on doing media studies at Stanmore, surrounded by people I didn't really get on with, doing something I didn't enjoy – or I could go and be a pop star. Tough choice.

Matt, James, Charlie and I arrived at the studio the following week and listened through some more rough cuts of the songs they'd been working on for their first album. I got on brilliantly with James and Charlie; even Matt seemed friendly enough. I loved all the songs and, if anything, I was even more excited at the end of that day than when Richard had offered me the gig. I remember the four of us going to Burger King – the band, together – experiencing the kind of camaraderie you only get with being in a band. It was something I'd never done before, and the feeling was fantastic. I remember walking to the station with Charlie, shaking hands and agreeing with him that this was the start of something awesome.

Which it was. For them.

I was over the moon. I got home and started telling everybody I knew that I was leaving college to be in this brilliant band. It was the best feeling.

Elation. Everything seemed to be slotting into place.

A couple of days passed. It was Halloween and my sister, Carrie, was having a party. We had loads of people round the house, including all my family, and kids everywhere. My mum answered the phone and handed it over to me, saying that Richard Rashman wanted to talk. I went upstairs to take it.

'Hello, Tom.' Richard's American drawl was as matter-of-fact as it always was. He's totally blunt. A guy who says things as they are. 'So we've been talking,' he said, 'and we've decided to keep the band as a trio. So we're really sorry, but we're keeping it as Matt, Charlie and James. You're not going to be in the band.'

I'd been flying high. Now I felt like I was in the gutter. Total devastation. End of the world. I'd had two days to enjoy the idea that I was going to be a pop star. Two days to gloat about it in front of everyone I knew. (Thank God Twitter and Facebook weren't around at the time.) Now I would have to admit that it had all been a mistake. And even worse than that, it looked like I was going back to college in the morning.

All these thoughts rebounded in my head. I was vaguely aware that Richard was still speaking. 'We really like you,' he tried to assure me. 'It's no reflection on what we think of you as a performer . . . we really like the kind of songs you've been writing . . . we'd love to keep working with you.'

Rubbish, I thought to myself. Richard was obviously just letting me down gently. I listened politely, but deep down I knew everything was slipping away.

'I go to LA tomorrow,' he continued, 'but I'm back in

a couple of weeks . . . you should spend some time working on some songs . . . maybe come over and talk things through, show us a few when I'm back . . . we can help you develop them . . .'

Yeah, yeah. I was totally sure I'd never hear from him again. I mumbled something down the phone and hung up. My dreams were well and truly shattered.

The two weeks that followed were horrible. I went from one of the biggest highs in my life to one of the deepest lows. Obviously Rashman had been stringing me along, and I don't think I even picked up a guitar in that time, let alone worked on any songs. So when the phone rang a fortnight later and a drawling American voice said, 'Hello, Tom, why don't you come in and see me tomorrow?' I was surprised and completely un-prepared. I was hardly a prolific songwriter. The first songs I'd written were for my GCSE music course when I was fifteen: two songs, both absolutely terrible. All I can remember of them is that one was a total rip-off of a Green Day tune. I don't think I ripped it off intention-ally, but I was just feeling my way around the edges of songwriting, learning how to structure melodies, so I guess it's not surprising that the stuff I was into at the time unconsciously ended up in my songs.

I desperately needed material for the following day – it wasn't like I could turn up and play 'I'm In Love With A Whore' five times back to back. Once was probably too many. I spent that night cobbling a few songs together. My short experience with Busted had taught me that it was possible to write decent songs about silly, youthful, teenage things, and given me a little bit of confidence that it was something I might be able to do. I can't honestly say, though, that I achieved it that night. The tunes I came up with were probably even worse than 'I'm In Love With A Whore'. The best of the bunch was called 'Hot Chicks Dot Com', all about the delights of finding photos of your mum on a porn site. Don't expect ever to hear it – I've conveniently blocked the details from my mind.

The following day, armed with a guitar and my handful of songs, I went to meet Richard and Fletch again.

I played through my songs.

Fletch looked at Richard.

Richard looked at Fletch.

Fletch looked at me.

And then he started to tell me, in excruciating and long-winded detail, just how crap they were.

Fletch didn't pull his punches – I subsequently learned that that's a trait of his – and I felt like each one was hammering me into the ground. He wasn't entirely damning, though. Fletch is a brilliant pianist and a great all-round musician, and he identified *small* sections of *certain* songs that were *potentially* good. He told me which bits could be turned into hooks, and talked to me about how songs should be structured. When the time came to leave, he gave me what was almost homework. 'Go and listen to hit songs,' he told me. 'It doesn't matter if you don't like them, it just matters that they're hits. Find out what they all have in common. Work out how to do it.'

I went away from that session with the feeling that Richard and Fletch were serious when they said they wanted to work with me. I also realized, however, that they weren't easy to impress. If I was going to get anywhere with them, I'd have to raise my game.

Back home, I threw myself into Fletch's homework with a lot more enthusiasm than I'd ever had for the work my teachers set for me at college. I listened to anything and everything – not just the stuff that was big at the time, like Backstreet Boys and Britney, but also the harder American rock music that I really loved, Limp Bizkit and Blink-182 and Green Day. I asked myself: Who are the greatest songwriters of all time? The answer was obvious to me and to everyone else I spoke to: Lennon and McCartney. I went out and bought every Beatles record and became obsessed with them. I was amazed that I knew every single song already, despite never having listened to a Beatles album before. These songs just seemed to be implanted in my subconscious, and now that I was listening to them properly, I decided they were the best thing I'd ever heard. It was Paul's melodies that did it for me, and through listening to The Beatles I began properly to learn what a hook was, and a middle eight (the section in the middle of a song – usually eight bars long – that brings in new ideas or chords to keep the listener interested). Gradually I tried to incorporate these features into my own songs. Slowly, they improved.

I kept in touch with Fletch and Richard. Every now and then we'd meet up. I'd play them the tunes I'd been working on; they'd give me some words of encouragement and tell me what was happening with Busted – they'd been signed by now and were recording their first album – and play demos of their music. I had mixed feelings listening to these updates. I was still gutted not to be in the band, but part of me felt pleased that I'd been involved in a small way, even if that involvement had only amounted to being in the band for two days before getting kicked out. As a result I had a creative way of possibly getting out of college. That alone made me hungry to improve, and keen to stay in contact with Fletch and Richard now that I'd seen that they really could make things happen.

I was keen to stay in touch with someone else, too: Giovanna. Even though we weren't together and she had another boyfriend, I'd cheekily send her the cheesy love songs I was writing. I can't imagine the bloke she was with at the time was very impressed, but hey: I might not be confident, but I am persistent.

Months passed. I kept writing and showing my stuff to my sort-of managers. Then, one day, I played them a song called 'Hot Date'. When I'd finished, Fletch turned to me and, rather than ripping it to bits like he normally did, said, 'Congratulations, you've written your first song that could do something.' It never did become anything, and thank God, because from time to time the boys in McFly will stick a demo I made of it on the speakers and rip the piss out of me. Thanks, guys!

Richard and Fletch weren't just leading me on. As my songwriting skills slowly improved, the idea was always to find a songwriting partner for me to work with, and one day Fletch told me he wanted me to get together with a guy called Gary so we could play through some of my songs and see how we hit it off. Gary was from

Newcastle, seemed an OK dude, and had a good voice. He was a hell of a sight trendier than me (not difficult), but I reckoned we could get along together all right. Gary came down and stayed at my parents' house, and for a period of a couple of months we were the beginnings of a new band. It was with him that I demoed 'Hot Date' and a couple of other songs called 'Leap Of Faith' and 'Anything'. I started to feel as though something was taking shape. We'd see the guys in Busted now and then too. They'd listened to our demos and the feedback was good. And despite the fact that I was still at college, everything seemed to be going well.

One day, Gary and I went to Richard's hotel to play him some new songs. We never got the chance. Out of the blue, Gary announced that he wasn't into what we were doing any more. He wanted to go back home. Maybe he was homesick, maybe it went deeper than that. Whatever was wrong with him, this was the first I'd heard of it, even though he'd been staying with me and my family for months. His dad was in the building trade, and Gary had decided that he wanted to go and work for him rather than spend any more time trying to make it with the band.

Brilliant. I was back to square one. Now what was I supposed to do?

Once again, I had nobody to be in a band with. It truly was a terrible time, made better only when James Bourne from Busted suggested to Fletch and Richard that now that I'd learned how to structure songs properly, he and I should get together to write them. I jumped at the chance.

Busted had just recorded their first album, but fame was still around the corner. They lived together in a flat in a swanky, exclusive development in north London called Princess Park Manor. I drove down there one evening in my crappy little car to meet with James, and my eyes nearly popped out of their sockets. It was by far the fanciest place I'd ever seen. The building itself is an old mental institution, with impressive architecture, its own high-end gym, and huge metal gates like something out of *Jurassic Park*. Busted's flat was uber-modern, with three en suite bedrooms, double-height ceilings and the biggest TV I'd ever seen. The idea of three guys being in a band and living together somewhere like that seemed to me the coolest thing ever.

But even cooler than that was the rapport that James and I had. Right from when we'd first met we'd just clicked. We loved all the same movies – eighties classics like *Back to the Future* and *Cocoon*, the sort of stuff that Mum had brought back from the video store all those years ago, and which nobody at theatre school would ever have admitted to being into. We were a couple of geeks together. I thought James was hilarious, and having arrived for that very first songwriting session at eight in the evening, I didn't leave till five in the morning. I think we both knew that we'd stumbled upon something pretty special then. We wrote a really good song together called 'Chills In The Evening', and made a date to get together again. And every time we did, the songs seemed to flow – so much so that I finally dropped out of college because I was spending every night round at the band house, writing with James and not getting home until the small hours.

Despite looking up to Matt Willis in a big way ever since I'd been at school, I think by now I'd realized that I had more in common with James. As time passed, I grew to realize that in James I had found an amazing friend and mentor. He taught me everything I know about songwriting, and I truly believe that he is one of the most underrated talents of our time – a genius with an amazingly contagious creative energy. And if it hadn't been for James Bourne, McFly would never have been born.

Busted were signed to Universal Records. When their first single and album hit the shelves, and it became clear they were going to be big, Universal approached Fletch and Richard to manufacture a more traditional boy band, rather than a guitar band like Busted. They told me I could be in it if I wanted, but I knew I wouldn't be happy in that kind of set-up. I wanted to do my own thing, write my own songs, have my own band, play an instrument. Instead, I went on the road with Richard and Fletch as they toured the country audition-ing guys for the band that would eventually become V. They paid me to go with them and help with the audition process, sorting the hopefuls' application forms and filming the auditions. Maybe, we all thought, I might find someone who could be suitable for the band I wanted to put together.

The auditions were held at different locations around the country. Since they were organized by Universal Records and the managers of Busted, it was hardly surprising that they were very well attended, by a lot of extremely strong candidates. This was real boy-band stuff, so you can probably imagine the type of person who turned up: guys with bleached-blond hair doing stretches in the corridor and singing Backstreet Boys and Justin Timberlake. Talented, but a bit hard to tell apart from each other. They were all too pristine for what I was looking for. And there wasn't an electric guitar in sight . . .

Until, that is, we got to Manchester. A young guy walked in, and he immediately caught my eye because he wasn't chiselled and muscly, or moonwalking across the warm-up room. He was dressed differently to everyone else, and of the hundreds of people we'd seen all across the country, he was the first to turn up carrying a guitar.

He looked kind of cool. His name was Danny Jones.

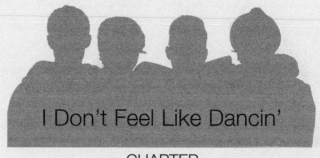

I Don't Feel Like Dancin'

CHAPTER

Danny: It's one of my earliest memories. I'm six years old at home in Bolton. My mum is flicking through the Yellow Pages. She looks up at me. 'Do you fancy guitar lessons?' she asks.

Show me a six-year-old boy who *doesn't* fancy guitar lessons, but I think I fancied them more than most. I was already obsessed. When I was very little I had a white plastic guitar that I carried around with me everywhere, like most kids carry a teddy. Now that I was six, I had my first proper guitar – a nylon-stringed beast from Argos – and in my head I was already Bruce Springsteen, rocking out in my bedroom like it was Madison Square Garden. Proper lessons with a real guitarist would be the coolest thing ever. The icing on the cake.

Mum rang the number and spoke to the guitar teacher, me looking up at her and hanging on every word of the conversation. She put the phone down. 'Sorry, love,' she said. 'He won't take you on till you're seven. Your hands won't be big enough yet.'

Seven? The teacher might as well have asked me to wait until I had a free bus pass.

We went to see the guitar teacher to try and persuade

55

him. He had a look at my massive hands and decided they were big enough after all. More importantly, I had the hunger. I'd have quite happily spent all day, every day, practising. Unfortunately, school got in the way.

School wasn't exactly the best thing that ever happened to me, but it wasn't the worst, either. Put me in a lesson that interested me and I'd be totally engaged, asking questions every other minute. Put me in a history lesson, or an RE lesson, and I'd be staring out the window, bored to tears. Which way I went was often down to the teacher. We had one brilliant music teacher called Mr Martin who would get everyone going, including those who thought they weren't really into music. Unfortunately my next music teacher – his nickname was Mr Pendle Bender – never really captured my imagination, which was frustrating because it was the one lesson I really wanted to be good, and to be good at. Mr Pendle Bender liked drilling us in music theory, but I was always more interested in performance. I used to try and find any way of performing, whether it was going onstage in school plays (I went for one audition and ended up with the lead role in *Bugsy Malone*), or playing lead guitar in the school productions of *Jesus Christ Superstar* or *Grease*.

Trouble was, playing guitar in my school wasn't very cool. I got picked on a bit for doing it. Spat on, sometimes. I wasn't much good at sticking up for myself. I just had to put up with the taunts in the corridors, not that they turned me off the guitar. Back home, if I wasn't practising in my bedroom, I was always out in the street with my friends, playing with our BMXs or kicking a ball around. I got quite good at football, and was offered a trial for Birmingham City under Trevor Francis, but it meant staying down there for a week, and we couldn't bloody afford it.

They were different, my mum and dad. As different as Springsteen and Pink Floyd, which was the music they listened to, and the soundtrack to my childhood. And although I don't have any memories of my early days being anything other than happy, I was never the type of kid to think about things too deeply. When I look back, I can see that the cracks in my family's relationships started to appear early on.

I had a good relationship with both my mum and my dad, endlessly talking music with my mum and going to the football with my dad. I found out later, though, that all was not totally well behind the doors of our little house in Bromley Cross. Dad was a prison officer at Strangeways, and a dog handler. He was a surfer in Newquay when he was young – a big lad who would have been a good bouncer. Perfect material, I suppose, for a prison officer. By all accounts, though, he changed when he started working at Strangeways. Hardly surprising, I guess. He worked in a stressful place. You sometimes felt like you were walking on eggshells around him. I remember him coming home from work, obviously in a strange mood.

'What's up wi'ya, Dad?'

'Ah, I don't want to talk about it.'

'No, go on, what's up wi'ya?'

And he'd tell me some horrible story, like the time he'd told an inmate to get back in his cell, and next time he saw him he'd had his radio aerial sticking out of his chest. 'It's just playing on my mind,' he'd say, before retreating into himself.

I was close to my dad. Closer than my mum and sister were, I sometimes think. And having a tough guy for a father had its advantages. If I ever went home and told him that some kid had spat on me in the corridor for playing guitar, he was always ready to stick up for me. One time, it went further than that.

I was about thirteen and had been out on the streets playing roller hockey with my mates. There was a little parade of shops a couple of minutes' walk from my house, and a bus stop where kids would hang out, maybe getting into alcohol, or a bit of drugs. It was quite intimidating walking past that bus stop on a Saturday when all the kids were there. On the day in question, my mate Sam and I passed it on our way into one of the shops to buy sweets. I felt a few of the kids' eyes on us, but that was nothing new. A moment later, though, I was aware that Sam was outside and it was all kicking off with some of them. Neither of us was ever the type to start a fight, but it turned out that a local kid who'd always been a bit of a troublemaker had given Sam some lip, tried to nick his sweets and generally caused a load of aggro. Sam had stood up to him and thrown his bike into some nearby bushes.

The kid legged it and we carried on rollerblading home. We were almost at my house when our way was blocked by another four kids – one of them quite young, two about sixteen and the fourth probably eighteen. They called Sam over to them, sounding all friendly and asking him the time. 'Sure,' Sam told them. But before we knew what was happening, they'd laid into him. Sam was taking a proper pummelling, and I didn't even hesitate. The second I realized what was going down, only one thought went through my head.

Dad.

I probably looked like a bit of a pussy running, but I knew my dad was just nearby, and I knew it was him we needed. I started thumping on our front door, shouting for him, yelling that Sam was getting done over. He didn't give it a second's thought: he sprinted out the house, me blading alongside him, until we found Sam. He was lying on the ground, totally kicked in, blood all over his face, so badly beaten that he didn't even know where he was.

Dad wasn't prepared to leave it at that. He bundled us into the back of his car. 'We're going for them,' he told us.

There was a V-shaped valley behind our house, at the end of which was an area called Sharples. Kids from Sharples were always fighting with us lot from Bromley Cross, and Dad knew just which estate to head for to catch them. It would take them ten minutes to get there by foot. We could do it in seven.

We got to Sharples and waited at the exit of a field where we knew the kids would emerge, Sam still laid out in the back, covered in blood.

Soon enough, they arrived.

Dad needed us to identify them before he did anything. 'Is that them there?'

I nodded.

'Right, lads, get down . . .'

Sam and I hunkered in the back of the car while my dad sat in the front pretending to read the paper. As the kids walked past the car, he slammed the paper down and jumped out. 'Oi!' he roared. 'You fuckin' kicked my son's mate in!' He let the younger ones go, but he grabbed the eighteen-year-old by the front of his shirt and started cranking him around the street, throwing him all over the place, screaming murder at him.

By now, half the street was out on the doorsteps, watching what was going on. I'd ventured out of the car too, thinking I was the dog's bollocks and egging my dad on. Word soon got around about what had happened, and from that day on kids in the area thought twice before jumping me or my mates. I never got picked on round my neck of the woods again.

That was the good side of having a dad like mine. But there were down sides too. As time went on, he and my mum stopped communicating and the arguments increased. He seemed unable to talk about the difficult things that had gone on at work, but it seemed it all came home with him anyway, and his frustrations would suddenly explode. It's sad, really, that he never felt able to share these things with my mum. His only way of chilling was to head off down the pub, leaving me, my mum and my sister at home.

Mum didn't take well to this change in Dad's character. Some of my earliest memories are of lying in bed and hearing the arguments that flared up between them. I remember my heart racing, my stomach turning over. It's stressful to hear stuff like that going on when you're a kid. Nobody wants to hear their mum and dad yelling at each other, after all. More often than not, the arguments would start off being about nothing at all – silly, petty, stupid disagreements – before spiralling out of control as months of pent-up frustration spilled out. It was horrible to listen to, but looking back I think I learned a lot from it. Mum and Dad struggled to talk about their problems properly, like adults. Now, I try to make sure that my girlfriend Georgia and I talk about *everything*, because I know I'm like my mum when it comes to letting things build up inside.

As time went on, I turned into the peacemaker of the family. When the arguments started, it was always me putting myself in the middle of them both, telling my dad to stop getting at my mum. The rows would always end the same way: Dad would storm out of the house and go to the pub, and I'd be relieved he'd gone and that my mum could relax for a bit while he wasn't there. To everyone else, Dad was totally chilled, but being at home seemed to bring out a different side of him.

I didn't want to admit to myself that anything was wrong, but in my gut I knew it was. And as time went on, it felt like the family was growing apart. Ours was a pretty traditional Catholic family. Sundays were the high point of our week. We'd go to church in the morning, then round to my nan's house just up the road for Sunday lunch. More and more, however, it seemed like Dad wasn't turning up to our Sunday lunches round my nan's. He was down at the pub instead. He loved it there. That time influenced a song I'd write much later called 'Don't Know Why'.

When I was twelve I got a red and white Encore guitar, and cried my eyes out with happiness. I used to spend all day on that guitar pretending I was Mike Oldfield playing *Tubular Bells*, while my dad filmed me. When I finally met Tom, we bonded over the fact that we both have videos like this of us growing up: Tom singing 'Kids Wanna Rock' by Bryan Adams in front of the Christmas tree, me playing Springsteen songs on my Encore. Springsteen was my idol. I wasn't much more than ten when I went to see him on his acoustic tour at Manchester Apollo. Mum camped out for front row seats and we got them. I was singing along all the way through his set, and at the end he told his guitar tech to give me his harmonica. There was an interview in the paper the next day where Springsteen mentioned how great it was to see a kid singing along to his songs. I think he must have been talking about me.

My sister Vicky was the better singer, though. As we got older, I used to back her with my guitar on pub gigs around the area, and she was always off auditioning for big shows, as she was a good actress, too. When I was fourteen, though, I saw an advert for a local talent show. Mum said, 'Why don't you go along and sing an Oasis song? You love Oasis.'

I didn't think I knew how to sing, but my mum was always really good at encouraging us and bigging me and Vicky up and making us feel like we could really achieve what we set our minds to – even when there was a possibility that it might end up being a disaster. She persuaded me to enter and, in the days before the competition, being a good Catholic boy, I was constantly saying my prayers: 'Please, God, don't let me forget the words to "Don't Look Back In Anger"!'

The day of the talent show came around. I was a little scally with a Ben Sherman shirt, almost fully shaved head and little round John Lennon glasses – what a sight. I sat like a rock on the stage of this weird Labour Club somewhere up north, playing my guitar and singing with all the expression and feeling you'd expect from a terrified fourteen-year-old. I reckon I must have sounded more like Noel Edmonds than Noel Gallagher. There was nobody in the audience apart from the families of the kids playing, and the whole show was like the worst ever version of *Britain's Got Talent*, with a ropey Abba tribute band and a few terrible magicians. Astonishingly, I walked away with a prize for second place. More importantly, I gained a bit of self-belief.

My red and white Encore served me well until one day, on the bus back home from school, I found a purse with a huge wad of money in it – £1,500. I ummed and aahed about what to do with it before giving it to my dad, who handed it in to the police. Nobody claimed it after a certain amount of time. The police thought it was drug money and they gave it back to me. So there I was, a schoolkid with one thousand five hundred quid to spend. I bought myself a beautiful Taylor guitar with the drug money I found on the bus.

When I was fifteen, I got a band together with a couple of other guys. We called ourselves Jinx, and entered another talent show, this time in Wigan. We won. I started to think that maybe I was OK at this music game, and I got up to a decent level on the guitar.

I knew that I wanted to go to music college, but to do that you needed to get a grade. I passed my Grade 6 with honours, but I really hated all the scales and music theory and classical stuff. It didn't seem to have anything to do with the kind of music I wanted to play, and I've forgotten it all now.

My mum and my sister were always aware of upcoming auditions. I was just turning seventeen when Vicky came across an advert on the Internet saying that Universal Records and the managers of Busted were auditioning in Manchester for a new band. She printed it out and showed it to Mum. Trouble was, we had a crappy old printer that used to miss bits out at the edge of the page. Thank God for that printer, because without it I'd never have given the advert a second glance. I can't remember the exact wording, but the gist of it was that they were looking for pop singers, not rock singers, so please do not bring guitars. Our printer missed out the word 'not'. I was big into Oasis and Ocean Colour Scene – a bit of a rock mod – and here, or so I thought, was an advert for rock dudes who wanted to be in a band to turn up with their guitars. Get in!

The day of the audition came around, and Mum took me and Vicky into Manchester. Whenever I get nervous, all I can do is think about getting away, and I don't easily remember what happened back then. Suffice it to say, my memories of that day are cloudy at best. I was nervous as hell as I waited in the queue, just across the way from the Palladium, clutching my guitar. I was the only guy there with an instrument, and people were giving me funny looks. Something was obviously wrong.

'I don't want to do this,' I told my mum. 'Let's go home.'

But Mum cajoled me into staying. 'It's Universal Records,' she said. 'You don't know what you might get out of it.'

I shuffled into a waiting room, clutching my guitar. All around me I saw these well-groomed teenagers doing stretching exercises like they were limbering up for the bloody ballet. I'd never done a stretching exercise in my whole life. I did a bit of a warm-up on my guitar, but soon enough I was muttering to my mum again, begging her to take me home. And again she encouraged me to stay. 'It doesn't matter if you get nothing out of it,' she told me, and she carried on boosting my confidence while I sat there like a fish out of water. I couldn't wait for the audition to be over.

We got called into this room in groups of six, and as I was ushered in, I was told to leave my guitar behind. Disaster! I felt sick – leaving my guitar behind was worse than leaving my mum behind – and before I knew it I found myself in front of the judges, X *Factor* style. They were all perfectly clean-cut and sharply dressed. They wore aftershave! People from Bromley Cross *never* wore aftershave. These were important dudes! They had an aura about them – after all, they came from London. I'd only been to London once, and that was to see Bolton in the play-offs against Watford at Wembley. For me, going to London was like going to Spain or Greece. A real event. What the hell was a kid from my neck of the woods doing in front of these fellas?

Auditioning, that's what. A guy in his twenties with

immaculate black hair – I'd later find out that this was Fletch – asked me if I could sing them a song.

'Sure.'

'So what are you going to sing us, Danny?'

I'd given this a lot of thought. '"Mr Writer" by the Stereophonics,' I said. I knew it backwards and it sounded cool on the guitar. Just one problem: my guitar was propped up against the wall in the next room.

Fletch didn't look impressed. Not surprising, really. This was *totally* the wrong kind of song for an audition like that. 'Do you know any pop songs?' he asked.

I looked round the room, racking my brains.

'Any Backstreet Boys? NSYNC?' Fletch pressed.

'Er . . . Paul Weller?'

Everyone laughed. I grinned along with them, secretly wishing I could be anywhere else but there.

In the end they let me grab my guitar. I sang 'Bitter Sweet Symphony' by The Verve – not exactly the world's poppiest, chirpiest song – but I must have done something right because they asked me to go away and learn something more appropriate. And to my surprise, they asked the young guy filming the auditions to teach me something. He was about my age and his name was Tom.

We found ourselves in a corridor with lime-green walls outside the audition room. We crouched down on the ground, each of us with our guitar, and Tom taught me 'I Want It That Way' by Backstreet Boys, line by line and with a bit of help from Vicky who knew the song really well. To my surprise, I *really* liked it. I'd never heard straight, clean pop chords like that, and I found them so satisfying to play. When we had it down,

I shook Tom's hand and wished him good luck for *his* audition – I really was that clueless – before returning to the audition room and playing through what I'd just learned for the panel and scarpering out to find my mum. 'Mum! They wanted me to play pop!'

'Well, that's all right. You like a bit of pop, don't you, love? A bit of Paul Weller? What's poppier than that?'

'That's what I said, and they all laughed!'

Mum just carried on being Mum, always optimistic. 'Ah, don't be silly, stay with it – it'll be all right . . .' We both did a good job of ignoring all the muscly fellas around us wearing leotards and doing their stretches.

Tom: Back in the audition room, Fletch and the others were discussing what they'd seen. They might have laughed at Danny, but they all absolutely loved him. He had charisma, and was obviously talented even if Paul Weller *was* as poppy as his tastes got. Fletch and I had a quiet word, and we both agreed that maybe he was someone who might be suitable to put together with me. In the meantime, everyone was looking forward to seeing him dance . . .

Danny: I was called in for the second round. There were more of us in the audition room this time, and I remember Tom lurking on the fringes with his video camera. Fletch explained that he'd like to see us all dance. Suddenly the room was filled with music and all the others were busting their best moves. I was standing next to a Liverpudlian guy, all baggy trousers and short-cropped hair, dancing like Michael bloody

Jackson, while the rest of the shiny-faced, white-toothed kids from *Fame* did the same. And me? I stood there and remembered my mum's words of encouragement. And I thought to myself: You're here now, Danny, you might as well give it your best shot.

You know when you see your dad dancing and it's the most embarrassing thing in the world? You know how he looks like the squarest person you ever saw? That was me. Nervous, freaked out, red in the face. In short, absolutely pathetic, and even more so when everyone around me was moonwalking. I remember looking through the glass panel in the door and seeing my mum and sister; they were wetting themselves.

Tom: Watching Danny try to dance was one of the funniest things I've ever seen. He was so obviously the wrong guy in the wrong place, and nobody could keep a straight face watching him. But he'd won the panel over anyway.

Danny: The dancing finished and the panel thanked us all for our time. They'd let us know if they wanted anyone to travel down to London for the next round of auditions. We filed out, but before I knew it one of the guys from the panel had approached me. He was older than Fletch, and had a drawling American accent. I later found out that his name was Richard Rashman. 'Hey, Danny,' he said, 'you got any original songs?'

As it happened, I did, so I played him a few. Richard kept me back for ages, listening to my tunes and chatting. Finally he handed over his card and suggested

I might like to come down to London to meet up. Cool, I thought. Why not?

Back home, me and my mum told my dad all about what had happened that day, and I said I wanted to take this Richard guy up on his offer to see him in London. Dad wasn't so keen. A young lad, travelling by himself down to London to meet a strange old dude in his hotel? I can totally understand why he was so against it – he was just being a protective dad – but I remember at the time sitting on the windowsill, listening to the conversation and getting more disheartened by the minute. Not only was Dad adamant that I shouldn't go down to meet some dodgy bloke in a London hotel, I was about to start college where I was going to study music production, and he didn't want me to throw all that away for some pie-in-the-sky idea of being a pop star. I could see both sides of the argument, but of course I just wanted to go for it.

Mum suggested that if I was going to meet Richard, then she would have to come with me, and that's how we resolved the situation. But even though I didn't really know *why* this guy wanted to see me, it was something I was desperate to do on my own. The last thing I wanted was my parents cramping my style every step of the way.

Mum and Dad talked it over and eventually they came up with a compromise. Mum would take me down to London and secretly book into the same hotel, where she could keep an eye on me and be on hand if anything sinister happened. Richard was to know nothing about it.

We took the train down from Bolton to London, and to this day I don't think Richard knows that my mum was there, lurking around the InterContinental in Hyde Park and keeping an eye on both me and him like a spy. As for me, I'd never seen anything like the InterContinental. It was like some big New York hotel you might see in the movies, with an old-world, regal charm and a slightly musty smell that now always takes me back to those early days. I went to meet Richard in the business lounge, ordered myself a Diet Coke (honestly, that was the best Diet Coke I ever drank), and sat there taking everything in. I was a million miles away from my life in Bolton, and even though I didn't quite know what I was there for, it felt good.

Richard started asking me questions. 'So, Danny, if you were in a band, would you want there to be five people in the band, or four people? Would you want to sing a lot? Would you want to *not* sing a lot?'

I don't think my replies were very illuminating, most of them being along the lines of: 'I dunno, mate – whatever!' I was genuinely open to anything, with one exception: 'Whatever happens,' I said, 'I want to play guitar.' Truth was, I didn't really care about anything else. I met with Tom again – we seemed to click just like we had done up in Manchester – but the next day I got the train back up to Bolton with my mum, her secret-agent role now over.

Tom: Richard called me that night. 'So, Tom, whaddya think?' By now, Fletch, Richard and Universal had narrowed the candidates for V down to about fifteen people, all of them super-talented. As far as Universal was concerned, however, only one of them was a dead cert: Danny. But somehow, that didn't feel right. V was the wrong band for Danny, whereas I knew we would get on. Richard agreed. We had to do what we could to snatch him from Universal's clutches . . .

Danny: I had no idea that all this was going on behind the scenes. What I did know was that a few weeks later, in October 2002, the *Smash Hits* tour was coming to Manchester, with Busted headlining. I got a call from Tom inviting me to come and see the show.

The night of the gig, Tom and Richard came to collect me. On the way to the venue, I was full of questions. 'Do you *know* Busted? Do you talk to them? You *talk* to them? *Wow* . . .' I couldn't get it into my head that Tom hung out with these uber-famous dudes. I felt like I'd stumbled into a dream world. And even as we watched the show, I still couldn't get my head round it. I kept turning to Tom, badgering him: 'So him, Charlie, him on stage, you *talk* to him? You *hang out* with him?' And when Tom just nodded, like it was the most normal thing in the world, I was seriously impressed. The songs that Busted were singing instantly grabbed me. And then, of course, there were the fifteen thousand teenage girls going mental. It was like my eyes were being opened to the pop world.

Richard was obviously trying to impress me with his 'come and see this band I manage' line. He succeeded. I had the same sensation I'd had when I'd gone to see Springsteen. I wanted to do what Busted were doing. I wanted to play on that stage. I wanted to have girls screaming at me. My heart was thumping with the excitement of it all, and I was seriously in awe of Tom that he hung out with guys like that.

A few weeks later, I was called back down to London again, this time so that I could take part in the final auditions for V at Pineapple Studios. They took place over a period of four days, during which time we all stayed in a hotel next to the studios. I found myself sharing a room with Tom, who was filming the auditions again. Funny that. We bonded even more by messing around like the kids that we were – stupid, childish stuff, like knocking on other guests' doors and running away. We weren't the only ones. Put a bunch of young guys together in a hotel and it's always going to be a riot.

Tom: James Bourne was hanging out with us for some of the time – he was pretty famous because of Busted by now – and I ended up topping and tailing in the same bed with him. He kept his socks on, and his feet, which were inches from my nose, absolutely *stank* . . .

Danny: It was quite intimidating. For a start I didn't know how to dress. All these dudes I thought I was up against were so cool. They were all good-looking, they had immaculate patterns shaved into their hair, they had proper suntans and were quite bosh, whereas I was just a skinny lad from Bolton. I tried to boy-band myself up a bit – my mum had even gone so far as to get me a fake tan – and I actually started to enjoy myself. I knew that if I didn't get into V, I'd still have Tom to write with. Either way, it was such an exciting time for me.

We would stay up all night in that hotel, listening to music, messing around, playing guitar . . .

Tom: James and I were pretty average guitarists back then. Our eyes popped out of our heads when we saw all the stuff Danny could do, straight from his guitar lessons up north. He knew how to play all the bluesy stuff I'd grown up listening to thanks to my dad – all the Rolling Stones and Eric Clapton I knew so well. And while he showed us his chops on the guitar, James and I were able to show him the pop chords we had been playing around with for the last year.

Danny: As we played together, there was an instant connection. Tom and I both seemed to know what the other person was going to do. And then, out of the blue, he'd start singing harmonies to my vocal lines. Harmonies? I was amazed – I didn't know how he did it, but I knew we had something special. Something that I wanted to show off a bit.

Tom: Most of all, though, Danny and I hit it off personally. He was cooler than me, and a lot more streetwise. More rebellious, too. It was always Danny who wanted to sneak a beer from the minibar, or try to get served in a pub – the sort of thing I would *never* do. And he was more sociable – the kind of guy everyone likes the moment they meet him. You couldn't imagine Danny hiding in the bathroom to get away from people at a party. But they say opposites attract, and we did. James could sense it too, I think, and he shared my excitement. He knew how long I'd been on my own, musically speaking, since my disappointment at not getting into Busted. He knew I'd been waiting to find the right person to form a band with. And like me, he knew I'd found him.

Danny: It was strange, going from those all-night sessions with Tom and James to the V auditions during the day, with Tom filming them behind the camera while I had to make some feeble attempt to do a fancy dance routine. My mum had told me that baggy clothes looked good for dancing, so I wore my boy-band jungle pants – massive, baggy army pants with shreds of material falling off them that you had to be David Beckham to get away with, not Danny from Bolton (looking back, I'm still cringing at the memory). I'd only got myself a pair because I thought they made me look like something out of New Kids On The Block, but I felt good in them, and I enjoyed hanging out with all the potential recruits for V.

I was a quiet kid back then, and at heart just a scruffy musician. To be in a room with these big personalities was intimidating, but I loved them all. The first guy I spoke to was Antony Brant, who went on to be a close friend of mine and the boys, even to the point that years later we'd fly him out to Australia to hang out with us when we were recording our fourth album because we dug his company so much. He's still one of the coolest guys I've ever met.

I tried to learn all these complicated dance moves to 'Everybody' by Backstreet Boys. I went along with it, doing my best, but every day I was on the phone to my mum, telling her I couldn't do it, I wasn't good enough. She was my rock. She told me to stick at it, so I spent my days busting moves in front of this panel of Universal dudes, trying to ignore the fact that I thought I was making a dick of myself, and totally unaware that the label had already decided they wanted me on board for V.

Tom: And the label were totally unaware that we had other plans for Danny . . .

V turned out to be such a talented boy band. Awesome singers. Good writers. A shame. It was the wrong time for them, and they never had quite the right songs, which meant they didn't make the success of things that they should have done. Looking back, I suppose it was partly down to McFly and Busted that they didn't succeed. We were proper bands, and I guess we made boy bands who just danced look a bit uncool. At the time, though, we didn't know what the future held for them. But I did know that I wanted Danny for my band, so we had to find out if he wanted to be in V, or if he wanted to throw his hat in with me.

Danny: It was Fletch who brought me round to their way of thinking. I remember him saying to me, 'If you want to be in a boy band, Danny, that's fine. If you just want to sing and dance, that's fine. They're a signed band. They've got a record deal. Tom's just a guy who writes songs. He has avenues, he has management, but there's no record deal. But think of this: You're in a hotel room in Germany, you're with five other dudes and you've not got a guitar. Would you be happy?' And the honest answer was the one I gave: no. That was when I realized that I didn't want to accept what was being handed me on a plate. I didn't want to be in V.

I turned them down, and returned to Bolton knowing that I'd taken a big risk, but also that I'd made the right decision. In the months that followed, I'd travel down to London and stay with Tom as much as possible, hanging out and playing music. Those times influenced a song I wrote in my little room in Bolton, called 'Not Alone'. When we weren't together, Tom would send me minidiscs in the post of songs he'd been working on (complete with the added accompaniment of his mum calling him downstairs for his tea). Busted were getting bigger and bigger. We both knew that everyone was waiting for the next thing to come along in the same vein – another guitar band to blow the regular boy bands out of the water. And as we got to know each other properly, and develop our own unique sound, we both hoped that the next big thing was going to be us.

Tom: When I wasn't hanging out with Danny, I spent a lot of time with James Bourne. James was a lot like me: a bit geeky, he didn't drink and he didn't smoke. His bandmates Charlie and Matt weren't quite so clean-living. With a Busted theatre tour coming up, James knew his bandmates would be partying harder than him, so he asked me if I'd like to come on tour with them so that he and I could start writing Busted's second album together.

I jumped at the chance, and that first tour was a massive event in my life, the coolest thing I'd ever done. I'd never properly experienced life on a tour bus before, nor that level of adulation from the fans. Busted had just had their first number one and were kicking off massively, so although it was a theatre tour rather than an arena tour, they had a crazy, hysterical fan base and there was mayhem everywhere they went – not to mention the hundreds of teenage girls (and their mums) hanging round the hotels and trying to get with them.

James was a bit oblivious to all that. He seemed more excited about being able to order room service in all the hotels we went to. While Charlie and Matt were out doing what pop stars do, the most rock 'n' roll thing James and I got up to was ordering milkshakes at 3 a.m., *even if they weren't on the menu!* We were entirely nocturnal. It wasn't uncommon for us to have breakfast with everybody else in the hotel who had just got up, and *then* go to bed. And during those milkshake-fuelled night-time marathons, we wrote, and wrote, and wrote. From a songwriting point of view, it was the most prolific time in my life. We'd write two or three songs a night, one after the other, and Busted's second album came together in less than two weeks. 'Crashed The Wedding', 'Air Hostess', 'Who's David?' – the songs just seemed to spill out of us.

One night, Charlie joined us instead of going out. Charlie and I never really hung out together very much. It wasn't that we didn't get on, but perhaps he felt a bit uncomfortable having me around. I don't know. That night, however, the three of us wrote a song called 'That Thing You Do'. It wasn't like Busted's other songs. It had a Beatles, Beach Boys vibe, full of three-part harmonies. You could instantly imagine jangly surf guitars in the arrangement. We loved it so much that we cracked up laughing every time we tried to sing it.

It was a brilliant song. Different, we thought, to anything else that was around at the time. And, crucially, it didn't sound like Busted. For the first time, we'd come up with something that was fresh and original that would be more suited to whatever *my* project was going to be. Sixties harmonies. Surf guitars. That song was the spark for everything that was to come.

We had half a band. We had the beginnings of our sound. What we didn't have was a name, and trying to *think* of one was doing my head in. Now that Danny was on board, we started to give it some proper thought. Rashman had a list of suggestions, and the name he was backing was, without doubt, the worst band name I'd EVER heard. If our manager had had his way, we'd have been called the Skate Park. Ask Rashman about it now, and he'll tell you it wouldn't have mattered – a name's just a name. But I'm pretty sure that with a name like that, our career would have been over before it had even begun. Game over. The other options on Rashman's list weren't much better: Cool Ethan, Abel Cain, Kevin (*Kevin?!*) . . .

Danny: One of my suggestions was Keeva. (WTF?)

Tom: They were all shockers. Without exception.

My favourite film growing up had always been *Back to the Future*, and our love of eighties films was one of the reasons James Bourne and I had hit it off so well. On tour with Busted, I was sitting at the back of the auditorium at Sheffield Arena, watching the band soundcheck their song 'Year 3000'. The lyrics to that song – about time machines and flux capacitors – all came from James's love of *Back to the Future*, and they got me thinking about DeLoreans and Doc Emmett and Marty McFly . . .

Marty McFly . . .

That was it. The word had popped into my head. The moment it did, I knew I'd got it. I ran backstage – the band had just finished soundchecking – and found James. 'I've got it!' I yelled at him. 'The band name, I've got it!'

'What?'

'McFly!'

James stared at me. His eyes widened. And then he went absolutely nuts. 'That's so cool, that's so cool! Quick, tell Danny . . .'

I told Danny the good news. 'McFly!'

Silence.

'McFlurry?' he asked.

Danny: I didn't get it. I'd never even seen *Back to the Future*. I honestly thought he was talking about ice creams. McFly was just a random word as far as I was concerned.

Tom: I couldn't believe that anyone could have not seen that film, so I told Danny that next time he came down to London, we were going to watch it together.

It was a couple of weeks later, round at James's house, that it happened. We were so desperate for Danny to like the movie, and to agree to the name McFly, that we went out of our way to turn it into a perfect evening, making amazing milkshakes and five-tiered sandwiches, before settling down in James's La-Z-Boys to watch the film. I felt almost jealous of Danny for never having seen it before, but most of all I just wanted him to agree with me, because in my head it was a done deal.

Danny: I started out enjoying the film well enough, although I still wasn't totally sold on the name. But then it got to the sequence in the movie where Bif is chasing Marty McFly and crashes into the manure truck. 'Whoa!' I shouted suddenly. 'Go back! Go back!'

The guys looked at me like I was mad, but I kept on at them, and they started rewinding the movie. We watched the horse manure jump off Bif's car and back into the truck. 'Pause it! There!'

On the side of the manure truck were the words: *D. Jones Manure Hauling.*

Fate.

'McFly's the name!' I shouted. Tom and James looked at me almost in disbelief. It was an amazing moment. The beginning of everything.

'McFly's the name!'

The Golden Ticket

CHAPTER

Tom: The Busted tour was finished and I couldn't wait to get writing with Danny again. James and I played him 'That Thing You Do', and with this new sound in our heads, we sat down as a threesome and, for the first time, wrote a song together. It was called 'Obviously'.

We would always take inspiration from stuff that was going on in our lives. I had told the guys that there was this girl called Giovanna who I was obsessed with – this was in the period when I was still trying to win her back. I was always trying to worm my way back in with her, but she had a boyfriend who was a lot older than me and in the police force. I hated my rival, even though it was my own stupid fault that Gi and I weren't together. The guys thought this was funny, and suddenly we had the basis of a song. *She's got a boyfriend . . . he drives me round the bend . . . he's twenty-three . . . he's in the Marines . . . he'd kill me . . .* He wasn't in the Marines, of course, but we agreed it sounded cooler.

That was the beginning of summer 2003. Danny stayed with me over the summer. We divided our time between my parents' house, the Busted house and a room on the third floor of the InterContinental Hotel where Rashman always stayed. During that time we wrote the majority of our first album. 'That Girl', 'Broccoli', 'Surfer Babe', 'Down By The Lake' and 'She Left Me' all came together in about a week while we were writing with James at the Busted house. The remainder were written by just me and Danny together. 'Room On The Third Floor' was the first tune we wrote just the two of us, all about going stir-crazy during our time in the InterContinental Hotel. And a little ditty called 'Five Colours In Her Hair' was based on a TV show called *As If*. We both fancied this character in it called Sooz – even though she was quite grungy, with different-coloured dreads in her hair. (Apparently Emily Corrie, who played Sooz, *hated* the song.)

We knew as we were writing them that our songs felt fresh. And they continued to feel different to the material I'd worked on with Busted. A bit less gimmicky. Everyone we played them to went nuts for the sound, and we knew something great was just around the corner.

Danny: We could have all the songs we liked, though. They weren't much good if we didn't have a band. We needed a bass player and a drummer. Finding the right guys was a lot less easy than we thought it would be.

Tom: We put the feelers out, going through all the regular processes to find people who we thought would fit in with us, both musically and personally. We went down all the usual channels, putting notices up in drum schools and advertising in the *Stage* magazine. It was tortuous. Hardly anybody turned up to our little auditions. Those that did were never right. We were choosy. Our new recruits needed to have everything. They needed to be good musicians, to look the part and to be people we thought we'd get on with.

Danny: And they needed to be hungry to learn. We'd already written this bunch of songs together, and we wanted our new bandmates to be as enthusiastic about them as we were. We met amazing drummers, guys who could play anything, but who didn't *look* right. We tapped up kids who *looked* cool, but who'd never picked up an instrument in their lives. We even approached a couple of guys in Top Shop and asked them if they played bass and drums. They didn't, of course.

Tom: While all this was happening, Danny and I carried on working on our material. Our songs continued to take shape. We recorded demos of 'Obviously' and 'Surfer Babe' with a young producer called Craig Hardy. We used to record in the spare room of his parents' house, and even though it was hardly a fancy studio, there's something so special about the sound Craig developed on those early demos. He went on to produce half of our first album, and if it hadn't been for him and the work he did on those demos, we might never have got signed in the first place.

We also worked out live acoustic versions of 'That Girl' and 'Memory Lane', and as things started to come together for us, and Busted's success continued, our management decided that the time had come to see what interest they could get from record labels.

We spent two weeks parading our stuff around the offices of all the major labels. Sony, BMG, EMI, V2, Warner Bros – we saw them all. That had to be the most nerve-racking two weeks of both our lives: we knew we only had one chance with these guys, and that if we screwed it up, our music careers could be over before they'd even begun.

Danny: We shouldn't have worried. Everyone's reaction was amazing, and they all seemed interested. There was a buzz going round about us. This was a time when the pop scene was dominated by boy bands like Blue and Westlife. Suddenly Busted had come along with their guitars and made guys who danced and sat on stools look extremely uncool. The next thing looked like it could be us, and given the relationship Rashman, Fletch and Busted had with Universal's Island Records, it stood to reason that we'd end up showcasing our stuff for them. And when they offered us a record deal, everything felt right. If we were on the same label as Busted, it would make it easier for us to tour with them. With a bit of luck, *their* success could become *our* success.

Tom: But we wouldn't have any success at all if we didn't have the right people to complete our band. Now, though, with a record deal in our arsenal, we could say that Universal music and Busted's management were looking for drummers and bass players. Potential recruits started to pay a bit more attention. We held an open audition in Covent Garden, and the response was slightly different to before. A couple of hundred people turned up, and number one in the queue was a very young-looking kid called Dougie.

Dougie: A very young-looking kid who was wishing he'd done himself a favour and stayed at home.

Home was a small town called Corringham in Essex. A quiet town. The kind of place where nothing really happens. Where everybody knows everybody else, and nobody seems to leave. If you were born in Corringham, chances were you'd live there for the rest of your life. Auditioning for bands in the middle of London wasn't the sort of thing kids from my home town did. Especially weird, uncool, unpopular kids, and I was as weird, uncool and unpopular as kids come.

I had a tiny group of friends. Skateboarding was our life. We'd skateboard every day after school, and at the weekends we'd head down to Leigh-on-Sea to skateboard some more. Mostly, though, they were a bit older than me, and I had no close friends my own age. I went to Gable Hall School, and I hated that place with a passion. For me, school meant constantly trying to avoid awkward, embarrassing situations. It meant running away from people who disliked me. It meant trying not to be tripped up in the corridor. It meant being bullied, and not having the guts to fight back.

I was a very anxious character back then. Shy. That had never mattered much at my primary school, but once I hit secondary school and everyone started dividing up into little cliques and defining themselves by what kind of music they listened to, things took a turn for the worse. Being into rock music and skateboarding was enough to make people hate you. All the popular kids were into garage and football. They wore tracksuit bottoms with their socks pulled over the top, and Nike caps. None of them liked me, simply because I didn't dress like them or listen to the same kind of music. It sounds silly now, but at the time it was anything but. Certain people wouldn't be seen dead with me. I got called 'grunger' on a daily basis. I was small, and I looked quite vulnerable, which meant I always got picked on. The bigger kids had a habit of picking the smaller ones up by the straps of their backpacks and swinging them round. The smaller you were, the easier it was, so I was a prime target. If you did anything other than walk on with your head down after it happened, you'd only be making things worse for yourself, so I never complained even though I burned with humiliation, and I never fought back. I tried to ignore the way all the hot girls laughed while the guys picked on me. And I was often too scared to eat lunch because the place where you had to queue up for food was where the seagulls used to hang out. If you got dumped on by a seagull, you were an instant target for ridicule. If you were Dougie Poynter and you got dumped on by a seagull, it was ten times worse. So I tended to go without, and as a result I used to pass out – literally – with hunger. For all these reasons, I just tried to keep out of the way and hoped people wouldn't notice me.

I was never a troublemaker at school, but I *was* always off with the fairies in class. I was forever getting caught copying other people's work (a speciality of mine), and I had a real thing about not doing home-work. The way I saw it, I spent six hours a day at school. Any time after that was my own. After all, I used to tell myself, I was *never* going to be a pro-fessional skateboarder if I wasted my time doing homework. And for a couple of years, before I got into music, that was where my ambitions lay.

I was more into ramp skating than street skating, mostly because it was safer. If we went street skating, chances were we'd be chased by some bunch of scallies trying to beat us up. It was amazing how, just because we had baggy jeans and skateboards, people wanted to have a crack at us. On one occasion we'd been skate-boarding at a skate park and were walking back to the train station when we heard a noise coming from behind us. I looked over my shoulder to see forty older kids pegging it full pelt towards us. They started shout-ing: '*We're going to fucking kill you!*' We shat ourselves. I honestly thought I was going to die. I remember my whole face going numb with terror. Somehow, we man-aged to get away, but those boys did get one of my friends eventually. They took his phone first so he couldn't call for help, then beat him up so badly that his face was mangled and bloodied and he ended up in hospital. There was no rhyme or reason behind it. He wasn't a tough kid, or cocky. He wasn't giving them grief. He just wore the wrong clothes and was into the wrong things. Like me.

I still remember the night I decided I wanted to be in a band for a living. I was in a woodwork class with one of my very few friends, Daniel Higgins. Woodwork classes were such a waste of time. I never actually *made* anything. Daniel and I used to spend an hour sanding down bits of wood and talking about music. I already knew I was into rock, but I didn't have much access to the Internet growing up, so it was hard to discover new music and work out exactly what my tastes were. I have a really cool aunt – my mum's sister – and she'd lent me some Nirvana and Pearl Jam, and bought me my first-ever Blink-182 CD. For me that Blink disc was the start of everything. I moved from those bands on to Limp Bizkit and Linkin Park – all the stuff that the rock kids were listening to back then. During this particular woodwork lesson, though, I persuaded Daniel to lend me his copy of *The Tom, Mark and Travis Show (The Enema Strikes Back!)*. It was a live Blink album, and very rare.

I remember that it was pissing down with rain that evening as I hurried home to check it out. I put the record into my crummy little hi-fi and sat there listening to it while I was supposed to be doing my homework, my clothes still wet from the rain. That record was the coolest thing I'd ever heard. It was the first time I realized that being in a band wasn't just about trying to be as hip as possible. It could also be about having as much fun as you could on stage. That, I realized, was what I wanted to do, and it was after listening to *The Tom, Mark and Travis Show* that I went to ask my mum if I could learn the electric guitar.

My mum worked from home as a beautician. Dad was a lift engineer. He wasn't around all that much because he left early and got home late, so I never had a particularly meaningful relationship with him. He was into Formula 1 and football. I hated both, so we didn't have all that much in common. My mum was a much bigger part of my life. She was always around, and was much easier to talk to. She could chat for England. I was obsessed with this one girl at school called Chelsea Dodkins, and I used to talk to Mum about her all the time. I think she knew, though, that as an unpopular, weird, skateboarding grunger I was unlikely to land myself a girlfriend – especially one called Chelsea Dodkins. But although Mum and I were close enough to talk about such things, she didn't share my vision of learning the electric guitar. She said no, not unless I learned the acoustic first. *What?* An acoustic guitar was no good to me. I'd have to think of something else.

Lizards were my hobby. I had loads of them, and I used to breed bearded dragons and sell them at reptile fairs. It didn't do anything for my popularity at school. A lizard's favourite food is a live cricket, but they were forever escaping and getting into everything – my school bag and pencil case included. There are ways to make sure people don't notice you. Ways to make sure you don't stand out as being different, or weird. Having live crickets jumping around you in the classroom isn't one of them. But breeding lizards *was* a nice little earner. Sometimes I'd make two or three hundred quid over a weekend, so I always had a fair bit of pocket money to spend. I used some of my lizard money to buy a crappy Hohner guitar with horrible nylon strings from Argos. I had no idea how to play guitar, but that didn't put me off. I sat in my bedroom for hours, listening to songs and trying to work my way around the fretboard.

A friend of mine who I used to skateboard with had started to learn guitar too, and one day I had an epiphany. Perhaps we could start a band! Surely we could find someone at school who played drums, and my friend persuaded me that playing the bass would be easier than playing guitar because it only had four strings. I was sold. I couldn't believe that I could just forget about the B and E strings on my guitar. It seemed too good to be true. I started learning bass lines on my Hohner until I'd sold enough lizards to buy myself a proper bass guitar – a Fender Squier that cost me a couple of hundred quid. That first ever group was called Ataiz – I've got no idea what it meant, but we thought it sounded cool – and, man, it was crappy. We didn't know *anything*. We didn't even know how to count a piece of music in, and we sounded absolutely terrible.

At the time, they were trying to turn my school into some kind of performing arts centre, and one morning they read out details of an audition for a bass player and a drummer that had been advertised in the *Stage* magazine. Like usual, I was late and missed the announcement. That would have been that if a kid who really hated me hadn't come up to me in the corridor later that day and asked if I was auditioning. I don't know why he did that – we loathed each other – but thank God for that kid. I went and checked out the advertisement. I saw the words 'Universal' and 'Busted' and was sold. I glossed over the bit that said you had to be between sixteen and twenty-one to apply. I was only fifteen, but that was near enough, right? The audition was the following weekend, and I asked my mum if I could go along. She said yes.

I thought it would be like *Pop Idol*, with thousands of people swarming around the audition venue, so when Saturday arrived I badgered my mum to get us there super-early. We arrived two hours before time, and as far as I could tell from a quick glance around the Covent Garden street, I was the only one there. It crossed my mind that we'd got the wrong day, or the wrong place. It also crossed my mind that I was about to make a total dick of myself. What was I *doing* here? I threw up while I was waiting. (I told you I was an anxious kid.) Mum had a little bottle of Rescue Remedy. 'There's no point coming if you're just going to be nervous, Dougie. Just put a bit of this under your tongue. Go on, a little bit more . . .' Whenever I smell that stuff it reminds me of that audition, and how nervous and pukey I was. But I'm glad my mum was there. Everything was so intimidating, and I would never have gone through with it if I'd been by myself.

We stood waiting outside the door of the venue, the only ones, for ages. I kept glancing round to see if I could spot anyone else who looked like they might be auditioning. After a while, I caught sight of someone. He was young and had bleached-blond hair that had turned slightly ginger. He definitely looked like the kind of person who might be there for the auditions, but he wasn't waiting outside the audition room like me. Instead, he was sitting in a café on the other side of the road, just watching. When, finally, a queue started to form behind me, he wandered over. I saw that he was wearing a Starting Line T-shirt. One of my favourite bands – and something to talk about! I plucked up a bit of courage. 'Mate, were you at the Starting Line gig the other night?'

He shook his head. 'It's my friend's T-shirt,' he said, and then he wandered off. Total blow-out.

The dude with the bleached hair sounded a lot posher than me, and he oozed confidence. He was a bit cocky, even. He never even introduced himself as Harry Judd.

Harry: Cocky? Well, maybe. I'm sure I was a lot less confident than I came across – why else would I sit in a café waiting for other people to form a line before I joined them? – but it is true that I was a confident kid, sometimes to a fault.

I was one of those children that's always on the go. By all accounts I was bouncing out of my cot at the age of nine months, walking at ten months and climbing to the top of the climbing frame before eleven months. I was full of energy, unable to sit still, and always want-ing to do something. I was also a bit of a perfectionist. Mum remembers me sitting down to do my homework and spending half an hour sharpening my pencil, then writing and crossing out the title because it wasn't neat enough. Not that schoolwork was really my thing. I loved being outside, playing sport and running around, and I needed to be constantly entertained. I was, in short, high maintenance, and my folks now freely admit that they sent me to boarding school at the age of eight because they couldn't handle me any more.

When the guys and I compare our schooldays, I have

the impression that they think I went to Hogwarts, and I guess to them Old Buckenham Hall in Suffolk wasn't far off. I still remember the Sunday night I travelled from home – Tenderings Farm in Essex – to OBH for the first time with my mum and brother. I'd already said goodbye to my dad. It was the only time I'd ever seen him cry, and I thought at first that he was taking the mick. I laughed at him, then felt really bad when I realized he was genuinely upset. OBH was about an hour away by car, in the middle of nowhere, a beautiful old building at the end of a long, elegant driveway. It was surrounded by land and sports pitches, and I think I must have been a bit wide-eyed as I turned up with my trunk and my tuck box, before being shown up to my dormitory and saying goodbye to my family, realizing that I wouldn't see them until the next holiday.

I was homesick for my first term, but soon got into the swing of things. For the most part I look back on my schooldays a lot more fondly than Dougie. I loved boarding school. I had all my friends around me, I could play all the sport I wanted. I had the time of my life.

It was at OBH that I properly got into cricket. Mum and Dad were very sporty, and I'd played at local cricket clubs when I was five or six. At prep school, though, I gradually started to realize that this was something I could really do. I was always in the first team, and I got sent for county trials when I was eleven. I used to do Easter cricket courses at Lords, and when I was twelve I was asked to trial for the MCC School of Merit, which I was accepted into. That meant I occasionally got to travel up to Lords for the weekend and play with some pretty epic cricketers – I always felt a bit out of my depth, but it was a great experience. I was fairly high-achieving in other sports, too – football, hockey, rugby, tennis, table tennis – but cricket was always my first love.

Academically, I was nothing to write home about. My attention span was seriously low, and I was too busy messing around in class. My reports always said the same thing: *Harry's always distracting the others in class, Harry must learn to concentrate, Harry could do better . . .* Every holiday, my brother, my sister and I would be called in one by one to read through our reports with Mum and Dad. I used to dread those moments, because I knew I'd always be in for a bollocking. I'd promise that next term it would be different, I'd turn over a new leaf. But when it came to it, I was always the first person out of the class when the bell went, sprinting to bag a cricket net before anybody else got there.

I started learning trumpet at OBH. There were two of us. The other guy was always the better trumpeter, but I beat him a couple of years running in the music competition because I held my nerve a bit better when it came to the performance. (Although I still remember the way my legs used to shake whenever I had to play in public.) I seldom let my nerves get the better of me – I always wanted to audition for school plays – and I think I enjoyed the challenge. Not that I was always success-ful. When I wanted to join the choir, I got together with the head chorister before the audition. He took me into a room, played some notes on the piano and got me to

Below left: Tom showing early promise.
Below right: 'Please sir, I need a wee.' When the time came to go onstage at the Palladium, Oliver's plight got even more desperate.
Bottom: Dad showing Tom how it's done.
Inset: Tom and his mum, Debbie, at a Bryan Adams concert.

Tom's first fans! Onstage with Dad – check out the
hat. It would be a few years before Tom could return
the favour at Wembley Stadium **(inset)**.

Above: Young Danny dreams about having guitar lessons.
Below left: First tattoos.
Below right: Danny with the Boss's harmonicas and his very own red and white Encore guitar.

Danny gets a taste for the stage in *Bugsy Malone*.

'Please God don't let me forget the words to "Don't Look Back in Anger".'

Left: Danny with his sister, Vicky, and mum, Kath.
Right: Brother and sister enjoy a night out.
Below: Having fun with Grandad.

Below left: The young Harry Judd relaxes in his doublet and hose.
Below right: The dog takes Harry and his wellies for a walk.
Bottom: Don't let the angelic smile fool you . . . Harry at Old Buckenham Hall School.

Above: The Judd boys playing cricket for
Uppingham School.
Below left: Harry with his Dad, Christopher.
Below right: Harry doing his best Danny Jones
impression.

Above left: Dougie's had some bad hangovers . . .
Above right: King of the Jungle.

Below left: Dougie's first six-pack.
Below right: Luckily when Dougie joined McFly, the guys were on hand to give him hair-styling advice.

Above left: Dougie getting in training for the X-Box marathons on the tour bus.
Above right: Dougie's always loved lizards – here he is with a big one.
Below: On the way to school (worst luck).

sing them back at him. 'You can sing,' he told me. 'You'll
be fine.' But I panicked in the audition, and the choir
master didn't share his head chorister's view. A promis-
ing vocal career, tragically cut short – I'd failed my first
audition.

My holidays were spent attending cricket courses,
trumpet courses, hockey courses . . . Looking back, I'm
sure my parents were just trying to keep me busy and
out of their hair. And when I was thirteen, I moved to
Uppingham School. I was still at OBH the first time I
went to visit my new school. It was like a much bigger
version of my prep school. The school itself is in the
main part of the town, but the fifteen different boarding
houses are dotted all around, and I was to be in a house
called Fircroft (there were actually only fourteen boarding houses when I was a pupil there but another one has
been added since then). It was speech day when I visited
with my dad. We arrived at Fircroft to see an area
cordoned off by police tape. There was a bloodstain on
the floor, with flies buzzing around it. The housemaster
was loitering nearby, looking like death warmed up.
Turned out that a couple of students had got themselves
all pissed up and laid into a third guy. They'd beaten
him to a pulp, so badly that he needed reconstructive
surgery. Welcome to Uppingham!

I might have been put off, but in truth Uppingham
was the polar opposite of that first experience. I loved
it, and I know how fortunate I am to have been given
the opportunity to go there. Fircroft was one of the
three 'hill houses', situated on one of the hills on
the outskirts of town. My house had ten boys from my

year, all from different prep schools around the country, but also much older guys, up to the age of eighteen. That was kind of intimidating, although it wasn't in my nature to *appear* intimidated. A kind description of the thirteen-year-old Harry Judd would be that I was a little over-confident. A more accurate description would be that I was a cocky little shit. I was cheeky. I was assertive. Anything I put my hand to, I reckoned I could do.

I was pretty popular at school – we always joke that I'd have got on with Danny, but not with Dougie, who by his own admission wasn't one of the cool kids. At least, I was popular until the end of my first year at Uppingham. I guess I just came across as being *too* confident. *Too* loud. Everybody turned on me. For the first time in my life I experienced bullying. Guys I'd been good friends with suddenly didn't want to be seen with me. I'd see them running away when I came into view, or pointedly choosing to sit at the other end of the table from me at lunch. Funny looks. Nasty comments. It got to the point where I wouldn't even want to walk past the beds of my former mates in the dorm because I knew I'd be asking for it.

At first I reacted to all this like my usual cocky self. 'Hey, guys, what's your problem?' But it didn't take long for me to be worn down by it. It spread from being just my close friends to being everyone in the year group. Only one guy stuck with me. His name was Ben, and to this day he's still one of my best friends. I remember asking him why everyone had turned on me. 'They're jealous, mate,' he said. 'It's just because you're so good at sport . . .' It was sweet of Ben to say that, but the real reason, I'm sure, was that I was just too cocky for my own good. I tried to put a brave face on it, but deep down I was badly hurt. Night-times were the worst, lying in bed, thinking of my friends at home, missing Mum and Dad and wishing that I could be anywhere else . . .

Thankfully, things changed when summer came around. It was all down to cricket. One week I scored 163 not out; the following week I made 180 not out. I was breaking school records and really starting to excel. One Saturday morning, my housemaster told me that one of the under-eighteen first team was ill, and would I like to take his place? That was my moment of glory: walking down to school in my cricket whites, knowing that everyone had heard the news that a fourteen-year-old second-year had been called up to the first team. I played for them for the rest of the term, and even ended up opening the batting. I was knocking out fifties on a regular basis, and I felt untouchable on the cricket pitch. Like I couldn't do anything wrong. It earned me a bit of respect around the school, and slowly my former friends started letting me back into their group. I went from being called Judd to being Juddy again – a sure sign that I was being accepted.

I'd learned a lesson that year. I was never going to be a shrinking violet, but I like to think I'd learned not to be quite so full of myself. Quite so cocky. My friendship issues resolved themselves, and I was totally happy for the rest of my time at Uppingham. Unfortunately, my cricketing career wasn't quite so solid. Just before the cricket season in my third year, I came down with glandular fever. (From kissing too many girls, obviously . . .) I had a shocking season as a result, and it was around then that the dreams I had of maybe one day playing cricket professionally were shattered. My confidence went completely, and although when my form returned, I knew I might score a couple of hundreds in a season, I also knew that there was a guy at Bedford School called Alastair Cook who was scoring ten hundreds in a season. I wasn't in that league.

But every cloud has a silver lining, because it was around that time that I first picked up a pair of drumsticks.

My musical career up until that point had been patchy. I got up to Grade 5 on the trumpet and played in school orchestras, and I reckon I could still crank out 'The Last Post', at least until it gets to the high notes. But I was never that into it. I gave up in my second year at Uppingham. I was always skipping my trumpet lessons, and it was such a waste of my parents' money. They didn't want me to quit, of course, but I managed to persuade them that I simply wasn't enjoying it.

About that time, though, I started getting into bands, and decided what I really wanted to play was the guitar. Of course, *everyone* wanted to play guitar, so I was only able to get a half-hour lesson on a Sunday afternoon, and even in that I didn't learn much more than 'Good King Wenceslas' and 'Twinkle Twinkle Little Star'. Nursery rhymes weren't exactly what I had in mind, so I gave that up too.

Soon, though, everyone in my year seemed to be in a

band. They had varying degrees of success and talent. Charlie from Busted was in the year above me; much later, word got around that a mate of his called Ollie Redmond was going to audition for a new band Busted's managers were putting together. I guess everyone thought they were in with a chance, just like Charlie. In the meantime, though, a couple of my friends – Josh and Tom, who played guitar and bass – had a little three-piece pop/punk band called Boy Genius, along with a drummer in the year above. When he left to join a different group they were bummed out at just having to jam together as a duo. I used to go and watch them sometimes, sitting at the drum kit down in the basement rehearsal rooms at school. It was there that the idea came to me. 'I should learn the drums!' I told them. 'Then I can join your band!'

I emailed the one guy in our year who played drums and asked him to give me a lesson. He taught me how to play a basic groove: bass drum on one and three, snare on two and four. Simple stuff, but I thought it was awesome. That one beat was enough to get anyone through a few punk songs, and enough to get me into my friends' band.

But then, as I do, I started to get a bit obsessed. I nicked the key to the school drum room with the best kit and stashed it in my blazer pocket so I could go and practise any time I wanted. I never went anywhere without my sticks. From that moment on, my whole life was about drumming and cricket – not that I was naturally nearly as good at the former as at the latter. I persuaded Mum and Dad to let me take drum lessons, which took me a good year of nagging after my abortive attempts at trumpet and guitar. My drum teacher was pretty cool. There were no grades or theory exercises or any of the boring stuff I didn't want to do. I just used to take in a bunch of CDs – Led Zeppelin, Red Hot Chili Peppers, Rage Against the Machine – and ask my teacher how to play the tunes I liked. I even talked Dad into buying me a second-hand drum kit. We drove to a service station near Leicester to meet the guy who was selling it. Turned out that there were some bits missing. There was no bass drum pedal, and the arms for one of the toms had gone walkabout. Small but important parts. Dad told this guy he'd pay him half now and half when he sent us the missing bits. He didn't look too sure, and I was so high about getting the kit that I tried to persuade Dad just to give him all the money. In the end he accepted half, and sure enough we never heard from him again – despite me calling him up on an almost daily basis, trying not to sound like I was fifteen years old while I threatened to sue him! I was left with a kit that I was so excited to own, but which I couldn't really play properly because it was incomplete. I knew nothing about the drums, really, so I didn't realize you could buy pedals and hardware separately, until my mum took me to a drum shop in Cambridge and got me all kitted out. I was away.

It was during one of the school holidays that my mate Josh made the trek down to London in an attempt to try and get his music career going. He eventually did. (He's now a songwriter for Alexandra Burke, among others.) Back then, he ended up playing for some guy called

Richard Rashman. Rashman told him he wasn't looking to take on any guitarists at that time, but that he did want a bass player and drummer for a new band he was putting together. Josh called me up. 'Mate, Busted's managers are looking for a drummer. You should go for it . . .'

I didn't really understand what he was on about. Why would *I* audition? I'd only been playing for eighteen months. The very thought made me feel sick with nerves. But then I put two and two together. This had to be the same band Charlie's mate Ollie Redmond was auditioning for. I was no prodigy, but I had decent coordination and a good sense of rhythm. Plenty of people had better chops than me, but I had a good ear and the stuff I could play, I could play quite well. I'd never have said it to anyone, but I was pretty sure I was a bit *better* than Ollie. So if he could audition, maybe I could too.

I decided to give it a go.

I had to get permission to come up to London on that Saturday morning, first from my parents, then from the school. My mum tells me now that she wasn't all that keen. What if I went to London and had my head filled with daft ideas of being a pop star when there were more important things like school and university to think about? 'For God's sake,' my dad told her, 'don't worry about it. Harry will *never* get into this band.'

My brother Thomas came with me on the train for moral support. It was a big deal, getting a train by ourselves, going to London. We really were just kids, and this was hardly the kind of thing we did every day. I remember sitting in that café, checking out the competition, and seeing a kid with spiky-blond hair standing at the front of the line with his mum. And when my brother and I eventually joined the queue, I remember an American guy – we didn't know at the time that this was Richard Rashman – came out of the building and walked down the line. The only people he stopped to speak to were me and the kid at the front.

Dougie: I kept my head down and let Rashman talk to my mum. My plan was to steer clear of talking to anyone who might ask me how old I was. Come to think of it, apart from my failed attempt to strike up a conversation with Harry, my plan was to steer clear of talking to anybody full stop. I tended to clam up in the company of strangers, and I don't think I'd ever spoken to a real-life American before. Except for Mickey Mouse in Disneyland, and I'm not sure that counts . . .

Harry: Rashman asked me if I could sing – I didn't know at the time that there was a kind of Beach Boys, four-part-harmony influence on the material Tom and Danny had been putting together, and he was on the lookout for musicians who had more than one string to their bow.

Tom: Rashman was like that. Always trying to find people who could play, sing, dance, do handstands . . .

Harry: I tried to sound as cool as possible. 'Yeah,' I lied, putting my abortive choir audition from my mind. 'I sing.'

My brother butted in: 'You know . . . he's more your . . . kind of . . . *backing* vocalist.'

And then Tom and Danny arrived, acoustic guitars in hand. I remember a ripple going through the queue: 'That's them. *That's them* . . .' Tom was wearing a long-sleeved stripy shirt and baggy pants with patches all over them, and half his head was shaved. Danny wore ripped black jeans and a T-shirt, and had spiky hair with a blond bit at the back. Epic moment, and talk about intimidating.

Tom: Intimidating for us, more like, walking past the queue feeling everyone's eyes on us and hearing them all whispering. I *hate* it when I know people are watching me. Maybe I'm in the wrong job. But I could see there was a good turnout, and I could tell at a glance from the way that some of them were dressed that they were on our wavelength. I remember seeing Dougie at the front of the queue and having pretty high hopes for him, and we knew in advance from the Uppingham grapevine that Charlie's mate Harry was coming along to the audition.

We'd sent down a bunch of forms on which the guys auditioning were to write their names, what instrument they played and a bit about themselves, as well as attach their photos. As soon as we saw these forms we could tell at a glance certain people who definitely wouldn't be suitable, but when we saw Harry's form we worked out that he must be Charlie's mate, and we already liked the look of Dougie. The hopefuls were divided into groups of five, and we started calling them in to the audition room itself. There was a drum kit and a bass guitar amp in the middle, with a video camera trained on them. Five empty chairs at the side and, in front of the kit and the amps, a long table for me, Danny, Fletch, Rashman and Louis Bloom from the record label. The first group of five to enter included Dougie.

Dougie: I was the first person in my group to stand up and audition. Nightmare. It meant I didn't know what to expect or what they'd ask me to do.

Fletch spoke first. 'OK, Dougie, why don't you tell us a bit about yourself?'

You know when your cheeks go numb with fear and you get that weird taste of anxiety in your mouth? You know when you're so nervous you feel like you're having an out-of-body experience? That was me. For a horrible moment I was an unpopular skateboarder again, being chased by forty scallies intent on killing me. I was absolutely bricking it, with all these adults looking at me as I lied to them about being sixteen, and muttered something about what school I went to. Other than that, I had nothing to say about myself.

Tom: Knowing Dougie as we do now, it must have been absolute torture for him. And that's what came across, so Fletch tried to move things swiftly on by asking him to play some bass for us.

Dougie: The bass was plugged into the biggest amp I'd

ever seen. I'd only ever had a tiny practice amp, so the big old Trace Elliot in the audition room was totally new to me. The strap on the bass was extra-high; I'd only ever played it really low, and now I couldn't even *look* cool. I was more highly strung than my instrument. Everything seemed to be happening in slo-mo . . .

'Can you play some pop?' Fletch asked.

Pop? I didn't *know* any pop. I'd planned to play some Blink stuff, a) because I thought it was really cool, and b) because it was super-simple, root notes only. What the hell was I going to do?

Hang on. The other day I'd been pissing about in my bedroom and had learned how to play the bass line to Michael Jackson's 'Billie Jean'. That would do . . .

I started playing. But I was only a couple of notes in when I remembered that actually I'd only *tried* to learn how to play it, but had got bored halfway in. All I really knew was the two-bar intro. Eight notes in all . . .

I played them. Then I played them again.

And again.

And again.

I must have played the two-bar intro to 'Billie Jean' for a full, excruciating minute, until . . .

Tom: Until we stopped him. I remember sitting there thinking, Er . . . when is this going to end? Is he going to move to the next part of the song? We had to put him out of his misery. 'OK, dude, that's enough!'

Dougie: Someone on the panel said, 'So, Dougie, can you sing and play the bass at the same time?'

I gave them a half-shrug. 'Well, I'll try . . .'

I'd written this song. It was called 'The Last Girl Story', all about being the last person alive and finding a letter. I thought it was completely epic (it was, in fact, completely crap), and I reckoned Tom and Danny would be totally blown away by the bass riff I'd come up with for it. I'd never heard them play, so I didn't know how good they were. In my mind, you had to be an adult to be a good musician. If you were a kid, like me, it automatically meant you'd be a bit rubbish. So why weren't they looking more impressed?

They stopped me quite soon into the song and I went to sit down again, completely crushed. Number two took the floor. He was a hundred times more confident than me. When he spoke about himself he even threw in a little joke. Damn! I should have done it more like that. And then he played some bass. He was literally up and down the fretboard, slapping the strings, playing all this amazing, funky stuff and looking pretty cool as he was doing it. I wanted to curl up into a little ball. I was way out of my league and felt like a total idiot for being there. The other three guys were drummers, and in all I reckon I was in that room for about half an hour with just one thought in my head: I'd totally blown it.

When I get nervous my whole body feels uncomfortable. I just want to unzip myself and jump out. I had that feeling then. Humiliated, like it was the most awful thing I'd ever done. When the audition was over, we were told to go and wait outside the room. I couldn't get out of there quick enough. I stood in the corridor, nervously talking to the really good bass player, waiting to be sent home any minute.

Tom: Back in the audition room, everybody was really disappointed. We'd had such high hopes for Dougie. He was so cool, with his blond spiky hair. He already looked like he was in our band (the same went for Harry when his turn came), and everyone had been praying that he was a great bass player.

Danny: Maybe, we told ourselves, Dougie had just been nervous. Maybe if we gave him a chance he'd settle into it and win us over. The other bass player was flash, but he didn't look very cool. He was over-confident, and somehow just didn't feel right.

Dougie: Rashman came out of the room and smiled at us all. 'OK,' he said. 'You, you and you . . .' He pointed at the three drummers. '. . . can go home, thank you very much for coming. You and you . . .' He pointed at me and the other bass player. 'We'd like you to stay.'

I thought he'd made a mistake. How the hell had I pulled *that* off? I felt a bit of confidence creep in. Maybe it was my kick-ass song that had done it! It sure as hell wasn't 'Billie Jean'.

Harry: For me, the audition process was a bit easier, although I don't think I was any less nervous than Dougie. I was in a group of five and one of the guys spent a fair bit of time telling me about all the flash things he could do on a drum kit. He went first, though, and didn't play that great, which gave me a bit of a boost. A couple of other guys took the floor. They were all really shy and lacking in confidence. As I watched them, I realized that I had nothing to lose, and that when my turn came around, I just had to sell myself.

They called me up. I think I did a pretty good job of hiding my nerves as I introduced myself, then I sat down at the drums and played. I was by no means the best drummer there, but I wasn't the worst either. One of the others was completely amazing, but he had long, greasy hair, a leather trench coat and looked at the floor all the time, so I knew I *looked* better than him even if I didn't sound better.

They'd asked everyone else in the audition whether they could sing. Everyone had said no. I decided I only had one shot at this, so when the question came I said yes.

'Do you know "Year 3000"?'

'Yeah . . .'

They sat me down in front of the camera with Danny, and I'm sure my vocal performance was the most cringeful thing I've ever done. I got all the lyrics wrong and most of the notes. But I'd given it a go, and, at the end of the audition, I was one of the guys they asked to stick around.

Dougie: For the second round of the audition, Fletch stood up. He started talking. 'This band,' he said, 'have been signed to a major record label. They're going to be on TV shows like *CD:UK* and *Top of the Pop*s . . .'

Harry: I looked around. There were only about ten other drummers recalled to the second audition. That meant I'd be able to tell everybody that I got down to the last ten of a band that was going to be on *CD:UK*. I was going to dine out on that story for the next five years at least . . .

Dougie: 'I want to give you a vibe of what the band's about,' Fletch told us. He played their demo over the PA system.

It was genius, like Green Day meets the Beach Boys. The moment I listened to that demo I got super-excited. I *had* to be in this band. But then we were called up to sing along with Danny. He started to play the guitar, and I swear I'd never heard *anybody* play as well as that – completely professional and completely better than I was. I sang along, feeling like I was outside of my body listening in, and not much liking what I heard.

Harry: When the auditions were over, Rashman and Fletch gave us the whole 'Don't call us, we'll call you' spiel. We went our separate ways. I didn't expect to hear from them again, but still: the last ten! How cool was I?

Back at school that Sunday evening I told everyone about it. 'They're the real deal, guys. They're going to be on *CD:UK* and everything.' And then I went back to my room and logged on to my email. There was a message in my inbox from Richard Rashman. Short and to the point. 'You're down to the last two.'

Oh . . . my . . . God . . .

I went absolutely mental.

Suddenly, there was a bit of a buzz all around school. It was the summer term. Exams were over and I had one more week of school left. The holidays arrived and the next week I was called to the final audition at John Henry's, a rehearsal studio in London.

I was up against a guy called Martin. Martin was a really great drummer, but I had an advantage over him. Before the audition, and without anybody else knowing, Richard Rashman had sent me the guys' four-track demo. I'd spent a week at home listening to it solidly, and loving what I heard. There had been plenty of kids at my school who were good – mostly classical – musicians. But I'd never heard anyone my age who could really sing like Tom and Danny clearly could. I was in awe of it all, and couldn't believe that I was potentially a part of this. I spent hours in our games room at home, where my kit was set up, trying to play along as best I could.

The audition lasted two days, during which time we concentrated on 'Surfer Babe' and 'That Girl'. 'Obviously' had a swing rhythm that I didn't really understand, so I couldn't play it, and it quickly became obvious that Martin was a much better drummer than me. He was a bit more serious, though, and straight-laced, so I knew I had that over him. I decided to play to my strengths and concentrate on getting along with everybody.

Danny: I didn't really get Harry's sense of humour, though. He and I came from such different backgrounds – me Northern working class, him a privileged public schoolboy. I'd never met anybody who oozed confidence like this guy, cracking jokes all the time that I didn't really understand. He was very sarcastic, and sarcasm was something I'd never come across before. My idea of funny was a lot simpler than Harry's, and although his witty, Uppingham banter soon got taken up by the band, at the time I thought he was . . . well . . . a bit of a dick.

Tom: I remember begging Richard not to make me share a hotel room with *either* of them in the InterContinental where we were staying that night. It would have been too awkward.

Harry: So I ended up sharing a room with Martin – a bit difficult, since we knew that only one of us would make the cut. That night the four of us played pool and went to the pub – it was local to the InterContinental, so the staff knew that Tom and Danny were underage and there was no chance of being served alcohol. At the end of the second day of auditioning, Fletch drove me and Martin to the train station. 'Well done, both of you,' he said. 'I guess this is a bit awkward. One of you is going to have a potential golden ticket to fame and success, and one of you is just going to go back to your normal life.' No messing around. Totally blunt. It was win or lose.

And then it was just me and Martin, standing outside King's Cross, wishing each other luck before going our separate ways.

Danny: Confession time: I was Team Martin. I wasn't really the type to think ahead, and was just looking at it from the point of view of who was the better drummer, whereas Tom, quite rightly, was remembering that we were choosing somebody who we'd hopefully be in a band with for ever . . .

Tom: It's true that Martin was the better drummer – we knew that already – but what impressed me about Harry was that he'd only been playing for just over a year, and he seemed keen to learn.

Harry: I had to wait a week before the phone call came. It was Fletch. And my God did he talk. I'd never come across anybody who could talk like him. He must have been on the phone for the best part of an hour, with me unable to get a word in. It's now known as being 'Fletched'. It would happen a lot over the next few years. The longer he talked, the surer I became that he was letting me down lightly. He kept telling me every-thing they'd had to take into consideration: how whoever they chose would have to be equipped to deal with life in the spotlight; how hard a decision it had been . . .
    'And so,' he finally said, 'to summarize . . .'
    I held my breath.
    '. . . that's why . . .'
    That's why what?
    '. . . we've come to the conclusion . . .'
    What conclusion?
    '. . . at the end of the day . . .'

Which way is it going to go . . . ?
'. . . to pick you to be in the band.'
Silence.

I exhaled very slowly.

I murmured some polite words of thanks, and tried to keep a lid on my excitement. But as soon as I'd put the phone down to him, I ran into the kitchen, screaming at my mum that I'd got into the band.

Moments later, I was on the phone again. All my close friends from school were together, on the bus going to the airport for a rugby tour of Australia. I shouted down the phone at them that I'd got into the band, and I heard the news being repeated: 'Juddy's got in the band . . . *Juddy's got in the band . . .*'

'So, what now?' my friend Browner asked me.

'That's it, mate. I'm leaving school. I'm not coming back.'

I'm not coming back. As I said it, I realized that from here on in, everything – *everything* – was going to change for me.

That night, my folks sat me down, their faces serious. They didn't know how to react – especially my dad, who had been so sure that nothing would ever come of all this. The bottom line, though, was that they didn't want me to do it. I needed to get my A levels, they said, then go to university and get a degree, or do an apprenticeship. My dad had worked in the City all his life, and I think he saw that as a future for me. In their eyes, I was throwing everything away – an expensive education, good prospects – in the hope that some unknown pop band might hit the big time.

They'd barely finished talking before I shook my head at them. 'You *have* to let me do this,' I told them. And when they were still reluctant, I became more stubborn. 'You can't stop me,' I said. 'You literally cannot stop me.' I suppose I could understand their concerns, but I knew I was doing the right thing. Even though I was just a naive seventeen-year-old, I'd heard the demo and I'd met Tom and Danny and seen how talented they were. It was completely obvious to me that they were going to be a success. 'I'm *going* to do it,' I said, 'and you *have* to support me.'

They could see I was serious and, thank God, backed down.

I went on holiday to Paxos the very next day with my mum, a friend of mine and his mum. Me and my mate talked about nothing except the band. Of course, every girl that crossed our path got told that I was in a signed band – I certainly wasn't above using my good fortune to boost my chances. There aren't many holidays, though, that you can't wait to get back from. That was one.

Dougie: An email from Richard Rashman dropped into my inbox the day after the audition too. It was back when everything on a computer took forever to load. I remember impatiently double-clicking on the message, trying to get it to open up quicker. Two hours later (or maybe it was two minutes), the email finally loaded.

It wasn't what I wanted to read.

This was a proper, serious act, Rashman explained to

me. I simply wasn't a good enough musician to be considered.

My heart sank. I'd offended them just by turning up. That's how talented I was.

I switched off the computer, ignored the bass propped up in the corner of my room, and started bawling my eyes out.

My mum came into the room and asked me what was up. I explained, and she put her arms round me. Then my dad came in and I told him why I was upset. He looked a bit confused. 'Well, what did you expect?' he said. 'Of *course* you're not good enough.'

Yeah, I thought, still on the edge of tears. What did I expect? Of course I wasn't good enough. End of story.

The Five-knuckle Shuffle

CHAPTER

4

Dougie: Looking back, Rashman's terse rejection email was a good thing, even though it didn't feel like it at the time. It made me get my arse in gear. The next day, once I'd got over the disappointment, I realized that if I really wanted to make it in a band, I would have to put in a hell of a sight more work on the bass. I could afford to pay for tuition with the money I was making from my lizards, so I booked in bass lessons every night and singing lessons twice a week. Then I emailed Rashman and told him what I'd done. I didn't expect anything to come of it, but he was a good contact, so I figured I should try to keep in touch.

To my surprise, Rashman emailed back. 'Keep me updated, Dougie,' he wrote.

I soon realized that playing bass wasn't the easy option I'd thought it would be. When you're playing guitar, your left hand occasionally gets to stay in the same position. On the bass it was all over the place. But I was determined to improve, so I practised as much as I could and started immersing myself in music a bit more challenging than the stuff I'd been listening to. I tried playing along to a Beatles record, and decided that Paul McCartney was the best bass player ever, and I did my best to accompany a Beach Boys CD too. Every now and then I'd send Rashman an email. After a few weeks, I had an email back. Rashman wanted me to meet him in his hotel. Maybe we could have a talk and I could play him some stuff without the stress of other people watching.

Tom: Danny and I had no idea that Rashman was in touch with Dougie. We'd already said no to him, and as far as we were concerned, Dougie was out of the picture.

Dougie: I arranged to go and see Rashman the following weekend. But that Friday, something happened that would change my family's life for ever.

I knew something was wrong the moment I got home from school. Various members of my extended family were at the house, and my cousins were all running around in the garden. There was nothing particularly strange about that, but normally we'd all meet up on a Tuesday, not a Friday. I couldn't understand what they were doing there.

I walked into the kitchen. My aunt was there. As soon as she saw me she started talking. 'OK, Dougie, now I don't want you to worry, but . . . one of your baby lizards has been killed.'

I blinked. If you have thirty baby lizards, as I did at the time, chances are one or two of them are going to die. It was totally normal. Surely half the family hadn't turned up for a dead lizard?

'Oh,' I said, totally confused. 'How?'

'Squashed,' she said.

I wandered out of the kitchen and into the front room. My mum was there. She was surrounded by family members, and she was crying. I was so confused. It was only a lizard. I had another twenty-nine of the fellas in my bedroom. Why was she so upset? Mum tried to say something, but she could barely speak through her tears, and I couldn't understand it.

She pointed at something on the side. I looked over and, sure enough, saw a dead lizard lying there. It took a few seconds, though, for me to twig that she wasn't pointing at the lizard at all. She was pointing at the letter lying next to it. It was a single sheet of A5 paper, with a note from my dad scrawled on one side. I didn't read it properly. Just skimmed it. I only remember a single phrase: 'I can't do this any more.'

He'd left us. He didn't want anything to do with my mum, my little sister Jasmine or me. He wasn't coming back.

It was a bolt from the blue. I'd always gone through life knowing that my parents would never split up. Up until that moment there had been no hint that anything was wrong. I'd never heard any arguments, never seen any sign that Dad wasn't happy. I found out later that he moved in with another woman. I don't know for sure if he'd been having an affair – if he was then he must've been bloody good at hiding it as none of us even suspected it. And now, in the space of a moment, we'd gone from being a proper family to being just me, my mum and my sister.

Everything seemed to be going wrong in my life. I'd

failed to get into the band, and now my dad had walked out on us. I felt like my whole view of the world had suddenly shifted. Mum made it clear that night that Dad wasn't coming back to see me and Jasmine. He'd always been the breadwinner, so now money was going to be tight. I decided there and then that I needed to stop squandering my money on all these bass and singing lessons. The cash I made from selling lizards would have to go towards supporting our little family. I had to let go of this stupid fantasy I had of making it some day. I had to grow up.

I still had this appointment to meet Richard Rashman in London the following day. Getting into town was a massive deal for me. I certainly couldn't go by myself, and my mum was clearly in no fit state to take me. I told her not to worry about it, and it was sort of a relief to have an excuse not to get stressed about being in a band. But my uncle was around and told me I should go through with the meeting, and that he would take me into London. I still wasn't sure, but reluctantly agreed.

The shower broke that night. My mum, my sister and I stared at it, wondering what the hell we were supposed to do now that Dad wasn't around to fix things for us. The whole house had a totally different vibe about it. It was quieter. Darker, somehow. Strange. I went to bed with the unnerving feeling that my childhood had just finished.

We got the Tube into town the following day. I took my bass and my acoustic guitar and we headed for the InterContinental in Hyde Park. I'd never seen a hotel like this before: marble floors, chandeliers, old school and grand. No broken showers here. To me it looked more like a film set than a real hotel, and as I walked into the reception area, I felt like Macaulay Culkin in *Home Alone 2*. Things only seemed weirder once my uncle had left me with Rashman, this strange man he'd never met before, although my uncle *had* programmed his own number into my mobile phone. 'If he touches you,' he said, 'hold down number two. It'll call me and I'll be right there . . .'

There was no touching, of course. We sat in Rashman's suite, just chatting for a while, and I started to relax a bit. I played him a couple of songs – this was before I knew how to play chords on the guitar, so I just used it to pick out root notes like a bass guitar. Rashman explained to me where I'd gone wrong in the McFly audition, and showed me Tom's and Charlie's audition tapes for Busted – cool for me, because Busted were massive at the time.

I was full of questions about Tom and Danny. How good were they? How long had they been playing for? Rashman explained how Tom had been on the stage in the West End in *Oliver!* and how Danny had been play-ing guitar since he was six. That made me feel like I had a long way to go musically, but Rashman told me that I also had to work on my confidence. My presentation. It was little things. In my part of Essex, nobody ever shakes hands. You just nod and say, 'All right?' Richard thought that was very weird, so he made me practise knocking on his door and greeting him properly. 'Hi, I'm Dougie Poynter!' Not exactly what I'd expected . . .

Finally he played me some more McFly demos. 'Now listen, Dougie,' he said slowly. 'I'm going to do something I'm not really supposed to do. I could get into a lot of trouble for doing this. I'm going to give you one of these CDs, and I want you to go away and learn it. And I think that if we haven't found a bass player soon, we'll ask you back to come and do another audition. OK?'

OK. Apart from feeling sick with nerves all over again.

Having that CD at home to listen and practise to was a welcome distraction from what was going on in my family's life. It kept my mind off my mum being so upset, and helped me shut out what was really happening. In any case, all of a sudden I was on a mission. I thought the songs on that disc – 'That Girl', 'Obviously', 'Surfer Girl' and 'Memory Lane' (it was the same demo that Tom and Danny had played to all the record labels) – were *hard*, so I paid for more lessons and took it along to my bass teacher, who helped me work out the lines. Apart from that, I barely stepped out of my room. Partly I didn't want to go out much because I felt guilty about leaving my mum and sister alone in the house; partly, of course, I knew I might have a second chance. I practised all day, every day. I got up early and practised before I went to school. At night I practised until I fell asleep. I might even have taken advantage of my mum in her fragile state: 'I can't go to school today, Mum. I'm just, like, too depressed . . .' And so I had a couple of days off school so I could carry on practising. After days and days of this, I still sucked at 'Memory Lane', but I just about knew my way around the other three by the time I received another email from Rashman. He explained that they had another bass player under consideration, but they wanted me to come down to a rehearsal studio in London and have a go at playing along with the guys.

Oh no. Not this again.

'And by the way,' he added at the end of the email. 'The band's called McFly.'

Oh my God, THAT'S SO COOL! I started practising even harder, and praying that nobody would ask too many questions about how old I really was.

Tom: We still had no idea that Rashman was in touch with Dougie. All we knew was that he and Fletch had put aside a week in a rehearsal room so that we could continue auditioning new guys. We had a number of possibilities lined up, and this time we spent more time with them individually, teaching them our songs and giving them a bit more of a chance than we had during the previous round.

Danny: We got all sorts. One goth guy turned up wearing a pair of steampunk goggles, leather boots and leather trousers – me, Tom and Harry got the giggles the moment he walked in and started trying to sing Beach Boys harmonies. He was the least appropriate of the guys we saw, but nobody was right, with the possible exception of one bloke. Good bassist, and he seemed a cool guy. It seems a bit unfair to tell you his real name or what he looks like, so to save his blushes let's pretend he was called Vladimir and that he was a midget with a pudding-bowl haircut. Which he wasn't.

Maybe Vladimir could fit in. Rashman, however, had

another suggestion. 'I think you should take another look at Dougie,' he told us.

We'd pretty much forgotten what Dougie looked like, but the moment he walked into the rehearsal room it was immediately obvious that he was just a bit cooler than Vlad. What was more, Vlad didn't have the advantage of having been given the demo by Richard, and taking it to his bass teacher every night. So it was that we found ourselves going through the same process with Dougie and Vlad as we had with Harry and Martin. A two-day audition, with us all staying at the InterContinental.

Tom: I shared a room with Vlad. He didn't do himself any favours. I was woken up at two o'clock in the morning by a regular slapping sound. I rolled over in my bed to see my room-mate, lying on his bed with his knees up, 'pleasuring' himself. I could hardly look him in the eye the next morning. I thought of all the times I'd shared a room with Danny. We'd *never* have done that.

Danny: At the very least we'd have nipped into the bathroom. ☺

Harry: Danny and I shared with Dougie. There was no way *he* was going to be bold enough to knock one off the wrist. He was hardly bold enough to speak. We tried to get him to open up a bit, asking him all the usual questions. 'When's your birthday?' 'What's your star sign?' This last question seemed to stump him. He shrugged, said 'Dunno', and went quiet again.

Odd, Danny and I thought, that someone shouldn't know their own star sign . . .

Dougie: What they didn't know was how much I was panicking inside. I hadn't wanted to lie too much about my age by making myself a whole year older. Instead, I'd shifted my birthday enough that they'd think I'd just turned sixteen. It hadn't even occurred to me to check the corresponding star sign. I had to plead ignorance and hope that they wouldn't twig.

I had chosen my clothes for that final audition very carefully. Jeans and a black T-shirt. Black would make me look a bit more serious, I thought. Like I meant business. And I was starting to think that maybe, just *maybe*, I was in with a chance. My bed in that hotel room was the biggest I'd ever seen. I was a whisker away from a lifestyle totally alien to the one I knew. And when it came to auditioning with the guys, I found, thanks to Rashman's timely intervention with the demo tape, that I could actually play the songs.

Back at the hotel, the guys wanted to have a band meeting, so Vlad suggested that he and I took a walk around Hyde Park. As we walked, we started confiding in each other a little bit. Vlad confessed to me that he wasn't massively into the music we were rehearsing. One secret deserved another. 'Dude,' I said. 'I'm only fifteen!'

Vlad's eyes widened. 'No *way*!' We high-fived, and I remember feeling sure that my secret was safe with him, as we were both in the same boat. Of course, he was the worst person I could have told . . .

Harry: We were deep in discussion back at the hotel. Just like Danny had been Team Martin, I was Team Vlad. After all, Dougie *didn't talk*! He'd barely said a word for two days. It wasn't like we hadn't tried to engage him in conversation, but he was monosyllabic, like Garth in *Wayne's World*. Talk about a bad call . . .

Tom: I was Team Dougie. There wasn't much to choose between his and Vlad's bass playing, but I knew who I'd rather share a room with. Don't get me wrong. I'm not saying Dougie got in the band *because* his rival had been doing the five-knuckle shuffle in the bed next to me, but it didn't do Vlad any favours.

Danny: Personally, whatever Vlad had been doing, I was in two minds. That's me through and through – always needing a bit of help when it comes to making big decisions.

Tom: Rashman, though, was desperate to have Dougie. As we sat in the hotel with him and Fletch, he showed us a video he'd asked Dougie to send him of his band playing a little gig back home. It was that video that tipped it. We pretty much decided there and then that Dougie was our man.

Dougie: The audition came to an end. We went our separate ways. And after all the help Rashman had given me, I figured that he would be the one to ring me at home and give me the news. I was in my bedroom when I took the call. When he told me I was in, I felt numb. I walked like a zombie into the living room where my mum was sitting by herself, staring miserably into space.

'Mum?'

She looked up at me.

'I got in the band. I'm leaving home.'

'*What?*'

'I've got to leave home. It's part of the deal.' A pause. 'Can I do it?'

In some ways it wasn't as big a decision for my mum as it was for Harry's parents. In other ways it was huge. I hated school, and I sucked at it. It wasn't like I was going to go on to have a high-flying job in the City. I wouldn't have the chance to do anything *remotely* this exciting. I could join a band, make some money and play sold-out concerts; or I could stay at school until I was old enough to get a job at Tesco. On the other hand, I was leaving home weeks after my dad had done the same. It was difficult, I think, for Mum to let me go, but it wasn't like I was disappearing to join some bunch of guys who were never going to make it. The band had half a million pounds in the bank already; they were signed to Universal; their managers managed Busted. I don't think there was any doubt in her mind that this was an amazing opportunity that I had to follow up.

Danny: At the same time, Vlad took a call from Fletch, thanking him very much for auditioning but explaining that we'd opted for Dougie. That was when Vlad decided to play his last card and grass Dougie up for only being fifteen. Talk about backfiring. His strategy ensured that we liked him a little less, and Dougie a little more. Dougie had tried so hard to get in the band, even to the extent of lying about his age, that we knew he was our guy.

And Vlad? Weirdly, he ended up working at one of the record companies. It was a bit awkward when we saw him, but he didn't stay there long. Perhaps they caught him wanking at his desk. Who knows?

Tom: And so, finally, we were a band. I had just turned eighteen. Danny and Harry were seventeen. Dougie was fifteen. Four young guys, completely unknown but with the feeling that something amazing was just around the corner. It doesn't take much to imagine how exciting that time was, and our management knew that they needed to keep us firmly on the straight and narrow. Not that I had any plans to mess things up. I'd been close to Busted, and I'd seen how, from the beginning, Matt and Charlie had devoted themselves to the party side of being in a band. James, on the other hand, was more aware of the amazing opportunity he'd been given to make a career out of his music. He was far more passionate about songwriting than about partying. Maybe that was the reason why he and I had such a great relationship, because I was just the same. I'd never done drugs. I'd never even *met* anyone who'd done them. I might have got pissed once or twice growing up, but I'd never rebelled against my parents in any way. I was a regular goody two-shoes.

Harry: Our management were keen to ensure that the rest of us were the same as Tom. For Fletch and Richard, Busted were a bit like guinea pigs for how they would manage McFly. Busted had their problems. They didn't always see eye to eye, and weren't the close-knit unit that we would eventually become. Whether or not Fletch and Richard thought this was anything to do with their rock 'n' roll lifestyle, I don't know. But once Matt and Charlie started going down that road, it was already out of their management's control. I think they'd learned from that, and from day one our managers were a hell of a sight tougher with McFly than they ever were with Busted.

Danny: There was a real hierarchy between us and the management. They were a mixture of parents and bosses, and we were a bit scared of them. The rules were the rules. You can't drink. You can't smoke. You can't go out late. You can't have girlfriends.

Harry: So there we were: four young guys, in a band, money in our pocket and fame just around the corner. Obviously, we'd be following our management's instructions to the letter, right?

Wrong.

The Grass Isn't Always Greener

CHAPTER

5

Tom: On and off throughout that summer, Danny and I had been staying at Princess Park Manor with James Bourne. Busted were there; V were there; our management were there. Great in some ways, less great in others. Even before Harry and Dougie were on board we knew that, like Busted, our band was going to live together in one house, but we weren't sure that we wanted to be in such close contact with all these other guys. It would be cooler to have our own space. And so, once we'd hired Harry and he was taking his holiday in Paxos, Danny and I went house-hunting.

We had a long list of potential houses to see, the first of which was a place in Whetstone, just ten minutes round the corner from Princess Park Manor. The moment we stepped inside it, we knew we didn't have to look at any others.

1526 High Road was, quite simply, the biggest house we'd ever seen. Both of us had grown up in small houses, and neither of our families had had a load of money swilling around. Now though, thanks to our record deal, we had some cash to play with. As we looked round 1526, our eyes popped out of our heads. There were five bedrooms, super-high ceilings, an amazing patio – for a bunch of guys living by themselves, it couldn't have been better. The master bedroom was massive, with walk-in wardrobes and an en suite bathroom; in the loft there was a slightly quirkier room with its own balcony. Having decided pretty much on the spot that this was going to be our band house, Danny and I played paper, scissors, stone to decide who got which room – Danny won the master bedroom, I got the loft – and we left the slightly smaller rooms for Harry and whoever was going to end up playing bass for us. I had a crappy old white Fiat Punto, which I crammed full of all our stuff, and together we moved in.

We needed to furnish the house. Chintzy sofas and mahogany dining tables? No way. I bought myself a bed with a mattress made out of material developed by NASA – for a space geek like me that was about the most awesome thing I could spend my money on – and we chose the biggest flat-screen TV we could find. When Harry got back from holiday, he joined us and we spent a couple of weeks attending to the really important aspects of being in a band, like signing up for a Blockbuster account, and lounging around this palatial house, watching DVDs and generally chilling out and getting to know each other properly.

Harry: The night I moved into the band house, we stayed up till the small hours, dicking about like children. We had pillow fights and played hide and seek. We'd pretend that we wanted to go to sleep, then two of us would creep into the third guy's room and scare the crap out of him. Stupid, stupid behaviour, but hilarious.

What Tom didn't realize, though, was that I fully expected being in a band to involve a bit more than pillow fights and silly games. And I had a feeling Danny felt the same.

Danny: I still didn't quite *get* Harry. He was always cracking these jokes that I didn't really understand. I still didn't get his sarcasm or his public-school sense of humour. I didn't get how he could be so confident. But we soon realized we had a lot more in common than we thought. We were both into sport, for example. And growing up, we'd both been a bit more rebellious than Tom – drinking and smoking, things that he'd never have dreamed of doing. I'd tried a cigarette when I was about thirteen. That was the norm where I was from. There wasn't much to do in Bromley Cross, so a lot of our time used to be spent hanging out in the local park drinking bottles of orange WKD that we'd persuaded older kids to buy for us.

Harry: And although Uppingham and Bromley Cross were poles apart, my friends and I had toyed around with alcohol and weed, so that was something I had in common with Danny that I didn't with Tom. One of the unique things about our band, and it was like this from day one, is that we all have very good, but totally individual, relationships with each other. It would have been natural, after I'd moved into the band house, for me to feel like an outsider with these two guys who'd known each other for ages. I never did.

We were young and hadn't worked out for ourselves

that smoking weed wasn't classy or cool. So it was that I broached the subject with Danny. 'Dude, do you smoke?'

Danny nodded. 'A little bit,' he admitted.

'Do you want to, maybe, do some?' I had a big lump of resin sitting in my wash bag, after all.

Danny: I was up for it, but with one proviso. 'Dude, you *cannot* tell Tom.' I'd spent enough time with Tom to know he'd be totally against it, and that if one thing was going to disrupt our fledgling band, it was this.

Tom: He was right to think that. Drugs, for me, were a *big* deal. It was black and white. All drugs were bad. There was no difference between weed and heroin, between a joint and a crack pipe.

Harry: Danny's warning held some weight. It wasn't that we were scared of Tom, exactly, but there was no doubt that he was the leader of our band. He was older than us, but more to the point he was the foundation around which McFly had been built. He called the shots, not just in the rehearsal room but in the band house too. I'd managed to get myself into the band, and I didn't want to mess it all up by pissing the main guy off.

But I *did* like my weed. I *was* young. I *did* want to have some fun . . .

And so, come three o'clock in the morning on that first night, after we'd been playing our stupid game of trying to scare each other for a couple of hours, I decided that the time had come for a crafty joint.

I sidled up to Danny. 'Dude, let's *really* leave Tom to go to bed now, so we can go for a smoke.'

We called it a night and went to our rooms. I fished the lump of resin out of my wash bag, rolled a nice fat joint and waited for the band house to fall fully quiet. Fifteen minutes later, I met Danny down by the side of the house to spark up.

We should probably have realized, I suppose, that Tom thought we were still playing the game.

Tom: I had no idea what they were really doing, but I decided it would be a very good idea to scare three kinds of crap out of Harry. I went and hid inside the cupboard in his bedroom. Any minute now, I thought to myself, he's going to come back to bed and I'll jump out screaming and scare the living daylights out of him. I crouched uncomfortably in that cupboard for ages, giggling to myself at the thought of my hilarious practical joke.

Five minutes passed.

Ten.

No sign of Harry. Where the hell was he?

Harry: I was staggering into the kitchen with Danny, stumbling over things, finding the noise hilarious, quickly shushing both of us, then cracking up again. We sat down at the table, eyes like saucers, stoned out of our tiny minds.

Tom: I heard a noise downstairs. They were still up! Right . . .

I sneaked out of Harry's cupboard, crept down the stairs and, avoiding the kitchen, slipped outside. I tiptoed round the side of the house until I was outside the kitchen window, and . . . BANG! I suddenly thumped on the glass.

Danny: We yelled. We jumped out of our skin, gibbering with weed-induced paranoia. And then Tom was in the kitchen with us, laughing his arse off. We were completely stoned, but we had to pretend to be sober because if Tom knew what we'd been doing, the shit would have hit the fan big time.

Tom: I wouldn't have known anyway. It wasn't just that I'd never been stoned, I'd never even *met* anyone who was stoned before. I just thought: Boy, they look tired! I went to bed none the wiser, totally unaware that with the arrival of Harry, McFly was no longer quite the clean-living band I'd always thought it would be.

Danny: We lived in the band house all the while we were searching for a new bass player, only decamping to the InterContinental for the auditions because we didn't want anybody staying in the band house unless they were actually *in* the band. Once we'd recruited Dougie, and the day came for him to move in with us, we all piled into Fletch's people carrier, went to pick him up from the station, and decided to have a bit of fun with him.

Dougie: I had nothing but an overnight bag, and after

I'd climbed into the car, we drove off. The guys had already told me what an amazing place they'd rented, and how much fun we were going to have there, but I didn't really know what to expect. We started driving through some dodgy parts of town, before pulling up in front of a rundown old tower block. 'There you go, Dougie,' said Fletch. 'This is it.'

Talk about a practical joke backfiring. It looked absolutely fine to me. I was Dougie Poynter, not Robbie Williams. Why *wouldn't* I be living in some tower block? I was climbing out of the car and making my way towards the entrance before they told me they were winding me up. I shrugged, a bit bemused, and got back in the car.

And *then* they took me to the real place.

Just like the others, I'd never even seen a house like it. I'd never seen ceilings that high, or a flat-screen TV that big. 'Sorry, mate,' the guys told me, 'you've got a crap bedroom.' I went to look – the one I chose was still eight times bigger than the room I was used to at home, and it would end up being the room we'd hang out in the most.

The following weekend I moved the rest of my stuff in. It fitted in a single box: a few clothes, some CDs and a handful of videos.

Tom: As soon as I saw that Dougie and I had the same *Star Wars* box set, I knew we'd get on. Did I mention that I'm a geek? We didn't get much chance to bond over our shared love of science fiction, though, because soon after Dougie moved in, Danny and I had arranged to go on holiday with James Bourne to Florida. For a while there was talk of Harry and Dougie joining us, but in the end the decision was made that they should stay in London and rehearse the songs that Danny and I had lived with for so long, while we headed to Walt Disney World. Sorry, guys.

Harry: We holed ourselves up in our rehearsal room with a session bass player called Ben Sergeant and for two weeks we practised the songs we found most difficult – especially the groove to 'Obviously' that seemed to elude both of us. Ben kept telling us to think about the vibe of the piece, the *feel*. I'm not sure we really knew what he was talking about, but slowly it started to come together. And it was during a break from practising that Dougie ran into the rehearsal room, his eyes shining. 'Mate,' he said. 'Guess who's downstairs. *Blink!*'

Dougie: My heroes were in the same rehearsal studios, practising for the Reading Festival. We hung around outside their room like the couple of fanboys that we were, hoping that we might get to speak to them. And we did. I can still recall that conversation with Mark Hoppus like it was yesterday. I tried to sound so laid-back as I squeaked at him that we were on the same label – like I thought that being in a signed band was the most natural thing in the world – and did what I could not to seem star-struck. But I was. Already, being in a band was as cool as I'd hoped it might be.

In the beginning, there were Tom Fletcher and Danny Jones.

Above: Fletch (*left*) and Richard Rashman (*right*) – McFly's secret ingredients.
Left: Although Tom didn't make it into Busted, he and James Bourne loved writing songs together – and being fellow geeks!

Dougie was only fifteen when he joined the band – it was Harry who taught him how to shave during their days in the band house.

The McFly band house was the coolest place for four young guys to live. Check out the 'babe wave' on the arch. Dougie's room was the smallest but the guys ended up hanging out there all the time (*below*).

In 2005, 'All About You' was the Comic Relief single and the band travelled to Uganda to make a film for the charity. It was an eye-opening and emotional trip that had a lasting effect – especially for Tom, who shouldn't have eaten that watermelon . . .

Above: The set for the 'Five Colours In Her Hair' video shoot. 'Man, we cringed at that video.'

Below: Celebrations as McFly hear the news that 'Five Colours' had hit the number one spot.

And 2005 just got better and better. McFly celebrate their BRIT award for Best Pop Act and, *right*, Billie from Green Day sets about pouring champagne down Harry's gullet. **Below:** Playing with Brian May was a career highlight for the band.

McFly in movieland. *Just My Luck* wasn't a huge critical success but Harry, Dougie, Danny and Tom had a riot making it. And a certain young starlet took a shine to Mr Judd . . .

Harry: And it was cool in other ways, too. I only had the crappy drum kit my dad had bought from that bloke in the service station, so while Tom and Danny were in Florida, Dougie and I made our way to Wembley Drum Centre and bought the best kit in the shop, and a whole bunch of cymbals. We set it up back at the band house, and it was pretty sweet going from nothing to having the best gear in town.

Dougie: I went to Denmark Street. It's full of music shops, and a Mecca for guitarists in London. I'd been there before, just to ogle the instruments, but they'd all been way too expensive. Out of the league of a kid buying equipment on the back of flogging lizards. But not any more. I bought myself a beautiful blue Fender bass that I thought was just about the hippest thing I'd ever seen.

Harry: And back at the band house, it was party time. I had different mates round every night, and I'd discovered that Dougie, too, was happy to join me in a smoke. I read him the riot act: 'Dude, you *can't* tell Tom . . . Danny said he'd go crazy . . .'

Once the others were back from Florida, we were super-careful to hide our habit from Tom. But as the weeks passed, we grew a bit sloppy. We started smoking by the open window in Dougie's room, feeling a bit bummed out that Tom wasn't into it and that we had to hide what we were doing. We were having so much fun getting stoned, and it sucked having to be so secretive.

Tom: I might have been naive, but it didn't take more than a few weeks for me to work out that something was going on, especially given that the whole house stank of cannabis. Not that I knew what the smell was, of course, but when I started to suspect that the guys were doing something they shouldn't be, I was ten times more alert to the little telltale signs. Why were they so obviously waiting for me to go to bed? Why did I suddenly feel a bit left out? And as Harry and Dougie were getting sloppier and sloppier at keeping things secret, I soon twigged what was happening.

I spoke to Danny about it first. 'Mate, I think Harry and Dougie might be doing drugs.'

He nodded, all wide-eyed innocence. 'Yeah, I know . . . shocker.'

The penny dropped. I sat in my room and burst into tears. Our band had barely begun, and already our drummer and bass player were a couple of drug fiends! What would our management say if they found out? What would my *parents* say? Even worse than that, I was worried what would happen if the public found out. We were still unknown, but I knew that it was just a matter of weeks before we would be catapulted into the public eye. If it leaked out that half our band was doing drugs, our career would be over before it had even started. I'd been around Busted. I knew what a big deal this stuff was in the world of pop. I'd seen artists carelessly admitting to smoking a bit of pot back in the day, and having to do huge anti-drug campaigns to save their careers. I bawled my eyes out that night as I battled with the suspicion that everything was already coming to an end.

What could I do? Talk to our management? No way. They'd do their nut, and in any case that would make me feel like I was betraying my new friends – like a kid telling the teacher and getting them into trouble. Speak to my mum and dad? They had enough stress on their plate without worrying that I'd moved in with a bunch of stoners. In the end I decided I had to confront them. Lay down the law. Make sure that if they were going to do this, they did it in such a way that it wouldn't compromise everything.

Harry: It was in the kitchen that Tom confronted us. We didn't try to deny it. He gave us a set of rules.

> 1) You're only allowed to smoke on Saturdays.
> 2) You're only allowed to smoke after 11 p.m.
> 3) You're only allowed to smoke outside.

Tom: I started acting a bit like a manager myself, trying to manage the situation so that our *real* managers wouldn't find out. You could smell the weed whenever the guys were smoking it, and I was paranoid that Richard or Fletch might come round, or my parents drop by unannounced, while the chuckle brothers would be skinning up in Dougie's room and the stench of whatever skunk Harry had picked up would be creeping downstairs. If I could limit it to Saturday nights, outside, then at least I could avoid the possibility of that happening. And maybe, if they were only smoking once a week, they'd lose interest after a bit.

Yeah, right . . .

Harry: I remember thinking, OK, this is completely fair. Tom's being absolutely reasonable. It's not cool that we've just joined this band and we're suddenly acting all irresponsible. Tom's the boss. He sets the rules, and we ought to abide by them. But the devil on my shoulder was *so* pissed off. We were young, we were in a band. Smoking a few joints was totally harmless, or so we thought. We weren't hurting anybody. Nobody needed to find out. Why the hell *shouldn't* we enjoy ourselves?
Dougie: We accepted Tom's rules. At least, we pretended to accept them. But the very next night we were on tenterhooks waiting for him to go to bed. As soon as he did, we arranged a rendezvous in Harry's room to have a smoke in fifteen minutes. I reckon I managed about five.

'Dude, is it fifteen minutes?'

'Not *yet*, Dougie! Get back to bed!'

We broke Tom's rules that very first night. No comeback, so the following night we fully intended to do the same. Danny was otherwise engaged with some girl in his room and this time, we arranged to meet at my place – a bit safer, because I had a lock on my door – to have a joint by my open window. We couldn't have been much less subtle – the stuff we were smoking absolutely stank, and Tom's room was right above mine. But we were too up for it. We couldn't stop ourselves.

We were halfway through our first joint when we heard Tom's footsteps coming down the stairs.

'Shhhh . . . *Shhhh!*'

The footsteps approached my door.

Silence.

And then a piece of A4 paper appeared under my door.

Neither of us said a word as I crept over and picked it up. It was a drawing of two stick men, each with a massive joint in their hand. And written underneath were the words 'Rule Breakers'.

Harry: Weed can make you paranoid. It can make you scared. Man, were we scared when we saw that drawing. We'd *really* pissed Tom off now. We'd broken the band rules immediately. What were we going to do?

Tom: I thought that at least they'd open the door to me, but it remained firmly locked. What they didn't realize was that I didn't much care about them smoking just then. I was bummed out for other reasons.

That night, I'd been out with James Bourne. All was not well in the Busted camp. There had been debates with Richard and Fletch – differences that were all cleared up in the end – but at the time James was freaked out. 'You four,' he'd told me, 'you've got to stick together. You've got to forget about the managers, and be a team . . .'

I came home with my head spinning. Fletch and Rashman were integral to everything we were doing. Sidelining them would have been almost impossible. I needed to speak to the guys about it. So after I'd posted them my silly drawing, I knocked on the door and asked to be let in.

I sat on the bed and explained everything James had said. My stoned bandmates looked as bummed out about what they heard as I did, and as I sat there, James's words kept going round my head. *You four, you've got to stick together . . .*

Clearly Harry and Dougie weren't going to stop smoking. They'd proved that already. But bands had split up for less. I didn't want to be constantly worrying that they wanted to get rid of me so they could go and skin up. I didn't want them to think that I was just there to stop them having fun. I didn't want to be a killjoy. So I came to a decision there and then: if you can't beat them, join them.

I'd never even smoked a cigarette before. I was as clean-living as they came. That night I sat with Harry and Dougie and joined in my bandmates' nightly pursuit for the first time.

Dougie: We turned our place from being a big family home into the coolest house for four guys to live in. It was every kid's idea of a dream home. We cut out pictures of hot girls and stuck them on the archway that went into the living room – we called it our 'babe wave'. We had a cupboard full of DVDs, and fairy lights hanging all around the place. When Christmas came, we filled the house with decorations, and then never took them down. We had all this money to live on, and all we had to spend it on was weed and toys. For the first time ever we didn't have to worry about having enough cash, so we decked out our rooms with all the coolest things we could find.

Tom: There was, of course, also the small matter of music to attend to. We were due to start recording our album at the beginning of December. So from the end of August, all through September, October and November, our days were spent in the rehearsal studio. We practised our songs day in, day out, playing through them again and again . . .

Danny: And again . . .

Harry: And again . . .

Dougie: And again . . .

Tom: . . . and while we were in rehearsal, the process started of getting word out to the media about McFly. Key people would come down to meet us. All of a sudden we had to get used to journalists and TV interviewers, and to the strange business of people taking an interest in us. I think we took to it fairly naturally. We didn't work too hard to impress. We tried to be ourselves, dicking around in the studios and cracking stupid jokes.

Dougie: Sometimes Fletch would try to direct us to act in a certain way, or to say certain things, but that always came across a bit cringeful. We discovered early on that the more we could be ourselves, the better impression we made.

Tom: It was around this time that Giovanna and I finally got together properly. This time it was for real. We weren't kids at school, and we didn't live with our parents any more. More to the point, we'd experienced life without each other for a couple of years and we both knew we were meant to be together. It was our density, as George McFly would say. In the first few years of the band, I spent every moment that I wasn't working with her. She had a flat in Sidcup where she was studying acting, and it would become the perfect escape from how mental our world was. I'd drive over there in the early hours of the morning and, while she went off to college in the day, I'd stay in her flat and watch movies, or put on a hat so that I was semi-disguised and wander around Bluewater shopping centre on weekdays when it was empty.

Management had made it very clear to us, however, that *our* house was a work house. A business. We weren't allowed girls over. It wasn't a place to invite our friends. It wasn't a place for parties. If Giovanna was round, she'd nip out in the car to Tesco, or wait outside on my balcony, or even hide in the toilet, if we thought Fletch was coming around. We were that scared of him and Rashman.

While our night-times in those early months might have been lost to a fog of smoke, we did work hard in the daytime, practising our songs, and, when December came round, recording our album.

Harry: The recording process was more intense for Tom and Danny than it was for me and Dougie. We weren't like some indie band that could get away with sounding a bit rough around the edges. The tunes that would go to make up *Room On The Third Floor* needed to sound crisp and clean. Proper pop. I'd been playing drums for less than two years, and to a click track for only one of those. I could just about manage to get down the drum tracks for 'Surfer Babe' and 'That Girl', but the rest of the songs on the album were recorded by a great session drummer called Ian Thomas.

Dougie: Same went for the bass. I'd been working hard on the McFly songs, but playing in a studio is a lot different to playing live. While Tom and Danny were more than capable of laying down the guitar and vocal tracks, Ben Sergeant recorded bass for the album. It was Ben who came up with the opening riff for 'Five Colours In Her Hair'.

Danny: Harry and Dougie have always been modest about their musical ability, but this needs saying: once the band got going, nobody worked harder than them at getting good. It didn't take long for both of them to turn into awesome musicians. (Whereas Tom and I, if anything, regressed!)

In any case, we didn't need to worry about musicianship for our first TV performance in the middle of December. *CD:UK*, just like Fletch had promised. It felt surreal that this moment had finally come, that we were genuinely going to be on TV. Exciting, too. We knew we had something good. Something special, that we couldn't wait to show to the world. Even though we were miming our instruments at the time – the TV

studio wasn't equipped to broadcast a band playing live
– I for one was looking forward to standing up in front
of the cameras with a guitar round my neck.

Dougie: Me and Harry were glad we were miming. We
were terrified. *CD:UK* was a big deal back then, one of
the most important music shows on TV. We should
probably have tucked ourselves up nice and early the
night before – we had to be up at seven for a car to take
us to the studio – but sober, early nights weren't really
our scene. Predictably enough, we spent the night before
our first TV performance getting stoned up on the
balcony in Tom's room. At five in the morning we were
still up, heads full of weed, giggling away and repeating
the *CD:UK* theme tune to ourselves for hours on end. It
was a bleary-eyed band that turned up at Riverside
Studios in Hammersmith a couple of hours later.

We were on the show with Busted and an Irish boy
band called D-Side. They'd released a couple of singles
and we'd heard of them. As we stepped out of the car,
we noticed a few girls hanging around. We assumed
they were waiting for the other bands, but suddenly
they approached us and asked for our autographs.
Surreal moment. How did they even know who we
were? And anyway, we didn't even *have* autographs.
We scrawled something for them before hurrying into
the studios to do the show.

That first live show was awesome. James Bourne
introduced us with a line that echoed *Back to the Future*
– 'You might not be ready for this yet, but your kids are
going to love it!'

Turns out they *were* ready. When the show was over and it was time to go home, we could hear a crowd of screaming girls outside the building. This, we decided, was going to be very embarrassing. Obviously they were all screaming for Busted or D-Side. We were going to step outside and none of them would know who the hell we were.

We couldn't have been more wrong. They knew *exactly* who we were. They were all screaming for us.

Tom: Meanwhile, we were still recording *Room On The Third Floor*. That meant Danny and I were needed in the studio to lay down vocal and guitar tracks more regularly than Harry and Dougie. Exciting times, but we'd still be raring to get home every evening so we could hang out together.

Unless, of course, it was a day off. And it was on a day off, when we were all in the house together, that the phone rang. It was Fletch, and he was uncharacteristically to the point. 'I want a meeting,' he said. 'Band house. Three hours. All of you. Nobody else can be there, and no excuses.'

We were bricking ourselves by the time he arrived. What was going on? What did he know? He was stony faced when he walked into the house.

'Sit down,' he told us. 'Now.'

Fletch took a seat on the sofa in the sitting room. The rest of us sat on the floor facing him.

'Is there anything you guys want to tell me?' he asked.

A pause.

'No . . .' Squeaky voices all round.

'Nothing?'

Silence.

'Anything about illegal substances?'

Shit.

My heart was pounding, and I almost felt as if I could hear the others doing the same. I glanced at them out of the corner of my eye. What were they going to say? Would anybody fess up?

It was Harry who broke the silence. He was clearly trying to play it down. To sound innocent. 'Are you talking about smoking weed?'

Fletch nodded. 'Yes.'

And then he embarked on his bollocking.

Harry: And I don't think any of us had ever *had* such a bollocking. It made those awkward moments when my mum and dad used to read my school reports pale into insignificance. What the *hell* did we think we were doing? Did we think that just because we were in a band, we could get away with doing this stuff? Did we think that we were too damn cool to follow the rules? Did we have so little respect for our management that we thought we could just ignore them?

I put my hand up, naively thinking I could deflect some of the heat from the other guys. 'Actually, Fletch,' I said quietly, 'you should probably know that I was smoking weed before I was even in the band.'

He glared at me. 'If we'd known that,' he said, 'you'd never have got in the band in the first place.'

That shut me up. And he was right, of course.

Dabbling with drugs was stupid. We were just too young to see that at the time.

Danny: Have we mentioned that Fletch can talk? Fletch can talk. Even if he was there to chat about the weather he could go on for hours. That bollocking felt like it would never end. By the end of it, though, Fletch had come full circle. 'You could be the biggest band in the world,' he told us, 'but it's up to you. Let's have a twenty-year career, make millions and buy an island. Then you can smoke as much weed as you like. But for now, cut it out . . .'

Tom: And so we did. Fletch's bollocking had done its job. I would never touch drugs again, and for me personally, the next couple of years – during which I barely even touched alcohol – were the best, most life-changing, of my life.

Looking back at those early days in the band house, we can all see how important they were in helping us bond as a band. It could have gone so wrong. Danny and I had picked Harry and Dougie after, literally, two days of knowing them. We could have all hated each other. We could have found that we had nothing in common, or that we resented the time we spent with each other. In fact, we had *such* a lot of fun. We weren't yet famous or successful, but already we were having the time of our lives. Even when we hit the big time, we didn't want to go out to clubs or celebrity haunts. Not our scene. For us, the best thing about being in a band was *being* in a band, *doing* band stuff – not all the trappings that went with it. We liked working on our music, and we liked hanging out together. All this meant we gelled more than most bands ever have the opportunity or inclination to do. Within a couple of months of moving into the band house, I had three new best friends. Their names were Danny, Harry and Dougie. No matter what the future held for us, our friendship was something we now knew we could always rely on.

And now, when people ask us how we can remain so close, we all think back to the time we spent together in the band house. It's impossible to have that much fun together and not end up friends.

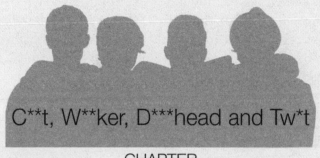

C**t, W**ker, D***head and Tw*t

CHAPTER

6

Danny: As far as we were concerned, McFly was going to be the coolest band out there. We had a fresh new sound, we wrote our own songs, we played guitars, we looked good and sounded great. We cared about our music and we reckoned the world would give us the kind of credibility we craved.

But that was before we turned up to the video shoot for 'Five Colours In Her Hair'.

Man, we cringed at that video.

In the early days, we had no say over how we were presented. We concentrated on our music; other people concentrated on our image. When the time came for us to shoot the video for 'Five Colours', we were presented with a video treatment and a director, and there was no question of us having any creative input. We knew, the moment that we arrived on set for the shoot (four hours late, admittedly, having got stoned the night before), that we were going to hate it. And as the crew got us to pretend we were jumping in and out of TVs and twatting around on Day-Glo sets, we felt more embarrassed about what we were being asked to do with each second that passed.

Everyone tried to reassure us. 'It's going to be great

. . . just wait till it's lit . . . just wait till it's colour-graded . . .' We allowed ourselves to be encouraged, but when the video came back and we saw it, all our worst fears were confirmed. It was colourful and garish and a bit silly: everything that we didn't want to be. We talked about getting ourselves a video camera and shooting a new video by ourselves, something that *we* liked. We didn't, of course, and in hindsight it would have been a massive mistake. We might not have liked that video, but our disappointment was sure as hell softened by the success it would eventually give us. Success that was just around the corner.

Harry: On 2 March 2004, Busted embarked on an arena tour of the UK. We joined them in a supporting slot. Exciting? Put it this way: our first proper shows were to be in front of sell-out audiences of ten thousand people. Ten thousand girls, all hopefully knowing who we were, all screaming at us.

Unfortunately, they weren't screaming at a live band. Tom, Danny and Dougie were singing live, but our instrumental tracks were pre-recorded. We tried to argue our case – we'd been practising hard for six months, and as far as we were concerned we sounded pretty good – but our management put their collective foot down. We wouldn't have time to soundcheck properly, they explained. We wouldn't be able to cope with the pressure. We'd be like rabbits in headlights. We were pretty depressed about this, but in hindsight, and even though it sounds a bit lame, it was definitely the right decision. This way, we could get used to performing on stage in front of big crowds without it affecting our playing. If we'd sounded terrible on that tour, it could have been the end of everything.

I didn't really know what an arena was. In my head, I thought it was a stadium. I pictured us at Old Trafford in front of seventy thousand people. When we turned up for the first gig at the Point in Dublin – one of the smallest arenas on the circuit – I remember feeling a bit disappointed at the size of it. And when we walked out on stage for our first proper live gig and the screams weren't *quite* as loud as I expected, it felt a bit awkward.

That tour, though, was the start of everything for us. As it progressed, the screams got louder. The buzz about McFly got buzzier. We were on the road for a month, and during that month our lives changed. We went from being four largely unknown guys who spent their time chilling by themselves at home, to being a recognizable pop act. To being, for want of a better word, famous.

Dougie: In the eyes of the press, McFly and Busted were best buddies. The truth is that we didn't really hang out with them as much as we do now. It wasn't that there was a particular problem with them, but we were such a close-knit band we just wanted to hang out with each other.

Tom: That's not to say, though, that we didn't realize how lucky we were to be on that tour. Matt Willis's seal of approval on our McFly material meant everything to me. A complimentary word from him meant more to me than from anyone else.

There must have been two hundred thousand people – all from the exact demographic we were targeting – who saw us on that tour. It finished with a gig at Wembley on 28 March. The following day, 'Five Colours In Her Hair' was released. Our first single. None of us were under any illusions about how important it was that the first single performed well. The world of pop music is fickle. If you're not a success when you first start out, people are reluctant to give you a second chance. But I think we all felt like the success of 'Five Colours' was meant to happen – like we were on a speeding, unstoppable train and number ones were just stops we would inevitably blast through on our way to wherever we were heading.

It was early in the morning on the Wednesday of the week our single was released that there was a knock on the door of the band house. It was Fletch, dragging us all out of bed. We congregated, bleary-eyed, in the hallway, totally confused. Fletch had a video camera. What the hell was he doing?

'Lads,' he said. 'I've got the midweeks.'

The midweeks are a big deal in the music industry. These are the sales figures, collated, strangely enough, around the middle of the week, which give you a general idea of how the charts are going to look the following Sunday. We'd heard people talking about them, of course, but this was the first time they had any relevance to us.

Fletch tried to keep us on tenterhooks. 'Well . . . you're . . . NUMBER ONE!'

The pressure was on. He was filming us. We had to

respond with whoops and hugs and cheers. Truth was, it was bloody early. As soon as Fletch lowered the camera, we mumbled: 'Could we, er . . . could we maybe go back to bed now?'

I don't think there was any arrogance on our part. If anything, we were a bit oblivious to it all. Nobody else around us made much of a fuss about being number one. Busted had already been there and done that, remember. I guess it wasn't so exciting to have us coming along and doing it second.

Dougie: It's not that being number one wasn't a big deal. It's not that we weren't stoked to repeat that success with our second single, 'Obviously'. It's not that we were blasé, when *Room On The Third Floor* was released in July, to find ourselves being given an award at the Barfly in London for overtaking The Beatles to become the youngest band ever to have an album debut at number one. It's just that we were suddenly so damn busy that we barely had time for it to sink in. We'd gone from being unknown, to appearing on a couple of TV shows and magazines, to supporting Busted on an arena tour, to putting our first single out there. Slowly but surely we were being eased into being famous, so when it came it wasn't a big shock.

All of a sudden, though, we *were* hot property. The teen press – *Smash Hits*, *Sneak*, *Top of the Pops* magazine – were all over us. Some days we would find ourselves doing five photoshoots a day; a million interviewers asking us a million questions. It was a whirlwind of constant work – we were lucky if our schedule gave us an afternoon off a week. But it never seemed like a chore. After all, we weren't at school, we didn't have to go and do proper jobs. What's not to like? We were having the most brilliant time, playing shows, travelling to amazing places we'd never have seen otherwise, like Japan, where, bizarrely, we had a couple of number ones in our first year. The fame and all that came with it we could take or leave. But being in a successful band? Complete awesomeness.

Tom: Our life had suddenly turned mental, and there's no way we would have coped if we hadn't had amazing people around us. Fletch and Rashman were central to it all. We owed them everything, and we still do. They're the reason we were a band, and they're the reason we still are. Richard has this uncanny ability to see the good in people that others overlook. He realized Harry was right for McFly, and sent him our demo so he'd have an edge at the auditions. He knew Dougie had something special, and did everything he could to help him get good enough to have another shot at joining the band. And it was Richard who constantly called me in those early days, encouraging me to write more, meeting me, listening to me, advising me, and teaching me all about the music business.

As for Fletch, he's incredibly talented in his own right – a great musician and songwriter. He's not the most organized manager in the world, but he's the most passionate by ten million miles. He's an incredible leader – when you have Fletch leading you into battle, you truly feel unstoppable.

Fletch and Richard were very strict with us in the early days, and they were damn right to be. We were only teenagers. Now, though, we have a unique relationship, and I'm not sure there are any other managers like them out there. For them, it's not about business or money or success – we truly are a team, and anyone who knows anything about McFly knows that there's another member of that team just as indispensable.

It became apparent very early on in our career that we needed someone to help us on a more day-to-day basis. Enter Tommy Jay Smith. Tommy's been with us from the beginning, and he has the hardest job in the world. Officially he's our tour manager; unofficially he's like a surrogate parent. He does almost everything for us, whether we're on tour or not. He organizes our diary, he wakes us up in the morning, and he tells us what we need to pack if we're going away. If we need to leave somewhere at 6 a.m., Tommy has to be knocking on our door at five. It's his job to make sure we get everywhere on time, and that when we get there we have everything we need. Tommy finds guitar strings when there are no music shops open; he books our doctors' appointments and dinner reservations. If something goes wrong at home, Tommy's there to sort it out. We see him more than we see almost anyone else – pretty much every single day, and certainly more than we see our parents. His is a high-stress job and he does it brilliantly. Without him, we'd never get anywhere or do anything. And in the pages that follow, you need to imagine Tommy there, all the time, in the background. What a legend.

There are more than four members in our band: it's impossible to imagine McFly without Richard, Fletch or Tommy. They love the band for the same reasons we do. Frankly, I'd rather get rid of Harry than one of them. ☺

Harry: The feeling's mutual!

Although we seemed able to take our new-found fame in our stride, that didn't mean there weren't moments that genuinely terrified us. Our first live stage performance springs to mind. There was no quiet warm-up gig in a little club in front of a hand-picked audience. No easing us into things, unless you count the Busted tour when we were miming anyway. Our first live gig was not only in front of Buckingham Palace and eighty thousand people. We also found ourselves having to follow a little-known artist by the name of James Brown. I'll never forget standing side of stage at the Olympic Torch ceremony on the Mall in June 2004, watching James Brown's massive band, with horn section and two drummers; or talking to Ozzy Osbourne, Rod Stewart and Ronnie Wood, those rock legends, backstage. I'd like to say we took it in our stride. Totally cool. Just another gig. Truth is, McFly were bricking themselves. When the time came to take the stage and play 'She Loves You' and 'Five Colours In Her Hair', we were so nervous that we rushed through them practically double time. When we came off stage, Danny was furious. 'That was *crap* . . . too fast.'

I didn't care. 'Mate, we got through it. For a first attempt, that wasn't too bad . . .'

Danny: For a *first* attempt, maybe it wasn't.

All of a sudden, we found ourselves being recognized in the street. At first, when we'd been on *CD:UK* a couple of times and had started to appear in the music press, we mostly got confused with Busted. All that changed after playing to packed-out arenas and having a hit single. And in those early days it was Tom who got recognized the most when we were out and about.

Tom: I think it was mostly because of my big chin. And terrible teeth. I did an experiment once. It was lunchtime in a busy street. I walked down the road with my chin covered and nobody recognized me. With my chin on display, I was recognized straight away.

We started to learn when and where it was safe to go out. Our fans were mostly teenage girls, which meant we could pretty much walk around without being mobbed during school hours. Once, Dougie and I made the mistake of going to McDonald's one afternoon at about four o'clock. The whole place fell silent, like the man with no name had just walked into a saloon. We quickly stepped backwards through the doors and made a run for it.

Harry: Mostly, if we were going to have groups of screaming girls chasing after us, it would happen when we were all together as a band. Individually, we could normally go about our business. Not always, though. I was coming out of the theatre one evening when a group of twenty-five girls recognized me. They started running in my direction like bees to honey. I had to leg it and hide in a pub to stop myself being trampled.

Tom: Being suddenly thrown into the public eye was something we were totally prepared for, and although it was by no means the best part of being in a band, we loved it. It wasn't without its down sides, though. We found ourselves in a strange situation: people loved us or hated us. There was no middle ground. Fans would scream when they saw us; and the adverse reaction we provoked in some members of the public was just as extreme. And the truth was, we didn't really blame people for hating us. We knew that the way we were being presented to the public wasn't a true reflection of the band we really were. We were (at least we thought we were) pretty cool, but we were being packaged up as this squeaky clean group to appeal to the masses. We were fully aware of how shocking the video for 'Five Colours In Her Hair' was. We hated it, and when people slagged it off we quietly agreed with them. People didn't believe that we were decent musicians. They didn't believe that we wrote our own songs. They thought we were just another manufactured boy band. It was weird, knowing we were in this awesome band and having to be all defensive about it in interviews.

Harry: We quickly became good at shrugging off stupid criticism – it was insignificant compared to all the amazing stuff that was happening to us – but sometimes you couldn't help but let it get to you. The *NME* printed a picture of us and labelled it: 'From left to right: Cunt, Wanker, Dickhead and Twat.'

Danny: I was 'c∗∗t'! ☺

Harry: You had to find yourself wondering what some middle-aged magazine editor really thought he was achieving, whether he felt good insulting a few teenagers because they'd had a hit record or two. It definitely fanned the fires, and as a result we did get a lot of grief, especially from other guys.

We were on the road one night and we stopped off at a petrol station in the middle of nowhere to grab something to eat. Some goth guy was behind the counter, and it was only once Tom, Dougie and Danny were back in the car that he gave me a look of recognition. 'I know you,' he muttered. 'I know you guys . . . *wait* . . . aren't you that band McFly?'

I was loving getting recognized by then. I gave him a modest little shrug and tried to sound as cool as possible. 'Yeah, that's right . . .'

He peered a bit closer. 'I *hate* you guys,' he said.

'Right. Thanks.'

But he was only just warming to his subject. 'You are *so* shit . . .'

Time for a sharp exit.

'You are *SO FUCKING ANNOYING* . . .'

I should have just put my head down and walked out, but I didn't. In a moment of bravado, I knocked over a stand of crisps and swiped a line of magazines off the shelf.

Silence in the petrol station.

We stared each other down.

His eyes started to glint. All of a sudden he looked completely psychotic.

171

NUTTER ALERT!

I sprinted out of the shop, across the forecourt, and dived into the car. '*Drive!*' I screamed, and we screeched out of there before the nutter could get his hands on us.

Tom: We all had similar experiences. Years ago, I had a friend and we were inseparable. After school, when I was going to college and hanging out with Busted, he got in a band. I used to see all the promo about him and his band, and was always texting him, suggesting that we went for a drink and telling him how great it was that things were happening for him. But I never got much of a response, and in time we drifted apart.

Unfortunately, his band never quite made it – they released a couple of singles, but their label dropped them before their album came out. We released soon after that, and our story was obviously a bit different. I can see that it must have been a bit of a kick in the teeth for him.

We were doing a magazine interview when I got asked about our friendship. 'Yes,' I said. 'We used to be close, but we kind of lost touch.' I didn't say more than that, and I didn't think anything more about it, either. Until, not long afterwards, Danny, Dougie and I were in Tesco doing some shopping. I was by myself in the cereal aisle when I sensed someone coming up towards me. And I heard a shout: 'You *bastard*!' I turned round and had a millisecond to register that this was my friend's mum. Then, out of nowhere, a cloud of white goo splashed all over me. Man, that woman had a fantastic aim with a pot of cream.

The pot splattered to the floor. I looked down. It was a big one. I didn't know they *made* pots of cream that big.

I stared at my clothes. They were white. My face was wet.

I looked at her.

'How dare you slag off my son?' she shouted. 'After everything you've been through.'

I stepped forward, hoping to calm her down. But then I slipped in the puddle of cream and ended up on my arse on the floor. She panicked, left her shopping, and sprinted from the store. I tried to chase after her, but it was difficult because my feet were all slippery with cream . . .

Dougie: I was paying at the checkout when Tom suddenly appeared, looking like Casper the Friendly Ghost. Cream was dripping off the end of his nose. 'What the . . .'

Tom: I was suddenly surrounded by the supermarket security guys. They thought I'd been trashing the place. 'Not me!' I shouted at them, and I pointed at the exit where this woman was running out.

Danny: I turned up then, and, with a couple of the security guards, sprinted to the car park to stop her. Too late. Her husband was already in the car. She jumped in and they screeched off like the Dukes of Hazzard.

Another time, during one of our infrequent nights out in a club, a bunch of guys started on us. We were getting ready to leave – a car was waiting for us just out-side – when one of these blokes punched me in the ear, right on my earring. It's not often that I lose it. I try to count to ten before I react . . .

Dougie: Trouble is, sometimes he gets stuck . . .

Danny: . . . and on this occasion I flipped. The guys had to pull me out of the club, bundle me into the waiting cab and scream at the driver to go. These lads were fully intent on beating us to a pulp, just because we were in the public eye.

Other bands took to hating us, too. Whenever we found our paths crossing with massive, successful artists, men and women without anything to prove, they were always super-friendly and encouraging. It was other current bands on the way up, or down, who seemed to have a problem with us.

Dougie: We went through a phase of being loathed by particular indie bands who liked to slag us off at every available opportunity. Like they defined themselves by hating McFly. Somehow, though, we managed to pull through, and although some people liked to think of us as C**t, W**ker, D***head and Tw*t, we had fans who more than made up for it.

Our first headlining theatre tour was in the autumn of that year. It kicked off at the Wolverhampton Civic Hall – a big moment for us. When the curtain dropped and the crowd screamed, the noise was so loud our sound guys had to max out the PA. In those days we had monitors on stage rather than in-ear mixes, and at times we simply couldn't hear what we were playing. And that's how it continued for the rest of the tour. There might have been people who hated McFly, but come show time it was easy to forget about them all.

Tom: Maybe we're deluding ourselves. Maybe it's not for us to say. But despite all the amazing things that were happening to us, the changes that were going on in our lives, I don't think we really altered all that much. Perhaps it was because we weren't very much into the whole celebrity scene. Perhaps it was because we'd always much rather hang out with each other, keep ourselves to ourselves. Perhaps it's because, although we were scared of our management, they were doing a good job of keeping us grounded.

Dougie: I changed more than the others. I had to do some growing up, pretty quickly. Almost as soon as I moved into the band house, the other three dudes had instantly become like my older brothers. Danny would do my hair if we were going somewhere; Harry taught me how to shave; all three of them taught me how to become a bit more confident. I think I was still pretty much in awe of them – not just because they were older, but also because Tom and Danny were these amazing musicians. It didn't take long for me to drift apart from my other friends. Without wanting to sound patronizing, they were still kids, doing kids' things, whereas I'd been caught up in this whirlwind of excitement. I tried to stay in touch with them. I genuinely wanted to know what was going on in the life I'd left behind. But our lives had become too different. We were poles apart.

Danny: We started to discover that when you're in the public eye, other people treat you differently. Not everyone – I had good, solid friends around me, and even my friends from Bolton seemed genuinely happy for me and everything that was happening in my life – but sometimes people just can't help seeing you in a different light.

Harry: A close friend of mine used to have parties a couple of times a year in a big barn where he lived. I always used to go to them and have a great time, but once we started having some success, events like that were a lot less enjoyable: seventy people constantly staring at you all evening isn't a lot of fun.

Dougie: And for me, even being at home could be difficult. When I first moved into the band house, I'd have to go home at weekends. Mum would come and pick me up from London on a Friday night and drive me back down to Essex. And it might sound churlish to say it, but I hated that. It wasn't just that I was living up in London with my three new best friends and we were having the best time, writing songs, playing music. It wasn't just that I was living every kid's dream.

It was also that home didn't seem like home any more.

It was two or three weeks after my dad walked out that I got in the band. The worst thing in my life had happened, followed by the best thing. It was a time of extremes. Dad made one brief reappearance after that, and I think my parents tried to work it out for a couple of weeks, but then he sodded off again. Mum had gone from having four people in the house to there being just her and my sister. Nothing seemed familiar there any more. I hated being brought back to reality. I hated the way going home didn't *feel* like going home: Mum didn't cook any more, she didn't have much money, things were falling apart in the house and she was really down. It was such a weird, alien environment.

I'd never been a particularly troublesome, moody teenager, never been the kind of kid to argue with my parents. But it was around now that I started acting that way. I was being forced to grow up so fast when I was with the band that I didn't *want* to have to be an adult when I went home. I wanted to have what the other guys had – a place where I could just go back to being ordinary Dougie Poynter with his family.

Mum and I started not getting along so well. It was entirely my fault. I found I didn't want to know what was going on back at home. I didn't want to think about how depressed Mum was. I think, deep down, she suspected that was the case, and would never let on to me that she was struggling. Sometimes, though, it just got too much. On occasion, my uncle would call me up and explain that Mum just couldn't manage, that she and my sister were living off Pot Noodles. At least I was in a position to help out financially, and I'd send her a few thousand pounds every now and again, which went some way to putting my mind at rest a bit.

Things improved with time, though, and now my mum and I are as close as we ever were. I also know that Mum found the excitement of the band's early years a welcome distraction from what was going on in her life at home, and that it helped her through the difficult times she suffered in the wake of Dad's disappearance. It gave her something to focus on.

Danny: Fletch did what he could to keep us on a short leash. He was constantly drilling it into us that we had to act professional, that our band was a business, that we needed to turn up on time for rehearsals or engagements, and that we should be back in the band house early when the working day came to an end. When Fletch said jump, we jumped. At least, we made it *look* as if we jumped. We were scared of him, and deep down I think we knew he had our best interests at heart. But it would be a lie to say it wasn't annoying. That we didn't feel as if our wings were clipped. We were young, but we weren't little kids, and we rebelled in our own way, even if we did everything we could to hide it from our management. Weed was one way of rebelling. Girls were another. I'll admit it now, even though I'm not that proud of it: with girls, I was like a kid in a sweetie shop. I was the polar opposite to Tom, who was a very good boy.

Tom: Once I'd finally wormed my way back in with Giovanna, I wasn't going to risk messing things up yet again. I'd been obsessed with her for years, and I think I knew, even then, that she was the girl I wanted to spend the rest of my life with.

Harry: Because Danny didn't have many friends down in London when he first moved here, he used to rely on me to provide the entertainment. I lost count of the times I heard the phrase, 'Mate, get her back and tell her to bring a friend!'

But as Fletch never tired of reminding us, the rules were the rules. We weren't allowed to have girls back to the house. We weren't allowed to be seen out with members of the opposite sex. And obviously none of us would be so stupid as to get with an older woman. An older woman who worked for a rival band. An older woman who worked for a rival band and was under Fletch and Richard's management. Would we?

It was during the Busted tour that one of the choreographers caught our eye. We all totally fancied her, but because we were so much younger we used to be pathetically gimpy around her. Showing off. Acting cool. Completely cringeful. It was a couple of months later, once I'd become single after splitting up with my then girlfriend, that Danny and I went out one night to a showcase for this girl band from Bolton, one of whom had been a girlfriend of Danny's. The choreographer, who we hadn't seen since the Busted tour, happened to be there.

That night we went to a club with the three girls, who were our age, and the choreographer asked if she could come along. We magnanimously agreed. Long story short, I ended up getting with her. Short story long, once we'd said goodbye to her, Danny and I went back to the girls' hotel. I got with one of them while Danny waited for the bed to be free, then Danny got with another. Then Danny's one started trying to drag *me* towards the bed, and I ended up getting with her too.

The next day we were playing at Wembley for the *Smash Hits* awards. The choreographer was going to be there, and I was fully expecting her to be a bit embarrassed about what had happened the previous night – she'd been a bit tipsy, not to mention that she was quite a few years older than me. Not a bit of it. She pulled me to one side and gave me her number.

This was a big deal. It was very cool, but also a bit scary. If Fletch and Rashman were to find out about this, I'd be in *serious* trouble. I told her not to tell *anyone*. But she was the forbidden fruit – not to mention that she was smoking hot – and I couldn't believe my luck.

Next day we were going to the première of *Phantom of the Opera*, all in black tie. We were never allowed to go to the after-parties to these things: Fletch was always telling us to go home and go to bed. (He thought he was being strict – he *was* being strict – but he didn't know that mostly it was fine for us because all we wanted to do was go home and hang out anyway.) It was the same story that night. I played along: 'Yeah, Fletch, I'm really tired, I'm going to go home.' In fact, I rang the choreographer, got her address, and went round, still in full black tie and with a rose behind my back. She had a house in a desirable part of London – I felt like I was in a movie all of my own. It was the beginning of an amazing affair, even more so because we had to keep it absolutely quiet.

Until one day, two months later, she rang me in a total state. 'Fletch knows!'

Turned out we'd been sloppy. The website Popbitch had run a story about us, and Fletch had his ear to the ground. Suffice it to say that he wasn't best pleased. We called it all off immediately, but I'd learned a lesson about how difficult it would be to keep private things private when you're in the public eye.

Danny: I learned the same lesson in a slightly less dignified way when the girl I lost my virginity to did a kiss-and-tell story in the papers. It wouldn't have been so bad if she hadn't revealed that I'd kept my socks on throughout. I denied it at the time, but what can I say: it was bloody cold!

Looking back now, we can all see that Fletch and Rashman needed to be strict. They weren't just there to look after our business interests, they were there to look after *us*, and we couldn't have had two better managers. But that's not to say that it didn't get to us. We weren't big into going out and partying; we were happy to work hard. But just now and then, we wanted to enjoy the upside of our success without having to be cloak-and-dagger about it.

Around the time that *Room On The Third Floor* was released, we were asked to play at the *Spider-Man 2* première – a little bit of light entertainment as the guests were walking up the red carpet. Bring it on. Premières were pretty much the only celebrity events that we enjoyed doing, and we were looking forward to this one more than most: a gig, a cool film and then an awesome party afterwards. Proper A-list. Hollywood stars. Tom had been to the after party for the final *Lord of the Rings* film, and had told us stories of how amazingly lavish it was. We were up for this one.

Fletch and Rashman weren't. 'You can't go to the party,' they told us. 'You have to go home, get an early night.'

Harry: It was one restriction too many. You could tell, because even Danny – friendly, easy-going Danny – kicked off in protest.

Danny: It seemed as if all we ever experienced was the work side of things. All we wanted was to have a taste of the glamour. I lost my rag, telling Fletch that we were all pissed off at missing out on all this cool stuff. It fell on deaf ears. Our car took us home. No party for us.

Harry: Except, of course, there was. Because although Fletch and Rashman might have thought we spent all our time at home watching telly, practising and catching up on our sleep, the reality was rather different.

Tom: We were four guys living the dream. Although we didn't much like the way we were being presented, or the way some people perceived us, it didn't matter because at the end of the day we could all go back to the band house and be together. We had hit records, we were famous, we were successful, but that really wasn't the cool thing about being in our situation. The cool thing about being C**t, W**ker, D***head and Tw*t was that, behind closed doors, we really were just four best friends, having the time of our lives.

Star Girl

CHAPTER

Tom: Valentine's Day 2004. Shit.

It was my first Valentine's Day since getting back with Giovanna, and I hadn't bought her a present. What should I do? Write her a song, of course. What could be more romantic than that? I grabbed my guitar and worked out a few chords and some lyrics. Personal lyrics, about her and me, about the first time we'd danced together, on the kitchen tiles of my parents' house, to 'Easy' by the Commodores. The song spilled out – it didn't take me much more than five minutes. It's not that I rushed it, but when I feel truly inspired my most creative songs fly out in minutes. I knocked on Danny's door and asked him to record it for me. He was already fascinated by music production – something he'd turn out to be awesome at – and we'd set up our own little studio in the band house.

I played him my song . . .

Danny: . . . and I *hated* it. It sounded to me like the sort of thing some dodgy barbershop quartet would sing.

Tom: But I recorded it anyway, on my own in Danny's home studio while he and the boys watched *Crimewatch* downstairs. Then I jumped into my car and drove over to Giovanna's to deliver her present. It was called 'All About You'. It was never intended to be a McFly song. It was never intended for anyone except Gi. It was the first song I'd written all by myself, without any input from James Bourne, or Danny, or Dougie. Just a personal song for my girlfriend that would end up becoming one of our biggest hits.

Fast forward six months. Busted had agreed to be involved in the recording for the Band Aid 20 version of 'Do They Know It's Christmas?' As a result, Fletch had got talking to Richard Curtis about Comic Relief. Always on the lookout for an opportunity, he broached the subject of us perhaps being involved in it. That was how we came to be sitting in Richard Curtis's office, knocking ideas around, trying to decide if there was something we could do together.

We'd already started writing for our second album, and the material we'd been coming up with was a lot less poppy than the songs we'd written previously, more influenced by bands like The Who and Oasis. None of that kind of thing would be suitable for Comic Relief, but I *did* have this song I'd written for Giovanna knocking around. Everyone went nuts for it. It was good and poppy, it had the right sentiment, and within a week everyone had decided that 'All About You' would be the Comic Relief single for the following year, with 'You've Got A Friend' as the B side.

In January 2005, we recorded the video for 'All About You', along with a plethora of celebs who had agreed to give their time for the project. Video shoots are never all that enjoyable, but there was something special about that one, although the day was tinged with regret: that morning, we heard that Busted had split up.

We owed Busted a lot – me especially, even though I'd been booted out of the band after just a couple of days. We didn't want to see them split. Charlie had decided, though, that he wasn't into it any more, and they had always agreed that if one of them wanted to leave, the group would all go their separate ways. Busted never had the same relationship with each other that we had. They were never best mates. Seeing them split was a reminder of how lucky we were that the four of us were so close. I wish that had stuck with me over the months that were to come.

Richard Curtis asked us if we'd be involved beyond recording the song for them. Would we go out to Africa and make a little film for Comic Relief? Of course we would. It would be another exciting addition to what was already looking like an eventful 2005.

It had been back on our first theatre tour that we were told a director from 20th Century Fox was coming over to watch the show at Hammersmith. 'You've got to play good,' our managers said. 'Be funny. Be cool around him.' We didn't really know why he was there at the time, but it was as a result of his visit that we were asked if we wanted to be in a Hollywood movie called *Just My Luck* with a young actress called Lindsay Lohan – one of the hottest stars in America at the time. When the offer came, we didn't realize what a big deal it was. It was just another thing that happened in the crazy whirlwind our lives had become. (Nowadays we'd be stoked.) Shortly after that, we learned that we'd been nominated for a BRIT. Our schedule was panning out nicely. A trip to Africa, the BRIT Awards and then some time filming in New Orleans and New York. Bring it on.

We flew to Uganda in January 2005. None of us knew what to expect. We'd been living the high life – we'd been on private jets and gone on five-star holidays, we were used to staying in the best hotels and had enough money to do or buy pretty much whatever we wanted.

And then we arrived in Kampala.

The moment our car drove us out of the airport, we felt we'd landed on another world. We were staying in their equivalent of a five-star hotel; fifteen minutes round the corner the poor of Uganda were living in the slums. Every day we drove into this area of indescribable poverty. Every day our eyes were opened just that little bit wider. And the wider your eyes are, the easier it is for tears to escape.

We were there to see the work that Comic Relief did, but more than that we were there to see how much more needed to be done. We were shown a clinic, funded by Comic Relief, to which people travelled from miles around, on foot. It was the only place in Uganda where you could receive treatment for malaria and HIV. It was a tiny place, not much more than a shack. Hardly enough to treat the thousands of people in that country who required its services. But it was all they had.

We met people our own age. They weren't living the

high life like us. They were dying of malaria. Crowded into this clinic, sweltering in the intolerable heat, there weren't enough beds for everyone who needed treatment. Many of them were lying on thin, dirty mattresses wherever they could find a piece of floor. On the stairs. In doorways. Waiting for the inevitable.

Danny: The worst thing was the smell . . .

Dougie: And the orange dirt that got everywhere . . .

Harry: And walking down the street to see stalls of putrid fish with flies buzzing all around them . . .

Tom: Kids with no shoes . . .

Danny: And open sewers . . .

Dougie: And little babies with stomachs distended by malnutrition . . .

Tom: We saw houses where the inhabitants had to shit into a hole that was connected to the place where they got their drinking water and washed their clothes. We visited the only freshwater pump in the vicinity. It was locked and guarded by a man from the government, who the locals had to pay in order to get fresh water. But none of them had any money. Comic Relief would give them the funds they needed to ensure they weren't drinking the same water that they pissed and shat in.

Danny: The kids were brilliant. Fun. We were human climbing frames for them. Curiosities too, and not just because we were white. They'd never seen freckles before, so they kept trying to scratch them off my skin. The same went for tattoos.

Dougie: And after following us around for a while, they all started copying Danny's Bieber-flick.

Danny: They had nothing in the world, these kids, but they didn't let it get them down, I suppose because they didn't know any different. There seemed to be an age limit on their happiness, though. We met sad children of fourteen who were the oldest in their family, forced to provide for their younger brothers and sisters. Forced to grow up before their time. The exact opposite of us.

Tom: I met a girl my age. She was HIV positive. The memory of her is enough to haunt anyone. She was just bones. Her bed was soaked in blood and urine. She was hallucinating, unable to stay lucid for more than a few minutes. Three days later, while we were still there, she was dead.

Danny: I went to visit a six-year-old with malaria. Her mum was by her bedside and I explained to her why we were there, and that we wanted to find out more about the harsh realities of life in Uganda. She seemed almost numb as she told me, in a matter-of-fact way, that her daughter suffered from constant fevers and excruciating pain in her limbs – by all accounts malaria makes you feel like your bones are on fire. Her little girl was one of the lucky ones – she was being treated – but you wouldn't have thought it when the doctor walked into the room. The kid started screaming. Bawling her heart out. She knew what was coming: painful injections directly into her joints. They were necessary, of course. They would, hopefully, keep her alive. But try telling that to a six-year-old. I held the little girl's hand, hoping to comfort her a bit. I'll never forget the look she gave me. I couldn't cope with it. I was crying too as I walked out of that room. Crying my eyes out.

Harry: When mealtimes came around, we were taken into a little hut to eat. It wasn't exactly five-star cuisine – Pringles, Kit Kats and not much else – but it was a feast compared to what most people had. The kids would surround that hut, eyes wide open and jaws dropping at the sight of this food, which we would gladly have shared out among them. But we were under strict instructions not to give anybody anything. It wasn't just that their stomachs wouldn't be able to cope with it. If we'd handed over a Kit Kat to one of those children, someone would simply have stolen it off them, beating them up in the process. That's what poverty does to you.

Slightly older children would beg us for help. They'd beg us for money. They'd beg us to take them away, to bring them back to England with us.

Tom: Uganda truly opened our eyes, but it also gave us moments that were memorable for good reasons. There was a single power point in the middle of the village where we managed to plug in a PA of sorts. They'd cobbled together half a drum kit, and we played a little acoustic set, teaching 'You've Got A Friend' to a crowd of two hundred African children with the sun setting in the background. Some moments you know you'll never forget. That was one. And it sounds like a cliché, but trips like that change the way you look at the world. Make you remember how lucky you are. And we were luckier than most.

Harry: When the time came for us to leave Uganda, we found ourselves surrounded by a couple of hundred children, all begging us even more vigorously for money, and to take them home with us. When we finally made it into the people carrier that was taking us to the airport, we sat in absolute silence for a few minutes, before Tom and Danny started crying. I could feel myself welling up, too. I looked over at Dougie. He was making a weird, sucking noise with his mouth. Completely emotionless, or so I thought, and for some reason I found myself laughing. In fact, because we were being filmed, he was trying to distract himself to stop the tears from flowing. Tom and Danny couldn't stop crying; Dougie and I were halfway between laughter and tears. We remained like that for a good couple of hours, the emotion of our visit and everything we'd seen finally spilling out of us. There was no sense of self-congratulation that we were involved in Comic Relief's work in Uganda; no matter what people might say in the future, it wasn't an exercise in cynical self-promotion. After seeing at first hand the realities of life out there, we just wished we could do more.

Tom: We arrived back in London towards the end of January, before immediately flying out to New Orleans to record some songs for *Just My Luck*. Harry and Dougie were playing so well now, and as the general consensus was that we were a pretty tight live band, our producer, Hugh Padgham, who had recorded most of our first album, was keen for us to dispense with the services of any session musicians. This was the first time we'd be properly recording together as a band. And it was doubly exciting because we were recording new material.

Danny: Hugh was a real old-school producer, and strict with us. We looked up to him. There was no turning up late for Hugh, no dicking around in the studio. The technology back then was very different to how it is now. We were still recording on to tape, for a start, and Hugh hated working with computers. He *was* the computer, climbing into the bass drum to dampen it just so, getting us to pull away from the mike when we sang certain words. And he wanted us to play our own music, to be the band *we* wanted to be. He was on our wavelength. Hugh had worked with everyone – Paul McCartney, Sting, Genesis, Freddie Mercury – and it was cool to be working with him in a fantastic studio in New Orleans, where so much great music had been made in the past.

Tom: And weird, too, to be there immediately after our experiences in the shanty towns of Uganda. I'd shared a watermelon with a little girl back in Africa just before we left. Bad mistake. I ended up puking my guts out in a New Orleans hospital and having injections in my arse. (Too much information?)

Danny: For me, being in the studio is like coming home. But while we were recording in New Orleans, I started to get the impression that something bad was going down at my real home back in Bolton. I kept getting calls from my sister. 'Don't you think Dad's acting a bit weird?' Truth was, I did. I thought he'd been acting weird for a long time. You remember I told you how my family used to go to my nan's of a Sunday lunchtime? And how, as time passed, my dad spent less and less time with us on those Sundays, and more and more time down the pub? That had continued once I'd got into the band. It was almost like the pub was his new home, the people there his new family. Once the band got busy, and the time I had to spend at home became severely limited, Dad was always wanting to take me to that pub whenever I went back to Bromley Cross. I was cool with that, and so was my mum, but she felt I needed to spend time with the family first. Predictably enough, it caused tensions. As always, I tried to be the peacemaker and split my time between them, but it just led to more and more arguments. And if ever I sided with my mum, Dad would just go off down the pub anyway.

Despite all that, I still had a good relationship with my dad. Real father–son stuff, where we could talk about footy and girls, and go drinking together. For my first Christmas in the band, as I had a bit of money in my pocket, I had taken my mum, my dad, my sister and my nan and granddad to Antigua, first class. I was sitting by the pool with my dad, getting blasted on cocktails and eyeing up girls, when he came out with it. 'She's really doing my head in, Danny.'

'Who?' I asked.

'Your mum. *Really* doing my head in . . .'

I didn't like the way he was talking, but it wasn't like me to make a big scene. I stuck up for my mum a bit and tried to move the conversation on.

My gut was telling me something wasn't right. It dawned on me that maybe I didn't know my dad the way I thought I knew him. I realized that our home had been slowly changing. It wasn't a family home any more. Dad was never there. Stuff around the house never got done. When my sister called me in New Orleans to say she was worried that Dad might be having an affair, I tried to put it from my mind and concentrate on the job in hand, but a little voice in my head told me something was going on. An hour later she called back to tell me it was true. My dad *was* seeing someone else.

For me, there was only one thing worse than knowing there was trouble at home: being on the other side of the Atlantic and unable to do anything about it. By all accounts, Dad was still sleeping at home, and Mum was devastated. I was so anxious – I kept experiencing panic attacks – but I did what I could to keep things in perspective. We'd just seen a young girl die of malaria;

this wasn't such a big deal in the grand scheme of things, was it?

When we returned to England, ready for the BRIT Awards the following week, the first thing I did was get a train up to Bolton. I realized on the journey that I was feeling scared to go home. When I arrived to see that all the lights were off, it seemed grimly appropriate. Nobody was there – Mum was round at my nan's – and when I heard the door open and realized it was my dad, I locked myself in the toilet, freaking out because I hadn't told him I was coming home and I didn't want him to get angry and think I'd been speaking to Mum and not him. But I couldn't stay in the toilet for ever. I took loads of deep breaths, opened the door with a shaking hand and stepped out into the house to face the music.

I couldn't stay silent. My mum was distraught, no doubt in floods of tears round my nan's. We sat down together. I was almost hyperventilating and he was holding on to my wrists, trying to keep me calm. I couldn't look him in the eye.

I kept trying to persuade him to sit down with Mum and talk to her, to explain and apologize for having fallen out of love with her but he didn't feel able to.

In the end, it was too much for me. I just lost it. 'Fuck you!' I shouted at him, and I stormed out of the house.

I'd always thought my dad was awesome. I'd always got on with him. Sadly, that was the last time I spoke to him face to face.

Like Dougie, all of a sudden I was the man of the house. But also like Dougie, I was almost never home. I won't pretend that heading back to the band house the following day wasn't an escape. But it's hard to explain the anxiety I felt, knowing that my mum and sister had to get used to this horrible new situation without me.

Dad didn't move out immediately like I'd asked him to. Back in London, I took a call from my mum, saying that Dad was coming back home to sleep in my bedroom. I spoke to him on the phone. Suffice it to say, the conversation was a bad one – so bad that I ended up punching a hole in the wall of the band house in my anger and frustration.

I don't know how we'd have managed if I hadn't had a bit of money as both Mum and Dad needed their own homes. I took over my mum's mortgage payments and my sister's student fees. Our little house in Bromley Cross changed from being a comfortable home to a sad place, and although I wanted to be there for my mum and sister, I didn't want to leave the bubble of McFly to face the reality of life in Bromley Cross. Who would?

The night of the BRITs arrived – perhaps the most exciting moment of our career so far. We were up for Best Pop Act and we knew there was a chance we could walk away with it. But it was cool enough just to be invited, let alone be there as a nominee. It was a reminder of just how insane our first year had been.

Harry: It's a bit trippy being on the red carpet. Not particularly enjoyable. You can't help feeling anxious before you arrive. You can't help worrying that you're going to climb out of your car and all the waiting press will wonder who the hell you are. None of us ever want to be the first to step on to the carpet, but that night was even more nerve-racking. Once we were inside, though, it was a blast. We were able to drool over Green Day's performance of 'American Idiot', and when the time came for Jodie Kidd to announce Best Pop Act, we all held hands under the table . . .

And the award goes to . . .

Tom: None of us like acceptance speeches, but the total buzz of winning made it bearable to stand up there and thank the people we wanted to thank while Fletch popped the champagne corks down at the table. Backstage we did the press run, and while we were in the Radio 1 room, Green Day walked in. I felt Dougie tapping me on the shoulder. 'Dude . . . *dude!*'

Dougie: The guys in Green Day shouted over at us: 'Hey, it's McFly! Who's the little dude with the champagne?' The little dude was me, a bottle in one hand, our award in the other, made up to be hanging out with some of our musical idols. Two minutes later, Billie was – literally – pouring champagne down Harry's throat. Could the evening really get any better?

Tom: Universal Records held a BRITs party afterwards. We rolled up pissed out of our heads and ended up drunkenly dancing with Girls Aloud and lapping up the compliments from the big cheeses at Universal, before heading back to the band house. Danny and I sat in our studio, listening to the demos of our new songs. They sounded awesome, we'd just won a

BRIT, we'd met Green Day. Everything was going right.

And on top of all this, there was the small matter of a movie to be made . . .

Dougie: The producers of *Just My Luck* were hoping it would be the next *Pretty Woman*. They were way off. But we had a cool time making it. Being on the set of a major movie was a bit like being in a dream world, like a movie all of our own. You can imagine the scene: a kid from a poor part of town is transported to Hollywood, and what follows is a montage of him in amazing places doing crazy things. That kid was us.

Danny: And like all kids, we had grown-ups telling us what to do. Our management had read us the riot act before we even stepped foot in New Orleans. It was orders from the top. No questions. No arguments. *No messing around with Lindsay Lohan. OK?*

Dougie: Even the instruction made us laugh. Like Lindsay Lohan would want to get it on with any of us. We were just there to have a good time and make a movie.

We didn't have any acting lessons. We definitely should have done. The idea was that it should all be natural and organic, that we should act the way we normally act. In practice, we needed a whole load of direction. We'd shot a few music videos before, but we'd never been on a proper film set, so we really didn't know what to do. It was also our first experience of being around someone properly world-famous, and without wanting to sound horrible, Lindsay Lohan was exactly how you'd expect a teen superstar to be. 'Complicated.' But she *did* make an effort with us.

Danny: More than an effort. During our first day on set she called me to her trailer. It was a massive Winnebago, stuffed full of hair products and perfume and other girly stuff, light bulbs around the mirror – you get the picture. I was nervous as hell, but then she gave me her number. I thought I was well in there – even more so when she asked us all to join her for dinner that night. Did we fancy going out in New Orleans with Lindsay Lohan? Hell, yeah.

Harry: A Hummer driven by one of Lindsay's younger brothers picked us up from our hotel that evening, and we were driven to a grand old New Orleans mansion in the French Quarter where Lindsay was hanging out with some friends. She kept us waiting in the Hummer for forty-five minutes before she turned up with her little sister and a friend.

We drove to the restaurant, but we hadn't even walked in before Lindsay started reeling off to me all the Hollywood A-listers she'd been with (my lips are sealed), before explaining that she preferred older men. 'You ever dated anyone older than yourself, Harry?'

I told her about the choreographer, and she seemed to think that was pretty cool.

Tom: Cool enough for her to want Harry and Danny to sit next to her at dinner, while Dougie and I got stuck at the other end of the table with her little sister, who couldn't have been more than twelve.

Harry: We ordered some food and wine. As we sat and ate, she told us all these stories – graphic stories about her sex life, enough to put us off our steaks. When the meal came to an end – Lindsay was a bit tipsy at this point – she decided that we should all head back to her hotel for some drinks.

We walked back out to the Hummer. I was about to climb in when I felt Lindsay's hand on my shoulder. 'No, Harry,' she said. '*You're* sitting next to *me*.' And then, in a slightly louder voice: 'Harry's sitting next to me, everyone!'

Back at Lindsay's hotel, her entourage was waiting, including her mum and her younger brother. There was some kind of high-school prom event happening at the hotel, so crowds of American kids were going nuts at the sight of her. And whenever anyone came up to her, she would jokingly introduce me as her boyfriend. At least, I *thought* she was joking.

Dougie: Weird enough, but not as weird as her family. Lindsay told her mum that we'd be going on to a club and that she should come with us. When her mum agreed, Lindsay's eight-year-old brother, understandably, started wailing and begging her not to go. Lindsay's mum comforted the kid, saying she'd stay with him, but then mouthed, 'I'm coming with you,' at Lindsay. Of course, the little boy saw her do it. Meltdown.

Harry: Lindsay's mum didn't join us in the end, but we met up with other members of the cast and crew at Club 360, a revolving penthouse venue overlooking the French Quarter and the Mississippi. I started feeling a bit out of sorts, and it was a trippy place, with the world spinning and the music loud. The fact that Lindsay was flirting with me made it even trippier.

I sat quietly in a corner of the club, but before long she had tracked me down. She started dancing in front of me. It was kind of awkward, knowing that half the eyes in the club were on us. And as she gyrated in front of me, I didn't quite know what to say. 'Er, you're a very good dancer,' I finally managed.

'Yeah?' she said, suddenly incredibly intense and a bit more drunk. '*Yeah?* I can dance anything. Tap, ballet, jazz . . .' Totally cringeful, but she redoubled her efforts just to prove it. I was feeling more and more uncomfortable, with the room revolving and Lindsay dancing. I retreated onto a kind of ledge that formed the circumference of the club, which remained still while the floor of the club rotated. I sat there quietly, but before long Lindsay had taken a seat, and it had revolved round to my stationary position. Almost out of nowhere, she was sitting opposite me, her face inches from mine.

'Kiss me,' she whispered.

Man, this evening was getting stranger and stranger. I looked round, then shrugged. Why not? Maybe it would make me feel a bit better. We kissed.

It wasn't much more than a peck, and I don't think anybody saw. It only felt like moments later, though, that everybody in our party seemed to be leaving the club. It was two in the morning already, but Lindsay was freaking out at the sight of everyone going. It turned out there was a house party happening nearby, and Lindsay was invited. She turned to look at me. 'Where *I'm* going,' she said firmly, *'you're* going.'

OK. Sounded good to me.

And so we all traipsed off to this house party.

I've no idea whose house it was. All I know was that arriving there made us feel yet again like we were in a movie all of our own. It was an enormous house in the heart of the French Quarter – traditional wood cladding, balconies, twinkling lights everywhere. As we stepped inside, the place was full of beautiful people drinking champagne. The ceilings were high and ornate, and a magnificent staircase swept up from the centre of the entrance hall. Under the staircase was a room, dimly lit with red lights. A bed in the middle, and on the bed a couple having sex, there for everyone to see. It could have been sleazy, but somehow it wasn't. Just cool. The kind of party bands *should* be going to.

I found myself out on the balcony of the first floor, where I befriended some random dude and we chatted for a couple of hours. If I'm honest, the thrill of kissing Lindsay in the club had worn off, she was nowhere to be seen anyway, and I was still feeling a bit out of sorts. I tried to buck myself up. Maybe I should hunt Lindsay down again, strike up another conversation, give it one last chance.

I found her back in the house and asked her where the loo was. Not my best ever chat-up line, but it did the trick. 'I'll show you,' she told me. She grabbed me by the hand and followed me into a bathroom. Then she shut the door behind us.

'Go on, then,' she said as she turned to the basin.

What? I don't need the loo. I didn't need the loo in the first place! I was just trying to get you in a room on my own . . .

I went along with it, pretending to have a slash while the noise of the running taps camouflaged my subterfuge. I gave the chain a decoy flush and then, as I turned around, she lunged at me. Nothing so chaste as the peck on the lips we'd had in the club. This was full-on, and it lasted for quite some time.

I pulled away, suddenly freaking out. 'We shouldn't be doing this,' I muttered at her. 'We've been told not to . . .'

Lindsay thought this was hilarious. I think it just made her want to do it more.

'Honestly, we've been warned . . .' I objected, even as she was undoing my trousers.

Suddenly there was a banging on the door. Shit! Trousers on. Nervous giggles. We brushed ourselves down, opened the door and hurried back out into the house.

Dougie: Danny and I had spent most of the party sitting on a sofa, drinking and watching wrestling on the TV – with the exception of the short amount of time Danny dedicated (successfully) to pulling Lindsay's friend.

Tom: I bumped into Harry just after he'd left the bathroom. He was slightly wild-eyed: 'Dude, you won't *believe* what just happened . . .' But we'd all seen the way Lindsay had been looking at Harry that night, so we absolutely believed it.

Danny: At about four-thirty in the morning, we all piled back into the Hummer to go back to her hotel. But somewhere between the house party and the hotel, nature called for Lindsay. Clearly, for someone of her elevated status, there was no question of crossing her legs and letting it off as steam, and even less question of her having a pee at a petrol station like an ordinary person. When Lindsay Lohan has to go, she has to go. She threw a bit of a diva fit, insisting that we stop the car and that her security guard knock on the door of some random member of the public to ask if she might use their facilities . . .

Harry: But when she wasn't kicking off, Lindsay was holding my hand in the back of the car. I tried to hide it, because I was scared that one of her entourage might clock what was going on, but Lindsay clearly didn't have any such worries.

And then we were in the corridor outside her hotel room. Things were looking up. Lindsay had a strop when her key card wouldn't work, so we were stuck outside her room for a bit while her security guy headed downstairs to sort out another key.

Tom: Dougie and I looked at each other. It was pretty clear by now that Harry was trying to get with Lindsay while Danny was still trying to get with her mate. We were just gooseberries, so we made our excuses and left them to it. We sat outside the hotel like a couple of gimps, looking up at the sky and having a spaced-out conversation about the planets while Harry and Danny were doing their pop-star bit back inside.

Harry: This whole time I was feeling dross, but even though the evening was getting increasingly surreal, I kept telling myself that I couldn't miss out on the experience – the story would be one to dine out on. When Lindsay's strop subsided and the security guy reappeared with a new key card, me, Danny, Lindsay and her mate bundled into her suite. Danny and Lindsay's friend took the bed; Lindsay and I ended up in the sitting room, making out on the floor. After a bit, we swapped over – Lindsay and I took possession of the bed.

She was doing everything she could to fuel my ego, telling me how she loved my accent and how she didn't get with actors any more, only musicians. It makes me cringe to think about it now, but I responded in kind. This was like *Notting Hill*, I told her. I was Hugh Grant and she was Julia Roberts. She loved that. She started explaining to me what, in her books, made a good kiss (an extremely full-on one, as I remember), and then things started to get a bit more serious.

A bit steamier.

One thing led to another. We moved from first base to second base . . .

And then, just as I was about to seal the deal . . . Danny walked in.

'Oh . . . sorry, mate!'

There was a quick scrambling and a grabbing of clothes. The moment had passed (cheers, Danny!), and we quickly made ourselves decent. Lindsay called down for breakfast, and before I knew it, the four of us had settled down on her bed.

Danny: It was one of those ones with a TV that rises up out of the end. *Sex and the City* was on continuous loop, but to be honest, watching telly wasn't really what either of us had in mind.

Harry: It must have been around 6 a.m. by now. For a while Lindsay and I carried on getting a bit frisky, but gradually she started to sober up. 'You've got to leave before eight,' she told us. 'My sister always comes into my room at eight, and you can't be here . . .'

I didn't really want to leave. We had unfinished business. But then she announced that she was tired, pulled one of those airplane eye-masks over her eyes and went to sleep.

So much for my romantic night of passion.

Danny and I set our phone alarms for 7.45 a.m. and caught half an hour's sleep. Creeping out of Lindsay Lohan's room just before eight was one of the more bizarre moments of our lives. Question was, what would happen next? How would Lindsay react the next time we met?

We were on set the following day. I decided that my strategy should be complete confidence with her. I'd walk up to her, give her a gentlemanly peck on the cheek, be friendly and polite. I went to her trailer, but her response was frosty, to say the least. If her eyes could have spoken, they'd have asked me what the hell I was doing, being so familiar with her, kissing her in public.

I backed off. Message received and understood.

It didn't take more than a day for the gossip to leak out that one of the McFly boys had been fooling around with Lindsay Lohan. Someone at the house party had blogged about it. Total panic. Everyone went into denial mode. Of *course* nothing had happened. It was a non-story. Nothing to see here. Move on. Needless to say, Fletch wasn't best pleased. He made me phone Lindsay up and apologize to her for my behaviour. That ranks pretty high on my list of most awkward conversations ever. I told her how sorry I was for the situation we'd got ourselves into, and assured her that I was absolutely denying it. She was really cool about everything by then, and even managed to laugh it off. But then, I guess she didn't realize at the time that our dalliance would one day be celebrated through the medium of song.

Tom: Weirdly enough, it was Fletch who, much later, persuaded us to alter the lyrics to a song we'd been working on for our third album called 'Please, Please' to namecheck Lindsay. We were sitting around in a hotel when he suggested it, and we all thought the idea was a bit lame. But Fletch has satanic powers of persuasion. Sure enough, by the end of that conversation, Harry's fling with Lindsay was immortalized in our lyrics. What girl could ask for more?

Girls Allowed

CHAPTER

8

Tom: It didn't strike me, even back then, that there had been a pattern to my life. I could go through phases of real creativity and enthusiasm, phases when anything seemed possible and nothing was out of reach. But for every high there was a low. I would experience such intense gloom that I couldn't get excited about anything. When I became intolerable to be with. When nobody could do anything right, including me. During our time in New Orleans, Giovanna and I went through a rocky patch. It was the most strain our relationship had ever felt, and it's incredible that we both pulled together to make it through that rough time. Looking back, though, I can see that it marked the beginning of one of my low periods.

Everything should have been so great. I had the best job in the world. I was doing what I wanted to do, and my bandmates were the three most awesome dudes I could wish for. Most of all, the band house – that amazing, super-cool, five-bedroom mansion – should have been every young guy's dream, and for a while it was. For a while, when everything was new, there was nothing any of us wanted more than to be back at home, all together. Gradually, though, that changed. It didn't help that we treated that house about as badly as a house could be treated. By the end of our first year, there was no getting away from it: the place was absolutely disgusting.

Dougie: We destroyed that house. We used to skateboard all around it, and the painted white walls were soon grimy with handprints. One night we invented a game called 'capture the pizza box'. It involved turning the whole house into an assault course by upturning all the furniture, switching off all the lights and dividing into two teams. The winning team was the one that got to the pizza box first, but to spice things up a bit, we armed ourselves with paintball guns. It's probably not too hard to imagine the state of the place after that. We never used to throw *anything* away, so the house was crammed with all the freebies we'd get sent as a matter of course. More to the point, we never washed up, we never cleaned, we never even threw our rubbish out. The laundry room was a sea of pizza boxes, mouldering there from when we first moved in. Fletch came over one day and was so shocked by the state of the place that he arranged a skip and some people to come round and bag up all our rubbish. They discovered that our bins were alive with maggots and cockroaches. Nice.

Danny: Enter Darrotta, our long-suffering housekeeper. She kept the place in order, replenished the fridge with the food we liked, and cooked us meals that could be reheated when we got home. She saved the day in so many ways – at least the place became liveable-in again.

Poor Darrotta. Sometimes she would come into the house to find her immaculately prepared meals were untouched and sitting next to a pile of empty pizza boxes, but that didn't seem to deter her.

Tom: We ate a *lot* of junk food. Pizza every night, burgers at lunchtime, fry-ups every morning. Of course, to start with it was awesome, having no parents to tell you what to eat, or to force fruit and veg down your throat. But it didn't take long for my diet to show. I put on two stone during that first year in the band house. The others ate the same, but didn't seem to pile it on like I did. Pretty soon, I became the fat one in the band. It didn't do a lot for my self-esteem. In New Orleans, we were larking about when Dougie managed to take a snap on his phone of me naked. I was shocked when I saw it. I looked like a shaved gorilla. It was hideous, and of course my weight didn't go unnoticed. Pretty soon I was fed up with the snide comments in the press, and fed up that I agreed with them. My mood went from bad to worse. From grey to black. And that black mood had its effect on our second album, *Wonderland*. It wasn't the only thing, however, that led to *Wonderland* being a very different record to *Room On The Third Floor*.

Danny: People called us a boy band. Well, we were boys and we were in a band, but we saw ourselves as a bit more than that. We hadn't been signed to look pretty and bust our moves on the dance floor; we hadn't been signed to sit on stools in a row, crooning; we'd been signed because we could write our own songs and play them well. As a result, even in the early days, our record label listened to us more than most boy bands ever get listened to. Ordinarily, a boy band will be given their songs, told to sing them over an arrangement that has already been decided on, and won't have much in the way of creative input. While they're off touring one album, the next is being written for them. Not so with us.

That said, we had a lot of respect for people around us, especially our producers. For our first album, we were very young and inexperienced, and we allowed ourselves to be influenced without questioning anything too much. When the time came to record our second album, however, we had very definite ideas about the musical direction we wanted to go in. While *Wonderland* was still very much a pop album, its undertones were a little darker. In our own little way, we were rebelling, sticking two fingers up at the band everyone wanted us to be. Rebelling against ourselves. We didn't want to be bubblegum. We wanted to be cool. Credible. The band that we knew we were.

The picture on the front of *Wonderland* is one of the worst I've ever seen of us. None of us are smiling; none of us look like we're enjoying ourselves. And it was daft. We were amazingly successful. Our first record had sold almost a million copies. People really liked us. But all we ever listened to was the negatives. For every ninety-nine people telling us they loved us, we listened to the one person muttering about how much they hated McFly, like the psycho in the garage who Harry had to run away from.

Tom: We were stupid to let it get to us. Stupid not to embrace what we were and enjoy what we had. Immature. But it was galling, when we'd worked so hard on our songs, that people refused to believe that we'd written them or that we were decent musicians. That frustration came out in the way we presented ourselves, and perhaps it came out in our music too.

That doesn't mean to say, though, that we don't feel fondly about *Wonderland*. It's still one of my favourite albums. The songs bring back memories of New Orleans and all the craziness that was going on in our lives around that time.

Dougie: And some of the songs were very personal to us. 'The Ballad Of Paul K' was inspired by mine and Danny's dads going through midlife crises and walking out on our families. Why Paul K? The song was named after a Greek kid I went to school with. He never spoke. It wasn't just that he was a bit quiet, like me – he actually *never* spoke. As time went on, he became weirder and weirder. He grew his fingernails superlong, and started to communicate with strange squeaks and grunts. If anybody stood in his way or tried to bully him, he'd scratch them in the face with his long fingernails . . .

Tom: 'The Ballad Of Paul K' was the first time we'd tried to write a serious song about 'life'. Even now I get guys coming up to me saying how well they relate to it.

Danny had got a bit more advanced with his production, so we'd started making full demos in his studio in the band house, and the process was exciting because the songs, to our ears, sounded that bit cooler compared to what we'd put out previously. We spent hours on those demos, staying up all night to work out the individual parts, and listening carefully to loads of different bands for influences and references. We were massively into The Who at the time, and looking back it seems amazing that a band with our demographic was given the freedom to pursue that kind of direction. 'She Falls Asleep' – another dark song, in two parts, about a girl committing suicide – was recorded with a big orchestra and cost a lot of money. Part 1 is two minutes long with no singing and would never be a single, but the label let us do it anyway.

Harry: It was when we were doing a live radio performance in Bristol with the orchestra that one of the violinists caught my eye. Her name was Izzy, and I started plotting my conquest almost immediately. The best-laid plans, though: a couple of days later we heard that one of the orchestra had come down with mumps. I knew without asking that it would be the gorgeous one that I fancied, and I was right. It was ultra-contagious – members of the orchestra started dropping like flies – and there was no question of any of us having contact with them. So my plans were put on hold. But when Izzy and I finally got it together, I had eyes for nobody else.

Izzy joined us on the *Wonderland* tour once her mumps had subsided, but at first we didn't really speak – the old playground thing, I suppose, where you end up never talking to the girl you fancy. It wasn't until the end of the tour that we spoke, and we kissed after a show in Cardiff on the penultimate night. I think I knew, even then, that it was a kiss which would change my life.

Once the tour was over, Izzy came over to see me in the band house. We joke now that she turned up that day and never left. In fact she did leave, a week later, to travel to Australia with her classical crossover band, Wild. When she was away, we spoke on the phone and she opened her heart. She wasn't sure this was the right thing. Izzy was fresh out of a relationship; she was two years older than me; she knew I was in a pop band and assumed that I had girls throwing themselves at me all the time, and that I'd want to play the field.

'You don't understand, Izzy,' I told her. 'I'm going to marry you one day.'

I was nineteen, I'd known her for a week, but already I was sure. From that day to this, we've barely spent a day apart. Izzy is even more important to me than McFly. I wouldn't even want to contemplate life without her.

Dougie: While Harry was getting loved up, we appeared on the front cover of *Smash Hits* with black hair and Mohicans and lip rings. I thought that was pretty cool. We were a number-one pop band. People expected us to be clean-cut and smartly dressed . . .

Tom: And more than ever, we found that our time was not our own. We literally didn't know what we were doing from one day to the next. Tommy would knock on our door and bundle us into a car or a tour bus or an airplane and make sure we turned up wherever we needed to be for whatever we had to do.

If we weren't rehearsing, we were recording. If we weren't recording, we were doing radio or TV promos. If we weren't doing promos, we were being interviewed by the press, answering the same old questions we were always being asked. 'What's your favourite ice cream, guys?' 'What's your most embarrassing moment?' When you're feeling frustrated about not being taken seriously, these aren't questions you want to be asked. Much better to let your music do the talking; then, as now, the best thing about being in a band was always the time we spent on our music. Nobody enters the music business because they want to talk about ice cream.

This was a dark patch in my life, but it didn't mean there weren't bright moments. In July of that year, we performed at Live 8 in both Japan and then Edinburgh – a crazy few days even by our standards. And not long after that, we had the opportunity to work with one of my musical heroes.

I was still obsessed with The Who at the time, the band that had hugely influenced my songwriting for *Wonderland*. We'd even covered 'Pinball Wizard' for a B side. I was nuts about them – they were all I listened to for about a year. So when the opportunity came up to record 'My Generation' with Roger Daltrey, we were all over it.

Dougie: The day we met him was the same day we heard that *Wonderland* had gone to number one. Awesome! We were set up in a live studio before he arrived, practising the song. There's a bass break in it, obviously first played by John Entwistle, The Who's legendary bass player. We'd just reached that part in the song when Roger Daltrey sauntered in. Shit. I'd been practising this break hard over the past couple of days, but to perform it in front of the guy who was used to hearing John Entwistle play it was about as nerve-racking as it gets. I just about pulled it off.

Tom: Dougie's too modest. He and Harry had really started to work on their playing. They were turning into an awesomely solid rhythm section.

Harry: There's a drum break in 'My Generation' too. Anybody heard of Keith Moon? As soon as Dougie had managed his bit, I felt Roger Daltrey's eyes on me. Deep breath . . . and it just about came together.

Danny: But Daltrey was no muso trying to catch us out. Like we've said before, it's always the guys who have made it massive who are the friendliest. He was no exception. And to be in the room with this absolute legend, performing one of his most famous songs with him, was a good reminder of how nuts – and cool – our life had become. He gave us some good advice about protecting our ears on stage – he'd seriously damaged his hearing the night Keith Moon set off a bomb in his bass drum, and while I don't think Harry has any plans to do that, we took his words on board anyway.

Dougie: A bit later we met Pete Townshend too. Odd-looking bloke. You know when you look at yourself in the back of a spoon . . . ?

Tom: But despite these brighter moments, I was still living under a cloud. I was a total nightmare to be around, and I even started wondering if I wanted to carry on with the band. I'd lost my enthusiasm for absolutely everything, and looking back it's a wonder the guys didn't deck me. Danny and Dougie don't do confrontation, though, so neither of them challenged my sour mood or my increasing lack of energy. It meant the only person who would ever stand up to me when I was being so hard to get along with was Harry.

To say Harry and I clashed during that period is an understatement. For him, being in a band was all about having a good time; for me, it was all about the music. We were both right and we were both wrong; at the time, just as it would wind me up that Harry was never around when we were working hard on our demos, it wound Harry up that I was dismissive of his desire to go out and have fun. I'd never really had close friends until McFly came along. For me, socializing meant getting together with Danny and Dougie in the studio. I guess I didn't get it that Harry had a social life outside of the band house.

Harry: Whenever I brought friends round, their reaction to Danny and Dougie was always the same: 'Legends!'

As for Tom, I'd always hear the same response: 'What's up with him?' And the antisocial side of his character seemed to be getting stronger and stronger. When I finally got it together with Izzy, she was convinced that Tom hated her, because he never seemed to make an effort.

Danny and Dougie would get just as baited with Tom as I would – we'd talk together about the way he was being – but they never backed me up when push came to shove. When I spoke to Fletch about the problems we were having, about how hard Tom was to be around, he thought it was all in my head because the others hadn't broached the subject with him. But they'd broached it with me, many times. And the arguments we had were very real.

Dougie had written a song before McFly was even a band, called 'Silence Is A Scary Sound'. The guys had made a demo of it, and Tom, being a decent drummer himself, had devised a drum track. We were in rehearsals for the *Wonderland* arena tour that was to kick off in September 2005, and we were practising this song. There was a part at the end that I couldn't play at the kit but which Tom, having written it, could.

Rehearsals had always been a tense time during this period. It felt like three against one, and that's never healthy for band harmony. But it all blew up during this one session. Because I couldn't play this part, I cooked up my own version of it – a bit simpler, but it still sounded OK. Tom wasn't having it. Every time I played it, he stopped the rehearsal: 'No, it's not like that. It's like *this*.'

I tried to keep my cool. 'I'll practise it,' I told him quietly. 'OK?'

But it wasn't OK. 'Why don't you do it like *this*? Like *that*? Just practise it, Harry. *Now!*'

'I *will* practise it, mate. But for now, I'll do it like this . . .'

Tom: Harry has an obsessive, competitive part to his nature. When he decides he wants to do something, it takes over his life. In time, drumming *would* take over his life. He was going to turn into an even more awesome drummer. But at this stage in our career, he had yet to grow obsessed with practising. While there's no doubt that Harry was a better drummer than me even then, the fact that I'd made a demo playing in my own style meant I expected him to be able to replicate it. I was being a complete dick, of course, but I think there was a tiny part of me that was pleased if Harry couldn't play something. It justified my (totally irrational) irritation that he wasn't there with us all the time in the studio, and that he'd chosen to spend more time out with his mates than working on demos with us at the band house.

Harry: Tom kept going on at me about this drum part. I was angry, and maybe a bit embarrassed. It was hard enough to take the fact that I couldn't play it, without having him needle me about it incessantly.

We took a break. Half an hour out to clear our heads and recharge our batteries. As I was chatting with

Dougie, I showed him a fancy drum fill I'd been working on.

And Tom *lost* it.

'I wish you'd spent as much time working on *our* stuff as you have on *that*!'

OK. Deep breath. Keep calm. Don't react.

Dougie went to the loo. Tom was on at me again. 'Go on,' he said. 'Practise it. Now. Practise the part.'

'Mate, I'll do it. I *will* practise it. But in my own time . . .' I didn't want to do it in front of him; I wanted the chance to work at it properly, on my own.

Tom sneered at me. 'It'd be all right,' he said, 'if you were a great drummer, but you're *not*.'

That was it. He'd been pushing me and pushing me, making me feel awful and stupid and like I didn't deserve to be in the band, and this was a step too far. I gave him the middle finger, threw my drumsticks across the rehearsal room and stormed out.

Tom: I didn't go back to the band house that night. I couldn't. I went to my parents' tiny house and slept in their minuscule box room, my own bedroom having been given over to my sister. I say slept; in fact I just cried and cried. It felt like the band was falling apart around me, and it was my fault. I needed to man up. Harry went away that weekend with some mates. I plucked up the courage to call him. I was so full of remorse. I told him the truth – that he was a *great* drummer and that *I'd* been being a dick – and he was cool enough to accept my apologies. But although that, for me, was a low point, I still had lower to go.

❖

Harry: Our arena tour in September was a massive step up from our theatre tour the previous year. Bigger venues. Bigger audiences. Bigger deal. We performed to hundreds of thousands of people over the course of that tour, including three nights at Wembley and three at the Manchester Arena. The first night of our first theatre tour in Wolverhampton had wowed us enough, but to step out on to the stage at Wembley and hear the screams was on a different level. We went all out with the production, too – pyrotechnics, huge inflatable legs, a piano that came up out of the ground, a revolving drum riser. We even filmed this crazy gangster scene to project as our intro. I dread to think how much money we lavished on that show.

Danny: And as the crowds who came to see us got bigger, so did the attention we received. On the *Wonderland* tour, it was impossible to get away from the fans. They'd follow the tour bus away from the venue; even though our hotels were booked under pseudonyms, they'd find out where we were staying and check in for the night; they'd always be in the hotel bars and the public areas.

We'd often arrive at airports to find fans waiting for us. And not just girls. We landed on one occasion to find, among others, a guy of about fifteen hanging around hoping to meet us. Let's not be too unkind about the fella, but he was a little bit odd. He tried to put his arm around us – a bit too aggressively – and so we started joking around a bit. 'Harry, he wants a hug! Dougie, give him a kiss!' Harry and Dougie obliged, and it was all very good natured. This lad had a big grin on his face as we all piled into the car that was waiting for us.

But as he stood there smiling, we saw he had something else, too.

He was wearing a kind of baggy shell suit, and it was suddenly obvious that either he had pinched one of Harry's drumsticks and put it in his pocket, or he really had been *very* pleased to see us.

Time for a sharp exit, as Boner Boy waved us off, his baggy trousers firmly erected around his nether portions like a tent.

Boner Boy aside, the vast majority of the attention we received was from girls. Sometimes it was a bit much. Sometimes we allowed ourselves to take advantage of what was on offer. But even from the early days, we considered it a bit uncool to work our way through McFly groupies just because they were there.

Dougie: These days, life on tour is a hell of a sight more sedate. As the years wore on, events occurred that would make us a lot less hungry for the usual goings-on that people always imagine a band get up to when they're on the road. You'll read about them later in our story. Nowadays, though, you're more likely to find us safely ensconced on the tour bus in the hours after a show, challenging each other in one of the legendary McFly Fifa tournaments on the Xbox, or hunkering down with a late-night movie in our hotel room, with the door firmly locked from the inside.

All told, though, the Wonderland tour was awesome. Playing to these massive audiences was the best thing ever, not because we were after the adulation, but because, as we've always said, the best thing about being in a band is playing the music. There was no bigger buzz than being able to play the songs we felt so passionately about in front of fans who were clearly as into them as we were. In short, the Wonderland tour confirmed the fact that, whatever else was going on in our lives, we had the best job in the world. Period.

Tom: By the time the *Wonderland* tour came to an end, I'd truly had enough of living in the band house. It was *so* cluttered. *So* messy. And our lives had moved on. We were so busy that we just didn't seem to hang out in the house as much as before. And maybe we'd grown up a bit too. It felt like the time had come for us to move on, and move out.

Princess Park Manor was the gated community where Busted had lived together, and where I'd spent time with James Bourne writing songs in the days before McFly. V, the band Danny hadn't joined, had just moved out of an apartment there, and together we made the decision to move out of the band house and into this new place. It wasn't a long-term solution. Our rough plan was that we'd live in *two* different apartments – Harry and Danny in one, me and Dougie in another. V's flat was the only apartment available, so the intention was that Dougie and I would move out when another became vacant. For this reason, Harry and Danny took the big, en suite rooms, while we moved into the slightly pokier spare rooms. I didn't even have a proper bed – just a mattress on the floor, a suitcase for my clothes and a keyboard on which to write songs.

Dougie: My room in Princess Park Manor was decked out with three enormous lizard tanks. I'd had a few reptiles in the band house – Ned the frog was a particular favourite – but now I shared my new space with two royal pythons, a Bosc's monitor, a salvator monitor, a bearded dragon and a couple of tortoises. There was enough space to walk to the bed, and nothing else.

Tom: While Dougie was getting all David Attenborough on our ass, I was still obsessing about being the fat one in the band. I wanted to lose weight, but rather than going about it the sensible way, I pretty much stopped eating. I'd go to Starbucks and order a Frappuccino and a blueberry muffin, and that was me for the day. Not eating apart from my daily Starbucks became my routine. Not only would I beat myself up internally if I consumed anything else, I'd be in a foul mood if we were working somewhere and there was no Starbucks. I *had* to have a Starbucks every morning. One day my car was in the garage so I got up extra early and walked several miles to our local town to get one. It was an obsession, and a deeply unhealthy one. There's nothing that makes you more depressed than not eating, and my black mood just got blacker. I became tired, grumpy, snappy, agitated with everyone – even more so than before. I had a constant headache, and any time I did succumb and eat something bad, I'd be racked with guilt.

Living in that tiny, spartan room; feeling bad about myself and everybody else; not eating. It wasn't a great time.

Harry: Understatement of the century. That was the period in our career when we argued the most. It was difficult to deal with because we'd always got on so well. But now, Tom was hard to talk to. Snappy. It felt like he was disagreeing with everything out of principle.

Danny: Whenever we went anywhere by car, he'd always have his iPod on, like he wanted to ignore us all, to shut us out. If we were discussing band matters, he'd be completely contrary, making a point of taking the opposite view to everyone else. His door was always shut.

Tom: I must have been awful to live with. I hated *everything*. I didn't want to do anything the other guys wanted to do. I didn't like the music they were listening to. I'd never been the most sociable of people, but now I felt more antisocial than ever. I'd lost my enthusiasm for everything. And the doubts I'd already been harbouring about whether I wanted to carry on with the band grew even stronger. I felt locked into my mood, and I didn't have any expectation of ever being able to break out of it.

Dougie: He even dyed his hair black. Whenever I see pictures of him like that, I remember that period when he was constantly down. Never smiling. If he ever dyes his hair black again, I reckon it would completely freak me out. None of us knew anything about depression, of course. Why should we? We just thought Tom was being a bit of a dick and tried not to let it get in the way of the complete awesomeness of being in the band. We didn't realize there was stuff going on in his head that even he didn't understand.

Harry: Tom's always been the leader of the band – not just because he started it, but because he's naturally a leader anyway. But now that he was being negative about everything, it had a knock-on effect on us all.

Dougie: Like if Leonardo from the *Teenage Mutant Ninja Turtles* started being all bummed out about everything. How were we going to kick arse if *our* Leonardo was wearing a black eye-band instead of a blue one?

Danny: I was baited about all the family stuff that was going on in my life, which put me in a bad mood, too. Tom and I were always arguing. Tom and Harry were always arguing. Dougie did the sensible thing and kept quiet. The three of us closed ranks a bit. Tom's mood changes were extreme, but because we'd never even come across the idea of depression, we didn't know what was going on. What the hell was Tom's problem?

Tom: I came to the decision that I definitely didn't want to live with the other guys any more. More to the point, I wanted to live with Giovanna. I wanted to get our relationship back on track. For the two months leading up to Christmas, I spent all my time looking for somewhere else to live.

Danny: Tom's issues aside, being in McFly continued to be a blast. At the Royal Variety Performance in November 2005, we met the Queen. I was so nervous. Me? Danny from Bolton? Performing for and meeting Her Majesty? It made me freak out. I downed a bit of booze to help me deal with it, then hit a bum note during our performance of 'The Ballad Of Paul K' . . .

Dougie: When you meet the Queen, a palace flunkey comes round and tells you all the rules and etiquette you have to follow. You're only allowed to speak when you're spoken to, and you *must* call her 'Ma'am' as in 'palm', not 'Ma'am' as in 'jam'.

So, we said to ourselves, let's get this right. 'Ma'am' as in 'spam' not 'Ma'am' as in 'palm'? 'Spalm' as in 'Ma'am'? 'Jam' as in 'ham'? Cliff Richard – obviously a veteran Queen-greeter – came up to us. 'Guys, it's "Ma'am" as in "palm" . . .' Cheers, Cliff!

Tom: Once the curtain had gone down, all the artists filed on to stage in a horseshoe formation. We were at one end. The Queen started at the other, pressing the flesh with artists whose careers she had no doubt been following carefully, like Ozzy Osbourne and Slash. I was stood next to Cliff with Harry, Dougie and Danny next to me.

Harry: As the Queen was working her way down the line, one of us suggested that when our turn came we should give her a fist pump and say, 'Yo, Queen!' That set us off. We started giggling. And the closer she came, the worse our giggling grew. By the time she was a few handshakes away, we were almost in tears.

Tom was trying to calm us down. 'Dudes, it's the *Queen* . . . Guys, *really, shut up* . . .'

Tom: I was worried we were going to be beheaded.

Danny: But the more he said that, the more it made the rest of us laugh. And it was impossible to stop – the worst laugh attack we'd ever had.

Harry: And then she was there. I saw her shaking Dougie's hand, and then she was shaking mine. I was just about to say, 'Your Majesty', when I heard Dougie try to suppress a snort of laughter. I put my head down so I couldn't catch her eye, and heard my voice rise a couple of octaves as I tried not to crumble: 'Your Majesteeeeeeee!!!'

Tom: She moved on to Danny. He'd obviously forgotten that you aren't supposed to speak until spoken to, because he immediately started jabbering away at her.

Danny: I didn't have any choice – I had to concentrate

on talking to her because otherwise I'd be concentrating on Harry and Dougie laughing. 'Enjoy the show, then?' I asked her.

'Oh yes,' she said. 'Very good.'

'Nice theatre, innit?'

'Yes, yes, beautiful place,' she agreed, before, thankfully, finally moving on. Happily I didn't end up in the Tower for breaking the rules. We never met Her Majesty again, but we did perform in front of her at an Olympics event and I managed to mess the words up – karma, probably, for us being such naughty schoolboys at the Royal Variety!

Dougie: Princess Park Manor had always been celeb central. Busted and V had been there, the footballer Ashley Cole was there, and so were Girls Aloud. Attractive girls, but a bit older than us, and because everyone fancied them we always ended up being a bit gimpy in their company. We were our own worst enemies around them, like a bunch of gawky teenagers around the coolest girls in the school. Of course, to get with one of Girls Aloud would be awesome, but that would never happen, would it?

Er . . . no. It wouldn't.

Danny: A few months earlier, I'd been on a night out with Antony Brant from V. We'd hooked up with a couple of girls and were bringing them back to his place in Princess Park Manor when we bumped into Cheryl

Cole and her mum. I don't know why, but Cheryl's mum and I didn't really hit it off – I felt like she was giving me a bit of an ear-bashing – but it was obvious that Cheryl herself had eyes for Antony. We took our girls back to his flat, but Cheryl invited him over to her place. It didn't seem fair that he was getting all this attention from one of Girls Aloud, while all I'd got was a few sharp words from Cheryl's mum. But it did at least make me realize that Girls Aloud weren't untouchable. Perhaps I could have a crack at one of them myself.

When *we* moved into Princess Park Manor, I decided to put my plan into action. Which one of them did I fancy the most? I decided on Kimberley. I reckoned I should send her a text to test the water. But how was I going to get her number?

Princess Park Manor came complete with a little minibus for anyone who wanted to get down to the nearby shops or to the station. All you had to do was phone one of the drivers and they would pick you up and take you where you wanted to go. There was one who was particularly friendly, a really happy-go-lucky guy. Always willing to please. And, of course, because all the residents of Princess Park Manor used the drivers, they had everyone's number. Including Kimberley's. When I asked this particular driver if he'd give it to me, he was happy to oblige.

I texted her. *It's Danny from McFly here. Got your number from one of the drivers. Wondered if you wanted to go for a few drinks. Be awesome to take you out . . .*

How could she possibly refuse such a gallant invitation? She texted back almost immediately. That had to be a good sign. I opened up her message.

First of all, I'm a bit annoyed he gave you my number. I'll have to have words with him about that. And secondly, no, I don't want to go for a drink. I've got a boyfriend.

She sounded *well* pissed off. Maybe Girls Aloud weren't allowed after all.

Dougie: It wasn't like the rest of us had exactly laid the best foundations for Danny. Practically every time we'd ever seen them in the past, we'd made twats of ourselves.

I loved being in the band so much, but if there was one tiny fly in the ointment, it was having to do the rounds of all the teen press and answer all the same old questions in interviews (I know – poor us!). We'd put all this effort into making our new album, but nobody ever asked us about the music; they just asked us what our favourite pizza topping was. Even worse than interviews were photoshoots. Whole days in studios, dressing up in silly scenarios. We wanted to talk about our new music; they wanted us to dress up as vampires for Halloween. Those photoshoots were so boring – and there were so many of them, because we were on the front cover of the teen press week in week out – that we started making ridiculous demands. We'd only do photoshoots, we said, if they became fun days. We insisted that the magazines take us go-karting and photograph us doing that; on one occasion I did a shoot surrounded by lizards and snakes. But it was more difficult to make interviews good fun, so the temptation to give stupid answers grew bigger and bigger. It was the only way to keep sane.

I was in the middle of one of these interviews when the question came: if you could set a trap for any other celebrity, what would it be and why?

I *tried* to answer it sensibly, but I couldn't really think of anybody I disliked enough! For some reason Nicola from Girls Aloud popped into my head. I don't know why – she is, by all accounts, a very nice person. Perhaps it was because a few other people had taken a dig at her, so I reckoned she'd be hardened to it, but I honestly had no beef with her at all. I was taking the piss out of the interviewer more than anybody else as I went off on one. I'd set this trap for Nicola – a big pit for her to fall in. There'd be spikes at the bottom, and if the spikes didn't kill her, then the snakes would. And if the snakes didn't kill her, an axe would chop off her head . . . It was a *really* daft question so I gave a *really* daft answer. My imaginary tortures for Nicola became more and more graphic, but I was obviously just having a laugh so I didn't think much more about it. When the issue came out, however, what was meant to be one throwaway answer to one throwaway question was splashed over the front cover and became a double-page spread in the magazine.

We were at our rehearsal studio a couple of weeks later, and during a break Harry and I wandered up to the cafeteria. Girls Aloud were sitting around one of the tables having a cup of tea. I'd forgotten all about the interview, but we still stood awkwardly in the doorway. *Uh-oh . . . Girls Aloud . . . hope we don't say something stupid . . .*

Which is when Nicola stood up. 'Here, Dougie, what's all this about a fookin' snake?'

I gave her a slightly perplexed look.

'You said you'd set a trap for me. What have I fookin' done to you?'

Oh. Shit.

I should have just apologized and explained what had happened. But I didn't. I panicked. I tended to do that in front of girls, especially hot ones. Everything became a bit of a blur and I remember seeing a can of Coke out of the corner of my eye. If only *I* was a can of Coke, I thought desperately to myself, I wouldn't have to deal with this awkward, embarrassing, excruciating situation . . .

And then Harry came to my rescue . . .

Harry: I thought I was a bit more streetwise. A bit smoother. A bit better at talking to girls. Leave it to me, Doug.

'Hey, girls . . .' I started to say. But then my powers of speech seemed to desert me. Dougie *had* said he wanted an axe to cut off Nicola's head. How the hell *was* I going to talk him out of that one? 'I, er . . . I don't think Doug *really* meant . . .'

They were staring at me, wordless.

'I mean, what he was *trying* to say was . . .'

They didn't look impressed. At all.

I could feel my face turning the colour of beetroot. I

looked over at the counter. 'Can of Fanta, please,' I squeaked.

Dougie: You know how, when you're at school and you've been sent from the class for being naughty, the walk to the door is the longest ever? That was us, heads hung, Girls Aloud smirking at us as we tried to make a sharp exit, but everything seemed to happen in slo-mo. Not our finest hour.

Harry: You'd think we'd learn, but there's something about them that turns us into buffoons. At the Pride of Britain awards that year, they were at a table near us. Danny and I had had a few beers and decided to go and say hello. I moved round the table saying hi to each of them until I came to Cheryl. 'How you doing?' I asked brightly.

'How you doing?' she said at exactly the same time. 'JINX!'

What are you, Harry? Eleven? What are you going to do next – tell her she can't speak until someone says her name?

Cheryl looked at me with a slightly strange smile. Her eyes moved left and right, as if she was looking for an escape route. I took a step back. 'Er, see ya!' I announced, feeling the blood rising up my neck.

We scarpered back to our table, and kept our heads down for the rest of the evening.

Tom: Our time in Princess Park Manor should have been fantastic, but, for me, thanks to my black mood, it wasn't. I had decided I wanted to get out of there, to buy a house of my own, but I didn't really know how much houses cost, and I certainly didn't know how much money I had. Up until then, I hadn't had to think about it. We had an allowance, and our rent was paid out of our band account. When I met with our accountant, I was pleasantly surprised. And when, just before Christmas, I found a house in north-west London, not a million miles from where I'd grown up, it felt right.

Dougie: Christmas was the only time we ever got off. We'd been doing loads of promo in the run-up to it, and Tom hadn't been in a good way at all. Maybe it was all down to the fact that we'd been working non-stop for a year and we all needed a break. From the band, and from each other. That Christmas, Danny and I took our families away on a cruise, Tom went to Florida and Harry to Thailand with Izzy.

Tom: For me, holidays are always very inspiring times, and for some reason, Orlando is a particularly inspiring place. Maybe that's why I try to go there every year. As soon as I arrive, I find my creative batteries recharging and I almost want to come straight back home and start working on new songs. Florida worked its magic then, too. I took my mum, my dad, my sister and Giovanna with me for Christmas and New Year, and it marked a turning point for me. I felt inspired to write – so much so that I wrote our song 'Bubble Wrap' while on the loo in Walt Disney World. (Well, it's a good time to sit and think, isn't it?) I came back feeling fresh (from Florida, not the loo). More positive. The darkness had started to lift.

Harry was still in Thailand when I returned, but Danny and Dougie were back from their cruises.

Dougie: We'd had a couple of weeks in the sun, and I came back feeling just as re-energized as Tom. And full of ideas. I had started getting into an artist called Drew Brophy. He makes cartoony, trippy surf art – bright and colourful, and the exact opposite to the imagery of *Wonderland*. It seemed to go hand in hand with the music Tom was getting into at the time.

Tom: Matt Willis from Busted had recommended to Fletch that we listen to a San Francisco band called Jellyfish. While I was in Florida I checked out their album *Spilt Milk*, and absolutely loved it. Even now I can't understand why it isn't one of the biggest albums ever. I came back to the UK feeling completely inspired by this new discovery, and to see Dougie enthused by his new-found love of Drew Brophy's work led to what I can only call an epiphany. We found ourselves massively geeking out, staying up all night, filled with a renewed enthusiasm for our work and for the future. Our musical outlook changed. From the darkness of *Wonderland* we saw ourselves creating something as bright as Drew Brophy and as poppy as Jellyfish.

Dougie: That night, I saw Tom's mood change in front of my eyes. The moment we started talking about accepting what kind of band we were, about concentrating on having fun and enjoying our music rather than trying to be cool and moody, it was like a cloud had been lifted from above his head.

Tom: And it had. Suddenly I felt determined not to sink back into that slump. Determined not to jeopardize everything by acting like a dick to the other guys. When you're depressed, you can't remember what it's like to be happy. But when you're up, you *can* remember the depression, and when it lifts the relief is so intense that you'll do anything not to get back into that state. Of course, sometimes you don't have the choice, and it wasn't for a few years that I learned that there were things going on in my brain that were more complicated than I knew. The alien was still tapping at my window. But right now, I felt like my head was in gear. Like the future was bright. Like I was back.

A good thing too, because now we had to start thinking about album number three.

It's Not the Size of Your Boat . . .

CHAPTER

9

Tom: *Wonderland* had been a reaction to *Room On The Third Floor*. Our next album would be a reaction to *Wonderland*. We had to get away from all the dark, moody stuff. We had to let the light in.

And we needed to write some songs.

Our publishers had suggested that we get together with some other songwriters and see what came of it. We weren't that keen – the whole point of McFly was that we did our own thing – but we went along with it. In early March of 2006, I found myself in a poky basement studio in Shepherd's Bush with a reasonably well-known songwriter who rejoiced in the name of Eg White. I tried to be open-minded, to approach this in the hope that something would come of it. But when Eg announced that he considered The Beatles to be over-rated, and that he was more of a hip-hop guy, I started to have my doubts about whether we were a good match. Suffice it to say I didn't return for the second day we had booked in together.

Danny: Dougie and I had a similar experience with another songwriter. Bollocks to this, we thought. We didn't *want* to write with other people. We were good enough to do it ourselves. So that's what we did.

Harry: I was due to travel to India on a cricket trip as part of Sport Relief – in its way as eye-opening as our band trip to Uganda had been, as we saw the devastation that the tsunami had had on the lives of the people there. You never forget these trips. It's sobering to go from the kind of five-star luxury I'd been enjoying on holiday in Thailand to witnessing at first hand how entire villages had been wiped out, and livelihoods destroyed.

Some people are cynical about the sight of celebrities taking over the airwaves for charity work. There's no doubt that it works two ways. We'd grown up watching the Spice Girls do the Comic Relief single; when we were asked to record it, we definitely realized what a big deal it was for our career. But it would be a deeply cynical self-publicist who wouldn't be moved by the grinding poverty I saw in India, and who didn't forget for a moment about what the exposure could do for them, and focus instead on how they could help the charity. We're by no means saints or missionaries, but having seen life on the other side of the fence, we're all happy to do our bit.

Tom: The only time I've ever lost it with a journalist is when one suggested our Comic and Sport Relief work was cynical and mercenary. Fuck. Off. Anybody who has spent any time working for these organizations knows what a witless suggestion that is.

Harry: The cricket in India *was* cool, though. I was going through a phase of rediscovering my love for the game. I'd play at any available opportunity, and started to recapture some of the form I'd shown at school. When the guys wrote a lyric in a song called 'Little Joanna' that went 'But only the music is bleeding when crickets replace the band', I thought they might be having a little dig. In fact, the line referred to insects, but there's no doubt that there were times that I found myself wondering if perhaps I should have pursued cricket rather than music.

Danny: While Harry was away in India, and after our abortive sessions with other songwriters, Tom, Dougie and I decided to hole ourselves away in the studio we had set up in Princess Park Manor. We wrote for ten days solid. We got up at eleven and worked till five in the morning. A few hours' sleep, then repeat. We barely stepped outside. Our housekeeper Darrotta brought us our meals, so we didn't even have to think about feeding ourselves. In those ten days, we wrote the bulk of our third album.

Tom: When we weren't writing, we were going through artwork and re-imagining everything about the band's image, dragging ourselves away from all the dark stuff that had gone before. In addition to listening to Jellyfish, I became completely obsessed with Queen, just like I'd been obsessed with The Who during *Wonderland*. And, most importantly, we were having a brilliant time again.

Despite all that, I didn't go back on my decision to move out of Princess Park Manor. I felt like I was on the cusp of a new phase in my life. Getting my own place, where I could be alone with Giovanna when I wanted to be, definitely felt like the right move. During our Christmas break, I had taken Danny and Dougie to see the house I was going to buy. I expected them to like it; I didn't expect them to like it as much as they did. Within half an hour of seeing it, they'd put down a deposit on a flat in the house next door.

Harry: I'd been getting ready to go on holiday in Thailand, so hadn't joined them. I got back from Thailand knowing that Tom would be moving out, but thinking I'd still have my boys around me at Princess Park Manor, only to find that all three of them were intending to relocate. I was a bit pissed off, and slightly freaked when the guys started on at me to come and check out another flat that was for sale in the same house as Danny and Dougie's. Long story short, Danny and Dougie ended up buying a flat each, one above the other, next door to Tom; I bought a flat just down the road. Bye-bye, Princess Park Manor. Now we all had our own space, but we were a stone's throw away from each other. A perfect set-up – best friends had become neighbours.

Tom: It was fun for everyone still to be close by, and convenient, too, because our days were filled with all the stuff that goes with being in a band. Like flying to LA, for example, to do some promotion for *Just My*

Luck, which was about to be released in the US. It was in LA that we came up with the title for our third album. We were hanging out eating burgers in a little diner on Sunset Boulevard with our mate George. George was regaling us with the story of some woman he'd shagged, and decided to share some wisdom about his sexual technique. 'It's not the size of your boat,' he told us. 'It's the motion in the ocean.'

Dougie and I looked at each other. We'd obviously both had the same thought at the same time. From that moment on, we knew *Motion In The Ocean* would be the name for album three.

It was on that trip to LA that we all visited a tattoo parlour opposite the Viper Room where River Phoenix died. We were getting on so much better now, and it seemed like a cool band thing to do. We each decided to have a word tattooed on to our feet, and chronically got the giggles thinking up stupid foot puns. In the end I had 'Big' tattooed on my heel.

Harry: I had 'Bare'.

Dougie: I had 'Athlete's'.

Danny: And I had 'Good Ef'. (C'mon, work it out.)

Dougie: I was trying to give up smoking, so although we *were* all getting on much better, I was a bit agitated for most of the time. Which is why, in LA, I ended up punching Harry in the face.

Harry: Dougie was suffering an unfortunate bout of halitosis, so I dubbed him 'poo breath'. Unfortunately, he was also suffering an unfortunate bout of sense-of-humour-failure, and didn't find it very funny. Tom and Danny, though, were in hysterics. Each time they laughed it just added fuel to the fire. Dougie got into more of a bait with every poo breath, which only made it funnier.

It was so juvenile. '*Stop* it, Harry.'

'OK, poo breath.'

'*Harry!*'

'Hey, chill out . . . *poo breath*!'

Dougie was in the front of the car, which meant we couldn't see how angry he was really getting. So I didn't take him very seriously when he gave me a well-deserved warning. 'Dude, seriously, say that one more time and I'll hit you.'

'OK, OK!'

A long pause.

I only whispered it: '*Poo breath*!'

Suddenly, Dougie twisted round from the front and launched his fist into my face. He gave me a proper smack. Can't say I didn't deserve it.

There was a shocked silence in the car.

'Whoa,' I said, rubbing my stinging cheek, 'chill out. Poo breath.'

We got to our hotel and I went up to my room. Almost immediately, the phone rang. It was Dougie, crying his eyes out. 'Dude, I'm *so* sorry for punching you . . . it was *so* out of order . . . I feel *so* bad . . .'

I tried to calm him down. 'Mate, don't worry about

it . . . I pushed you too far . . . water under the bridge . . . all friends . . .' He eventually stopped sobbing and hung up.

Tom: Thirty seconds later, I got a call from Harry. 'Guess who I had on the phone in floods of tears,' he said. 'Only poo breath.'

We performed a promo show in LA. It was the first time we'd ever played properly in the US, and although we weren't trying to 'break' America, it was slightly surreal to realize that we had fans out there. Not enough, though, to pull off the stunt that the film's publicity people had cooked up for the première of *Just My Luck*.

If we're not performing a show, our biggest nightmare is having the spotlight on us. Presenting awards, public speaking, walking down the red carpet – they're hell for someone who hides in the toilet during parties, and the other guys feel the same. Which made the LA première of *Just My Luck* one of our most excruciating moments ever. The prospect of turning up and being the centre of attention was bad enough. When it was suggested that we should arrive on an open-top London bus, our response was unanimous. No. Way.

But then we got Fletched.

Our manager talked us into it. (Verbally beat us into submission, more like.) So when the day came, we found ourselves standing on top of a double-decker, festooned with the McFly logo and a Union Jack, frankly wishing the ground would swallow us up. Nobody knew who we were! We might have pulled it off in London; in LA, a town used to Hollywood A-listers, nobody understood all this pomp and circumstance. We were fighting each other not to stand at the edge, so we could hide our embarrassed faces.

It was every bit as bad as we expected. Some fans had turned up, but they were miles away behind a cordon; a few press members had been briefed about us, so they half-heartedly snapped a few photographs. Other than that, bemusement all round. We couldn't wait to get off that bus.

Harry: Not that what awaited us on the red carpet was much better. None of us had seen Lindsay since New Orleans. Meeting her again for the first time on the red carpet in front of half the American press corps was hardly ideal. Clearly it wasn't something she was relishing either: she barely made eye-contact as we said hello and posed for photographs together. Even her little sister made a point of ignoring us. Blown out by a twelve-year-old. Sweet.

Tom: In any case, we were more excited to see Brian Wilson from the Beach Boys on the red carpet. Never mind that he seemed too spaced out even to know where he was, let alone who the hell *we* were – we had our photograph taken with one of our heroes, and moments like that never get old. And it's good for people in our position to be fans ourselves once in a while. It reminds you what it's like, keeps you grounded and helps you empathize with the fans who get a bit star-struck when they meet you.

Dougie: And then we watched the movie. We'd already had a screening in London, so we knew it wasn't the coolest film in the world. We knew it wasn't *Citizen Kane*. We sat there with the rest of the cast watching it through our hands . . .

Danny: The movie was proof that, really, we'd be better sticking to our music. Back in the UK, that's just what we did.

One of the most important decisions a band can make is who's going to produce them. Hugh Padgham had played a blinder on *Room On The Third Floor* and *Wonderland*, but we felt the time had come for a fresh set of ears and a new pair of hands on the mixing board. Around this time we met Jason Perry. Jason had been lead vocalist in a band called 'A', who'd been big on the Kerrang! scene, and had had a big hit with a song called 'Nothing' – a favourite of all of ours back in the day. Pretty cool, then, when it transpired that Jason was a big McFly fan, who saw us as serious musicians and not just bubblegum pop.

Dougie: I was a bit star-struck myself meeting Jason, but excited that he wanted to work with us.

Danny: It was immediately obvious that Jason had something new to bring to the table. The recording process for *Motion In The Ocean* was different from what we'd experienced before. For a start, we had a period of pre-production – rehearsals with our producer, specifically for recording. This meant that before we went into the studio with Jason to lay down the songs, we had all our individual parts worked out very precisely, so that our studio time was spent getting the performance and the sound right, and not orchestrating our songs as we went along.

In June, recording started for the new album. Jason and his co-producer, Julian Emery, wanted us to go away to record. Get out of London, away from any other distractions, so all our attention could be focused on recording. We went to Grouse Lodge, a residential studio in Ireland in the grounds of what used to be the Guinness family estate. The studio had its own little pub where the best Guinness in Ireland was supposed to be poured. Our bar bill at the end of the recording trip was several thousand pounds. This was the first time we'd worked with a producer whose strategy was to make sure we were having fun. If we weren't feeling it in the studio, he was happy for us to go and watch football or have a pint.

When we were recording 'Bubble Wrap', my vocal track clearly wasn't doing it for him. Jason asked me if I fancied a pint. Of course I did. Cut to half an hour later, I had a beer in my hand and the studio was in total darkness apart from the candles that he'd lit all around me to get the mood right. Jason and Julian did everything they could to make us happy while we were recording. Unlike when we'd been working on our previous two albums, there was never a moment when it felt like work. It was exactly what we needed.

Tom: Jason and Julian were writers as well, and we started putting a tune together. Its working title was 'Jelly Belly' and the lyrics were absolutely awful. We knew we had to change them, which is one of the most difficult things to do when a lyric is already stuck in your head. We liked the song, though, and recorded the instrumental tracks without really knowing what the final words were going to be.

And then, one night, I had a dream. In my dream, we'd written a song about falling in love with an alien (yeah, yeah, I know) that had become the biggest song ever in the history of the universe. The next day I told Dougie about my dream, and he suggested that we actually try to write this song, and base it on 'Jelly Belly'. The next job, of course, was to sell this slightly whacky idea to the other guys, but they were up for it, and the result was 'Star Girl'. Our record label took a bit more persuading – for some unfathomable reason they were in two minds about the line 'I fell in love with Uranus' – but we stood our ground. Good thing too. 'Star Girl' went to number one. It wasn't the biggest song in the history of the universe, like in my dream, but its airplay did breach the measly confines of Planet Earth. When Twitter became a major force, we started accumulating followers numbering hundreds of thousands. Being the geek that I am, some of *my* favourite people to follow were astronauts on the International Space Station, NASA and other space-related tweeters. One particular Twitter feed informed me every day what music the ISS crew had been woken up to. One day I re-tweeted this information, with an off-the-cuff comment: maybe we should try to get a McFly song played up in space.

It was a throwaway remark, but our fans took up the gauntlet. They went absolutely mental on Twitter, bombarding NASA with thousands and thousands of tweets, clogging up their email servers with requests to send a McFly song into orbit.

A week later, an email landed in my own inbox, from somebody at NASA. It was to let me know that our fans' bombardment hadn't gone unnoticed. They'd be in touch soon. Two weeks later, a bloke called Burt, one of NASA's head guys, called me up. He was amazed at how relentless our fans were, and we started talking about all sorts of possibilities. Maybe we could play at the last ever space-shuttle launch; maybe we could film a video at one of their facilities. At the time, NASA was running live sessions with the astronauts where you could tweet them questions and watch them online. And it was during one of these sessions that 'Star Girl' got played on the ISS while it was hurtling round the earth. It wasn't quite a dream come true, but it wasn't far off.

That summer was one of the best we've ever had. We returned from Ireland to our new homes, where Dougie had a skateboarding ramp erected in his garden, and we finished off recording vocal tracks for *Motion In The Ocean* in Danny's home studio. It was blazing hot, and we were reinvigorated as a band. The songs, I hope, reflected that. They were bubbly and summery. We felt good about the album, and we were back on track.

When the time came to tour *Motion In The Ocean*,

Heaven is a halfpipe.
When Dougie
moved into his own
place, he built a
skateboarding ramp
in his back garden.

Barbados. It was supposed to be a working holiday but there was definitely more holiday than working. Dougie and Danny's hair had a great time, too.

Above: Just checking for sharks . . .
Below: On reflection, climbing the Sydney Harbour Bridge
with a monster hangover probably wasn't such a good idea.

The calm before the storm . . . Danny, Harry and Dougie prepare for their next show.

Danny and Harry take advantage
of a break between dates on tour.

Harry gets ready
to greet the South
American fans.

At last, some time
out in Disneyland.

The band trip to Atlanta to work with Dallas Austin.

we made sure that our stage set reflected the upbeat, summery feel that we wanted the album to capture. We decked the stage out with Cadillacs and hammocks. We even had a beach hut so that we could invite fans up to watch us on stage. We had to stop doing that, though, because the rest of the audience would boo them. And it was on the *Motion In The Ocean* tour that we got to play with one of our musical heroes.

We'd had a number one earlier in the year with a Queen cover: 'Don't Stop Me Now'. Brian May had sent us a bottle of champagne to congratulate us, and asked if we would perform the song as part of the musical *We Will Rock You*'s sixtieth birthday celebrations for Freddie Mercury. We didn't need asking twice, and so we found ourselves in rehearsal with Brian May – the sweetest, most gentle man you could ever hope to meet. He politely listened to me geeking out about space (he has a PhD in astrophysics), and was really kind to all of us, as he still is to this day. It was like the stars were aligned. During *Wonderland* I'd been obsessed with The Who and had got to play with Roger Daltrey. Now I was obsessed with Queen, and here we were jamming with Brian May.

One good turn deserves another. Halfway through the *Motion In The Ocean* tour, we thought it would be a great idea to ask Brian if he wanted to come on stage with us. Whenever we have to do anything like this, we make Danny ask. He's by far the most affable, sociable member of the band, the kind of guy who can chat with anybody. Everybody likes Danny when they first meet him – it's only when they get to know him that they think he's a dick ☺. Danny popped the question – did Brian fancy doing a number at our Wembley show? He said yes. To be honest, he's such a nice bloke I can't imagine him ever saying no to anybody. He even delayed his holiday by a day or two to fit us in.

To announce Brian May on stage for our encore of 'Don't Stop Me Now' was definitely a career highlight. The crowd went absolutely wild for him, and it was a big moment for us when he later stated that he thought we were one of the best live bands in the country. Maybe people were beginning to take us a little more seriously after all.

Not that we were immune to criticism. It seemed there would always be people who wanted to assume we were nothing more than a manufactured pop band. Sometimes you can't help it getting to you. When a critic for a national newspaper wanted to give us a five-star review for one of our shows, her editor insisted that she make it four stars. Obviously they couldn't be seen praising McFly too much. One particular journalist slagged off our lyrics, but had the gall to misquote them. That *really* pissed me off. I wrote to her. It was fine not to like our lyrics, I said, but at least get them right before you criticize them. A reply came back almost immediately. She'd copied them out of our official lyric booklet. Further investigation revealed that Danny, who'd transcribed the lyrics for the booklet, had got them wrong himself. Nice one, Danny!

These days, if anyone misquotes us, it's easy enough to correct them on Twitter. And it's not a bad way to make sure they don't do it again. We've so many fans following us that they soon bombard the culprit with accusing messages.

All in all, though, life started to settle down a little for us after the release of *Motion In The Ocean*. We were all settled into our own places, and even Danny, the enthusiastic womanizer, found himself in a long-term relationship. We still tended to shun the celebrity lifestyle – our idea of a good night out wasn't cocktails and cocaine in a London club, but a few pints at our local old-man's pub, the Rose and Crown. Or so we thought.

Everything was good, even if our next career move didn't exactly turn out the way we wanted. Or maybe it did, because it paved the way for what happened next, musically speaking.

Bands and their record labels always have differences of opinion. What picture should go on the front of your album? What should be the first single? These are things that bands care deeply about, but they generally get resolved to everyone's satisfaction. The release of our *Greatest Hits* album, however, was something that we disagreed with from the moment it was mooted. Record companies love Greatest Hits records because they cost them nothing. To us it made no sense at all. We'd only released three albums, and we were constantly coming up with new material. A Greatest Hits after a decade's worth of albums would have been cool; to release one then seemed like a bit of a mockery. We worried that people would think we were following the usual manu-factured pop-band trajectory: a few albums, a Greatest Hits and then split up. In every interview we did around the time, we were asked if we were splitting up, and even when we said we weren't, nobody really believed us.

In the past, we'd always been given a lot of respect by the people around us, and a relatively free hand to do the things we wanted to do as a band. This was the first time we'd experienced being forced into something we opposed. It didn't sit well. But we tried to look on the positive side. Putting out our *Greatest Hits* did, at least, allow us to tour – that, for us, was always the light at the end of the tunnel. And also we were, despite what everybody thought, continuing as a band.

Because, no doubt about it, we felt we still had plenty up our sleeves.

Elton's John

CHAPTER

10

Danny: At our first ever show at the Hammersmith Apollo, my mum got chatting to a family in the bar. They were called the Sewells – Al and Deb and their two daughters. My mum hit it off with them, and they became friends. In time, Al would become a bit of a father figure for me. He and Deb were also lifelong friends of Rod Stewart, and so I got to know him too.

In November 2007, we went to Ireland to perform at a Childline show. Rod was playing the same night and had a private jet waiting to take him back home. He told me he had three spare seats, so three of us could fly back with him if we wanted to.

Tom: Obviously Danny had to go because he was Rod's mate; it was Dougie's birthday, so we decided that he should have a seat; which left only one. Harry and I played stone, scissors, paper for the pleasure. Harry lost, so I joined Danny and Dougie.

Harry: That's the way it goes, but to soften the blow England were playing in the Ashes, so I was able to go back to the hotel and watch the highlights. Simple pleasures . . .

Danny: We met Rod at the airport. When you fly on a private jet, you don't go through the usual airport security, so we had to hand over all our passports before we boarded. He's a bit of a joker, Rod. A bit of a naughty schoolboy. But we didn't think twice about handing over our documents, got on the plane and enjoyed a cool flight back to London.

Rod had a car waiting for him on the Tarmac. Before getting in, he said goodbye and handed back our passports. It was only as his car was driving away that we looked in our passports and saw that he'd used a permanent marker and drawn dicks all over them. I had one on my photo, sticking out of the top of my head! We rang him later and he was cracking up at his own little joke. No doubt he'd have been cracking up even more when he saw the trouble we had after that, using dick-graffitied passports to travel the world. Customs officials aren't known for their sense of humour, and I've lost count of the times they told us how juvenile we were, and how they really weren't amused by Rod's doodles. We all had to get new passports in the end.

Tom: The following year, we were asked to do the Children in Need single. They always want a cover song that everyone will know, so we thought about recording 'Stay With Me' and seeing if Rod fancied collaborating on it. He said he'd sing on the single with us, but somehow it never happened, and we ended up recording the track by ourselves, Danny and I both singing lead vocals. It was a tricky song, but we nailed it and performed it live on Children in Need. We opened the show, so it was quite a big deal.

We were on an arena tour at the time, and so we had to be flown by helicopter from Children in Need to our own show in Birmingham that evening. The chopper landed, we piled into the tour bus and Danny's phone went.

'Lads!' he shouted. 'It's Rod!' We all gathered round while Danny put him on speakerphone. 'Danny, mate,' Rod said, 'it was great – but why didn't you sing all the vocal yourself? That other guy, his voice just isn't rock enough . . .'

Cheers, Rod.

I was in such a bait for that Birmingham show. Nothing like having Rod Stewart slag you off just before a gig to take all the fun out of it.

Our *Greatest Hits* album was released against our will. Frustrating, to say the least. Now we found ourselves wanting to take back a bit of control, so when our management suggested that one option would be to go independent for our next record, we jumped at it. If we released an album under our own record label, we'd have full creative control over it. There'd be no interference from outside parties. We could do what we wanted.

It was risky. We would have to fund the whole thing ourselves. Recording, publicity, everything a record label would normally do, and do expertly, would be our responsibility. But we felt up for the challenge. So obviously, we'd be approaching the whole enterprise like proper businessmen. Watching the pennies. Bearing thrift in mind.

Well, not exactly.

First off, we all needed a holiday. But we also needed to work on songs for our next record. Why not combine the two? We flew to Barbados. The idea was that our girlfriends should come out for the first week for a holiday, and when they went home we would knuckle down to work. The first part of the plan went perfectly, and we had an amazing band holiday. Once the girls had gone home, however, I don't think we even *spoke* about our new album, let alone started work on it. We just messed around on the beach and got pissed at night. We shared rooms, and one night Dougie got so drunk he wet the bed. He failed to tell Harry about it, though, so the next night our drummer stumbled on to a delicately scented mattress. Maybe some alarm bells should have started ringing, if Dougie was getting so battered that he couldn't control himself. But they didn't. We were just having fun, and who wants to think that something might be wrong, when everything seems so right?

Harry: It was the last weekend before Christmas when we were asked to play at the Miss World contest in Johannesburg, sharing the bill with Alesha Dixon. Just a flying visit, out on Friday, back on Sunday, but you can imagine that our girlfriends said goodbye to us with slightly forced smiles. No need for them to worry as far as we were concerned – we couldn't imagine wannabe Miss Worlds even bothering to speak to four English gimps in a band.

The show went well, and afterwards we attended a

dinner at the hotel where the Miss Worlds had been staying for the past two weeks. They'd all had a nine o'clock curfew, and a strict no-booze-and-no-boys policy. Now they were ready to let their hair down, and the only guys of a similar age to them were us. Dougie, Tom and I were very much spoken for, and had no intention of straying. It was nice to look, but no way were we going to touch. By the end of the meal, however, loads of them were coming up to us asking for photographs. Our strategy was simply to stay put at the table, but Danny had other ideas.

Tom: The Miss Worlds were attracted to Danny like moths to a flame. As coffee was being served, he had six or seven of them surrounding him, fighting for his attention. If he'd died at that exact moment and gone to heaven, he'd have woken up in exactly the same spot.

Danny: It's true. I was in a relationship back home, but I wasn't happy in it, and was too much of a pussy to break it off. Now here I was in a room full of the world's most beautiful women, and I was determined to make the most of it.

Dougie: Once the meal came to an end, Danny wandered off while the rest of us stuck together. We went to a club within the hotel with Fletch and the awesome Alesha Dixon. I'd just had my nose pierced; when I joked with Alesha that she had a laugh like a frog, she gave it a cute little tweak and it gushed blood all down my front. Nice. We had a few drinks and a bit of a dance (Harry and I performed our party trick of dancing *very* gaily to Wham!), but it was all under control.

Harry: Miss Kazakhstan asked me for my room number. I gave her a false one . . .

It was ages before Danny reappeared, hand in hand with Miss England, grinning like the cat that had got the cream.

Danny: I was grinning for two reasons. It was cool to be getting with a 'Miss', but it also gave me a way out of my relationship. I didn't do anything more than kiss her, but back home I told my girlfriend that I couldn't possibly continue with her after being so miserably unfaithful. She was willing to give me another chance, but I was taking the coward's way out. The relationship came to an end in the messiest possible way.

You might have the impression by now that I haven't always treated the women in my life that well. You'd be right. I was young, single and just wanted to have a good time. I didn't know it back then, however, but that night at Miss World would lead to me meeting somebody who would turn the old Danny into somebody entirely new. Unfortunately, I still had more than a year to wait before that happened.

Dougie: Fletch had always said that for the price of recording in London, we could go to Australia and record. And *we* had always said: 'Fletch, that's rubbish.' It was like a red rag to a bull. Now that we were on our own, he went out of his way to make it happen. And so, to record the album that would become *Radio:ACTIVE*, we flew ourselves to Australia for ten weeks. What's the point of being the boss if you can't treat yourself now and again?

We flew to Sydney in January 2008. The plan was to start looking immediately for a cool place to live for the next ten weeks. Instead, we started drinking almost the moment we touched down. Our first day there was lost in a haze of beer and shots. We lost count of the number of bars we were forcibly evicted from – literally grabbed by the scruffs of our necks and hurled out of. Harry got in a fight with a bouncer, and had the scratches to prove it. By the time we got back to our hotel that evening, we were ready to pass out. When we woke up the next morning, everything felt grim. We couldn't shake off the bizarre sensation that Australia hated us.

We made the rather strange decision to work off our hangovers by doing the Sydney Harbour Bridge Climb. So there we were at the top of Sydney Harbour Bridge, listening to our guide tell us how many people had died during its construction and exactly what would happen to you if you fell off. Hardly what you want to hear when you're hanging like we were. And over the next four days, in between looking for somewhere cool to live, we were the perfect English gimps abroad, catching the commuter ferry to Manly Beach carrying beach towels and wearing flip-flops, only to turn lobster-red in the company of a seafront full of buff Aussies. All in all, the first week of our new enterprise was not an unqualified success.

Things started looking up, though, once we'd found ourselves a cool place to stay. It was in Manly, a suburb to the north-east of Sydney, and right on the ocean. It was amazing. One entire side of the house was a big window looking out to sea, and you could open the whole thing and let the outside in. The interior was state-of-the-art, the kind of place you normally only see in magazines. Even the toilets had sea views.

Tom: I'm not sure how I felt about that – windows work both ways, and some moments are best kept private . . .

Dougie: We had a forty-minute daily commute into the city to the recording studio that we were using. As commutes go, it wasn't bad – over Sydney Harbour Bridge, past the Opera House. It wasn't quite like jump-ing on the tube to get across town. And it was always sunny. We treated ourselves to some surfing lessons, so each morning we'd go for a surf, before making our awesome, scenic commute into the studio for about one o'clock. We'd record till ten or eleven, then drive home with the windows down and the breeze blowing. And apart from our bender on the first day we were clean-living. We hardly touched booze, because every day there was something to get up for that didn't involve drinking. Harry started training for the London marathon, and we even joined him for some of his train-ing sessions. It was a new-look McFly.

Harry: We invited Antony Brant to stay, and also our girlfriends.

Tom: And to top it all, we were recording exactly the music we wanted to make. No interference or meddling. Just us and Jason Perry, who had come out with us and whose enthusiasm was as infectious as the laid-back lifestyle we were living. A friend of Jason's was a stage hypnotist. I'd been reading Derren Brown's book in which he explains all about hypnosis and the type of person most susceptible to it: ones who quite like being the centre of attention, and who just need a bit of encouragement to show off. Which put me in mind of one person: Harry! 'Dude,' I told him, 'you are *so* the kind who'd be easy to hypnotize.'

Harry: I wasn't sure if this was a good thing or a bad thing, but I agreed to go along to one of this hypnotist's shows. Dougie and Danny were too scared to go up on stage, but Tom agreed to do it if I did and, together with Izzy and Giovanna, we put ourselves up for hypnosis when he asked the hundred-strong audience for volunteers.

I did *try* to relax as the hypnotist attempted to get us into a hypnotic state, but it was when the girl next to me fell asleep on my shoulder that I realized it wasn't happening for me. I looked to my left, where Tom was sitting, and could see that he was under. When the hypnotist told us that we were all holding the best-tasting ice cream in the world, Tom's face broke out into ecstasy as he licked it. I caught Izzy's eye and realized that she was wide awake too. We sloped off the stage with the few others who weren't affected, and left Tom and Gi to it.

Dougie: What followed was just about the most entertaining half hour of our lives. When the hypnotist realized that Tom and Gi were a couple, you could see his eyes light up, but Tom was the star of the show. The hypnotist had him ballet dancing across the stage like the sugar plum fairy, then punching the air every time the *Rocky* theme came over the loudspeakers. Best of all, he had him falling in love with another male volunteer who was dressed up as a woman, and every time this dude lifted up his skirt, Tom fell in love with him even more. Tom had to confess all this to a hypnotized Giovanna, who got more and more baited as it emerged that Tom wanted to leave her for this bloke in a dress.

'Right, Tom,' the hypnotist said to him. 'See that guy in the front row? He's stolen your willy.'

Tom looked at him. 'Mate, can I have my willy back? No, really, mate, haven't you got your own?'

'And now,' the hypnotist announced, 'you've got your willy back and it's double the size!'

Cue a big grin from Tom as he pats his enlarged manhood and struts around the stage like a dog with two dicks.

Danny: As a grand finale, Tom was in among the crowd, performing a striptease for me, Dougie and Harry – swinging his shirt in the air, rubbing himself up against us and totally getting into it while we threw him money. Nobody in the audience knew who we were, and half of them thought it was a set-up, because Tom had put on such a good show. It was almost too funny to be true.

❖

Harry: When you record, the bass and drums are done first. Once they're finished, the rhythm section's job is done. There wasn't much point us hanging around while Tom and Danny recorded their guitar tracks, so Dougie and I booked ourselves a surfing trip together.

Dougie: We'd go to several beaches in any one day, just bumming around in the water and having a great time. On one occasion, we were on our last beach of the day and storm clouds were gathering. The water looked grey and a bit eerie; the waves we were surfing were growing a little rougher. Harry and I had paddled out and were waiting for a wave when we saw two fins appear, then disappear again.

I knew a bit about sharks. I knew that, unlike dolphins, they have vertical tail fins that can appear above the water. That was what we'd just seen: the dorsal and tail fins of a shark, about to have a drummer and bass player for dinner.

'HARRY!!!! *SHAAAAAAAAAAARK!!!!*'

I've never moved so quickly. We paddled back in like maniacs, shitting our shorts as we genuinely expected to feel jaws round our ankles. We were totally terrified . . .

So why were the Aussies on the beach laughing at us?

Turned out it wasn't one *shark*, it was *two* dolphins. Did we mention we were typical English gimps abroad?

Danny: While Harry and Dougie were living it up, we were hard at it in the studio. As far as jobs go, ours is the least job-like around. However, spending every day in the studio, knowing that the onus is on you to create something, is about as close to work as it gets. It's a long, slow process, and can be disheartening sometimes if your creative juices aren't flowing. But Australia was a good environment for us to record in. Chilled. Slowly but surely, *Radio:ACTIVE* started to evolve.

Tom: We'd learned something about songwriting. The more personal you make a song, the more people are likely to relate to it. Try to write something that everyone's going to understand, and you'll end up diluting the sentiment. 'All About You', for example, was very specifically about me and Giovanna, and it turned out to be one of our most popular songs. *Radio:ACTIVE* was very consciously an album about us. About being in a band.

Around the time we were on the *Wonderland* tour, I'd written a song called 'One For The Radio', about all those people who liked to slag us off, even while they were humming our tunes. I'd played it to Dougie when we were working on material for *Motion In The Ocean* and he hadn't been that into it. No biggie. When you're working on songs, some just don't make the cut. But every now and then I look back over old ideas, and I did this when we were writing for *Radio:ACTIVE*. It was actually, I thought, a pretty good song, and the lyrics resonated with the way we were feeling at the time: a little frustrated at not being taken seriously as a band, even by people who secretly liked our music.

I played it to Richard Rashman. Stony face. 'You gotta change those lyrics, Tom. Nobody's going to relate to that.' But I knew they would. I knew it was exactly the kind of song our fans would get behind. Turned out they did. More so than any previous record, *Radio:ACTIVE* was very personal. The lyrics are informed by the high points and the frustrations of our lives, and we found, when it was released in July 2008, that it united our fans like none of our previous albums had done before.

Danny: Even though we were releasing this album independently, we didn't record it with our business heads on. We didn't set out to write the most popular songs for the widest audience. It was an album for us and for our fans. The record *we* wanted to make, not the record other people thought we should. And it seemed that everyone got behind us for that reason. We were given A-list radio play – not easy to get – and the feedback from the press and the industry at large was positive.

Tom: The release of *Radio:ACTIVE* was groundbreaking, in its way. This was at a time when the music industry was changing. The download revolution was in its infancy, and sales of physical records were plummeting. To download music legally, you needed a credit card; to have a credit card, you needed to be eighteen. A lot of our fans were younger than that. Almost overnight, there was an obstacle to our fans getting our music. So we had to get creative.

We gave the album away free on the front of the *Mail*

on Sunday. We were the first current band to release a new album in this way, and it felt like the eyes of the industry were on us. Was it a success? Hard to say. Certainly it got two and a half million McFly albums into people's homes at a time when album sales were declining rapidly, and the subsequent commercial release was perfectly acceptable. And it opened up a whole new fan base – we suddenly found that a lot more guys were turning up to our shows, whereas before our demographic had been resolutely female. Maybe *Radio:ACTIVE* had turned people on to the fact that there was a bit more to us than bubblegum pop. Maybe by listening a bit harder to our own instincts, we were getting ourselves some of the credibility that we wanted so badly.

Harry: It was also the first album that we took abroad. We'd always wanted to tour to different countries, but it was never a priority for our record label because labels make no money from a band's touring schedule. Now that we were calling the shots, it was something we could do. We did shows in Europe and Japan and, after one of our live DVDs had randomly performed well in South America, a promoter out there took a punt on us. He put a few shows on sale, and they sold out instantly. He put a few more on. Same deal. It even hit the news in Brazil that McFly fans were queuing up in São Paulo to buy tickets. We didn't even know we *had* fans there. Far from it. When we landed in Brazil for the start of our little tour, there were five hundred fans at the airport to welcome us; and as our vehicles escorted us safely off the airfield, our song 'Lies' came on the radio within about two minutes. It's awesome enough to hear your song on the radio in England, let alone halfway across the world. And on the way to our hotel, we saw massive billboards all over the city for our show. Seemed like McFly was a bigger deal in South America than we'd ever thought . . .

Different countries have different fans. In Japan, for example, we always found them to be persistent, but uber-polite. When we left on one occasion, we said goodbye to a group of girls who had congregated outside our hotel, and they all burst into tears. In Brazil, though, we discovered a totally new kind of fan. Passionate, to say the least. Even at the height of our early-days craziness in the UK, we'd never seen anything quite like it. This was our first taste of super-fame. It felt like being in The Beatles in 1964. Leaving our hotel room to go down to the bar was totally out of the question; at airports we had to bypass the security checks and be escorted straight to our plane; a group of fans had camped outside the venue we played in São Paulo for fifteen days before show time, and the queue was so long the news networks had helicopters flying overhead to film it. The fans knew where we were every minute of every day. If we had a day off to chill by the pool, they were there with their cameras. Go shopping? Forget it. On the way to an interview in São Paulo we had fans jumping on to our people carrier, opening the doors and trying to get inside. Step out on to your hotel balcony, there are fans in the road outside screaming at you. Go to the gym to work out, there'll be a line of fans standing there watching you on the treadmill. In Rio de Janeiro we stayed in a beautiful hotel on the beach, but it was simply impossible to get down to the sand because it would have meant battling through a Maginot Line of fans. We took a trip to the Amazon and they were there waiting for us in the rainforest, guitars in hand, singing McFly songs.

Dougie: The shows in South America are awesome. As intense and passionate as the fans. Barely a soul in the venues who isn't either crying or screaming. It's like a completely different world. There's no crowd safety in most of these South American venues, so they're rammed full of diehard fans, kids flying all over the place, and the noise is relentless. Add to this the fact that we don't go there very often, and it all leads to the most incredible atmosphere you can hope for during a show. There's nowhere else in the world where the experience of a McFly gig is even similar.

Danny: Bands are supposed to trash hotel rooms, right? Chuck TVs out of windows. It's in the rule book. Not for McFly. We've never been ones for the Led Zeppelin way of life. With one exception, that I don't look back on with any great sense of pride. It happened in South America. Chile, to be precise. We had a full day of press the following day, so Tom, Dougie and Harry had turned in early. Very sensible. It was the birthday of one of our road crew, however, so I stayed up to have a few drinks with him. Not very sensible.

There's a Chilean drink called pisco. I had no

intention of getting drunk, but shots of this stuff were being passed round, and before I knew it I'd downed more of them than was good for me. The rest of the evening is a blank. I can only piece together what happened from what other people told me afterwards. When the bar shut, I invited everybody up to my room for more drinks. A security guy told me it wasn't on, so I got all lairy with him and started pushing the poor guy around. One thing led to another, the police were called, and by all accounts I tried to push them around as well – just because I couldn't have a party in my room. I'm embarrassed even to think about it, because that's not me at all.

It was Tommy who woke me up the next morning. He was standing at the end of my bed, shouting at me. My eyes shot open, and it took a few moments to take in the devastation all around me. It looked like a bomb had gone off. Spaghetti was hanging off the ceiling from where I'd chucked a plate of the stuff upwards; standard lamps were bent at an angle; I'd smashed the top of a thick glass coffee table; it was like I'd turned into the Incredible Hulk in my drunkenness. I'd apparently ordered a shedload of room service, then not opened my door when it arrived. Even worse than all that, there was a letter of complaint from the front desk, stating that the hotel were intending to press charges against me, and that the police would be coming round again that afternoon.

I was so shaken up. What a twat. I'd never been like that after a few drinks, and I hope I never am again. I went down to the front desk and bawled my heart out apologizing. They let me off, thank God, so I legged it back up to my room and did what I could to clean the place up, while Tommy was left to deal with the small matter of the bill for all the damage I'd caused. To this day I've still got a big bottle of pisco in my freezer, but I'm too scared to touch the stuff.

All in all, though, *Radio:ACTIVE* was a positive experience for us. It felt good to be masters of our own destiny, and although it wasn't our biggest-selling album by a long chalk, it consolidated the fans and allowed us to go in the direction we wanted. So much so that by the time we were on our *Radio:ACTIVE* arena tour in November 2008, we were already playing around with new material for our next album, with the intention of releasing that under our own label too.

It was a memorable tour. We had a cool stage design, which only got cooler when we started wondering if there was an epic way for us to get from the main stage to the B stage in the middle of the audience. We'd done that once before simply by legging it, but then we got to thinking: What if we could actually *fly* to the B stage? And when nobody looked at us like we were a bunch of mentalists, we got to thinking some more . . .

We ended up with a see-through platform that flew above the audience and took us from the main stage to the B stage. *Spinal Tap*, anyone? And gimmicks aside, the show was great: by now we had four albums' worth of songs, lots of which had been hit singles, and our set list was getting better and better. And we were stoked when, halfway through that tour, Fletch announced that the same studio in Australia was available for us to use again. And so, in early 2009, after a brief trip to Japan for some shows, we headed directly down under. We had some creative momentum, and we wanted to keep it up.

Tom: You know how it is when you try to recapture a moment and it doesn't quite live up to your memory? Our second trip to Australia was like that. We had rented another lovely house on the next beach along to where we had stayed the first time round; Fletch and Jason were waiting for us, and it was massively exciting to be back. But when it came down to it, the spark wasn't there like before.

It didn't help that we weren't very well prepared. We'd started work on a few songs, but we'd landed on the other side of the world without much of an idea of what this next album was going to be. We had scheduled a week of pre-production before allowing ourselves four weeks of recording time, but it gradually became obvious that our half-written songs weren't gelling together very well. A hotchpotch of different styles. The songs themselves were good, but the project as a whole had no direction. By the time we left Australia we had the instrumental tracks for ten songs in the bag, which we could certainly have finished off and released, but which didn't feel right. They were the McFly album that never was.

Two songs – 'End Of The World' and 'I Need A Woman' – felt different. Slightly funkier. A new direction, maybe. Other than that, we felt like we weren't in very good shape musically, and it wasn't a great feeling. We had a summer of not doing much. For me personally, there's nothing worse. We'd wasted our recording trip, we had nothing to get excited about, and suddenly it felt like our career was going nowhere. We made a half-hearted attempt to complete the material we'd started on, but we knew it wasn't happening.

Danny: There are times in your life when you know you have to make a difficult decision. This was one of them. The producer of a record is a key figure. Like the director of a film, he has as much influence over the sound of an album as the musicians themselves. Sometimes more. So, if the sound wasn't right, perhaps we needed a fresh pair of ears and a different set of hands at the control desk. We decided to take Jason off the project and investigate the possibility of working with some new producers. Jason was devastated. We felt terrible. He had done two and a half albums with us and had become a close personal friend of the band. He tried to persuade us not to go through with it, but we'd made our decision. In retrospect, perhaps we should have given it some more thought.

Tom: We scrapped the majority of the songs we'd recorded, and treated 'End Of The World' and 'I Need A Woman' as demos. We were still independent at the time, but our experiment in self-promotion was about to come to an end. During the *Radio:ACTIVE* tour, Fletch and I had started working on a musical together. (Remember I told you he was a great musician?) Around this time he was meeting with Universal Records to discuss it, and the subject of McFly came up. Fletch explained that we were working on a new sound and played them these two demos. The record execs went nuts for them, and made us an offer we couldn't refuse. A totally new kind of record deal. We could still retain the autonomy we'd had before, but we'd have the oomph of a major label behind us. This could help in certain ways, not least that they could help hook us up with some of the best producers in the world: when the head of a major label rings, everyone takes the call. The idea was that we should collaborate with a few different people, and see what came of it.

And that's how we ended up working with Dallas Austin.

Dougie: Dallas Austin had worked with everybody. Britney, Madonna, Michael Jackson, Pink, TLC. Just reading a list of his previous work was intimidating. He agreed to hook up with us at his studio in Atlanta at the beginning of December 2009. Because this was a writing trip, Harry stayed at home while Dougie, Danny and I flew across the pond to meet with Dallas.

Harry: I stayed in London for other reasons, too. Izzy and I had been going through a rocky patch and we'd just split up. In time, we managed to sort out our problems, but I was an emotional wreck just then. The others could go and party stateside, but for now I just wanted to be at home.

Tom: Party? Well, yeah. Partying goes hand in hand with work as far as Dallas Austin is concerned.

We arrived in Atlanta in the late afternoon, and went straight to his studio. We didn't know what to expect, or even if Dallas would be there, and were a bit disappointed to see that it was in a slightly weird, not very nice area of Atlanta. Stepping inside the studio itself, however, was a different matter. It was one of the coolest, most creative places we'd ever been. The walls were plastered with gold and platinum records from the millions and millions of albums he'd sold; there was artwork everywhere, and amazing graffiti; there were interesting old instruments all over the place. And when Dallas himself turned up half an hour later, he was the picture of cool. We played him our demo and he instantly seemed to dig it. He liked that we were a young band writing our own stuff, he seemed to *get* us, and half an hour later we were working together on new material.

Dougie: We hadn't been working for much more than an hour when Dallas started receiving a bunch of text messages. He seemed a bit distracted. 'Guys,' he said finally, 'I forgot, I'm supposed to be meeting someone for dinner.'

That was fine by us – we were jet-lagged to hell and happy to catch some sleep – but Dallas wouldn't hear of us going back to our hotel. 'Let me see if you can come along,' he said. He exchanged a couple more texts. 'So, guys,' he said finally, 'you want to come and have dinner with Elton John?'

Like, seriously?

Yeah, seriously.

Half an hour later we were walking into a busy, vibey, dimly lit restaurant. Through the crowds of people you could just see Elton John sitting at the back with a young, good-looking guy and some old rocker with long hair. As we approached the table, we saw that he was halfway through his steak (somehow we'd never imagined Elton John eating a steak), with a non-alcoholic beer at his side. He and the others were at a small table, and there was a bit of a kerfuffle as we all pulled up more chairs to join them.

We got chatting. To our surprise, Elton knew exactly who we were. Not only that, it turned out he'd grown up near where we lived, and had played his first ever gig in the pub at the end of our road. It was immediately obvious that Elton was one of those people who's not afraid to say what he thinks, and at first we felt a bit intimidated sitting in the company of this legend – scared of saying the wrong thing. But the more we chatted, the more it became obvious that he was just a really lovely guy. He explained that he lived in Atlanta for a couple of months a year, before asking us what we were doing the following Monday.

Er, nothing planned.

'Why don't you come round to my place for dinner?'

Hell, yeah!

Danny: We drank a cocktail or two with Elton, then headed back to the studio with Dallas. It must have been ten or eleven at night, and we assumed that our evening's work was coming to an end. Dallas thought different. We did some tequila shots, then continued working on some songs. A couple more hours passed before Dallas suddenly announced that it was time for him to go and DJ at a local club. So we all piled into the waiting cars and were escorted into the VIP lounge of this bar while Dallas played his set. Once he'd rejoined us, we started getting some more shots down. We could take our alcohol back then – especially Dougie, for reasons that will become clear – and we got Dallas truly smashed. It was three in the morning by then. So surely the night was coming to an end?

Nope. Back to the studio with a bunch of people who'd been at the club. The party continued. I tried my hand at DJing for the first time, mixing Tina Turner with NWA. I loved it, and instantly knew it was something I wanted to do more of. The drinking continued; our demo went on; now and then Dallas would send one of us into a recording booth to sing a line or two. But mostly we just dicked around. By the end of the night we were giving wedgies to this big-shot producer who we thought we were there to impress, wrestling with him, hiding his shoes in the fridge – basically acting like a bunch of overgrown kids and having a hilarious time. And Dallas was having a laugh too: 'You guys, you're my boys, I'm your fifth member, you've *got* to do your next album with me . . .'

So that was that. It looked like we had ourselves a new producer. We stumbled back to our hotel at five in the morning, woke up disgustingly hungover, made our way back to the studio and did exactly the same thing all over again.

Tom: Monday night came. We had a dinner date with one of the biggest pop stars in the world. No biggie.

Elton greeted us at the door of his massive Atlanta apartment dressed in a slightly shiny Adidas tracksuit, gave us all a big hug and showed us into the most insane place we'd ever seen. The entire floor of this big apartment complex was given over to his living quarters, and he had a separate floor just below simply to store all the works of art and other stuff he'd accumulated over the years. But the living quarters were like a museum in themselves: rammed with paintings, sculptures and ornaments. There was a beautiful coffee table in the middle of the room, but there was no question of putting a coffee cup on it, because it was covered with tiny knick-knacks. Everything was pristine – including the perfect white sofas, so when Danny and Dougie asked for a glass of red wine, I was so anxious they'd spill their drinks I almost asked if they could have a straw too. Or, at the very least, if *Danny* could have a straw with it. (I'm reminded of the time he spilled egg all down him, before shouting: 'Of all the bloody vegetables . . .')

Dougie: Our drinks were served by two very young, very good-looking male waiters; and of course Elton had a personal chef to prepare the food. We drank some cocktails, and then Elton offered to show us round. The apartment was vast, and about as over the top as you'd imagine. Each room was scented by different candles; in the middle of the apartment was a life-size sculpture of a horse. The place was littered with Ancient Greek statues, including a Venus-de-Milo-type figure that Disney had given him for writing *The Lion King*. There was loads of photographic art on the walls too, including one that was a close-up of something . . . indistinguishable. We asked him what it was.

'Oh,' he replied nonchalantly, 'just jizz.'

Just jizz? We looked at each other. Then we started looking a little more closely at everything around us. Were we seeing things, or was half the stuff in this apartment actually cock-shaped? Penis sculptures started jumping out at us, alongside pictures of young lads on the beach and men wearing not very much. Even the jizz picture was one of a series of close-ups. We didn't ask if each specimen was supplied by the same donor, or if it had been a group effort, or even if they belonged to a friend.

He took us into his bedroom. 'Want to see my wardrobe?' he asked. He led us into a room that contained all the outfits he'd ever worn – clothes we all recognized from his videos and other appearances. 'Check this out,' he said. He pulled open these large drawers to reveal *all* his glasses. Big pairs, little pairs, pink pairs, sparkly pairs, crazy pairs – hundreds of them. It was like a museum to Elton John, with Elton as the curator.

Tom: Dinner was served. He'd already told us that we were having Mexican, and we were fully prepared for something special. When the food arrived, though, we were presented with your average, out-of-the-box, supermarket tacos. It didn't matter – we were having too much fun. We all sat around having a good old chat and a few drinks, and one thing soon became apparent about Elton John: he knows *everything* about the current music scene. This wasn't an old rock dinosaur living in the past and pretending he was down with the kids. He had a massive music collection, he knew exactly what *was* and what *had been* number one. He knew all about McFly and how I had written songs with James Bourne from Busted all those years ago. Take that, Rod Stewart! When the time came for me to nip to the loo – which was just as ornate and ornament-strewn as the rest of the apartment – I couldn't resist taking a photo of myself in the mirror. I mean, how often do you get to take a slash in Elton's john?

Danny: Elton was probably the coolest famous person we'd ever met. As we said goodbye, he asked us all for our addresses. That Christmas each of us received cards 'From Elton and David'. Believe me: there aren't many people with his kind of standing in our industry who'd take the time to do that.

We went back to recording, and of course back to partying. Atlanta is the home of strip clubs, and Dallas is one of their most enthusiastic clients, as were we for the short time we were out there. The club he took us to, The Cheetah, was not only a strip club par excellence, it was also one of the best restaurants in Atlanta. At about ten o'clock the girls all came out in their little black dresses and it looked like a line-up for Miss World, and being with Dallas Austin meant they all flocked to our table and started dancing for us. Almost every night we found ourselves there. Well, working on demos is hard work, and we needed a break . . .

Tom: Back in the studio, and despite our occasional excursions, we worked hard every night on our demos, determined to have a good four or five songs to take back to London with us. On the last night, Dallas suddenly remembered a song he'd written with JC from 'NSYNC that had never got used. It was called 'If U C Kate', and it had this funky, Prince-like vibe that was exactly what we were looking for. We went nuts for it: that song, we decided, would serve as the inspiration for our new record. It was perfect – and unprecedented for us to get so excited about a song that we hadn't written. We listened to it non-stop on the twelve-hour flight back home, and spent that Christmas partying and dancing to those demos. 'If U C Kate', in particular, became the soundtrack to our lives. And after our abortive trip to Australia, we were finally feeling more upbeat about our musical direction and what the future held. Our burgeoning relationship with Dallas was the start of something good.

In the new year, Dallas came over to London so that we could start making our new album together. Dallas being Dallas, we turned nocturnal. With Harry now, we all stayed together in the same hotel, where we'd set our alarms for the afternoon and head to the studio at about

6 p.m. before working through till dawn. I say working. We *did* work, but we interspersed it with trips to clubs and heroic quantities of alcohol. Our supper would be breakfast back at the hotel, where the other guests had just got up. And, now that Dallas was in town, all manner of people were forever dropping into the studio while we were recording, including some girl we'd heard a few whispers about called Jessie J.

Dougie: Sweet girl. Came back the next day with her girlfriend and cooked us lasagne.

Tom: But despite all the partying (and despite the temporary absence of our drummer, who'd managed to drunkenly fall over in a club, split his lip open and end up on a drip in hospital – nice one, Harry!), a load of songs for the album that would become *Above The Noise* took shape during Dallas's trip to London, and everybody from our record label was uber-excited about what we were coming up with. We allowed ourselves to get excited too. We ignored the little voices in our heads that kept questioning whether Dallas's producing style was quite suited to the kind of band that we wanted to be, or the sound we wanted to achieve. We'd made the decision to experiment a little, and that was what we were doing.

Harry: We were changing direction in other ways too. We'd learned throughout our career that being a successful pop act isn't just about the music you make. It's also about the image you project, and around this time, after looking at photographs of ourselves taken over the previous six years, we came to another decision: we needed to smarten up.

Radio:ACTIVE had by no means been a failure – it was always going to be an album for the fans, and we managed to sell out a big arena tour on the back of it – but it would be a push to say that it was as commercially successful as we'd wanted it to be. We had a problem to solve: how were we going to be *massive* again? Not looking so damn scruffy would help. Looking like pop stars instead. We should try to get in shape.

Tom: Nice idea, I thought, but it was never going to happen. Us? Down the gym? Get real. But it turned out I was wrong. Harry, who had moved out of north-west London by now and into Putney, got himself a personal trainer. We were in Portugal for a show when I first noticed a difference in him while he was getting changed in his hotel room. 'Dude, you're *massive*!' Cut to ten minutes later, Dougie, Danny and I were all in his room doing press-ups like something out of *The Benny Hill Show*. We all wanted to be like Harry! We started working with a personal trainer ourselves, and enlisted the help of a nutritionist to get us eating healthily. Even when going to the gym wasn't practical – like during Dallas's trip to London, when we were totally nocturnal and constantly drunk – we tried to make sure that at least the food we ate was doing us some good.

Danny: But our main focus, of course, was the record,

and that meant returning to Atlanta for a final recording session with Dallas. This time we had Harry in tow, and we couldn't wait to show him all our former haunts: Cheetahs, the studio, and of course Dallas's house . . .

Dougie: Dallas's house *is* a spaceship. The most insane home you've ever seen. Clean concrete lines and spiral staircases covered with graffiti; cubbyholes everywhere; a bar area with a window behind it looking *into* the infinity pool so you can see people swimming; a glass corridor to his bedroom. He doesn't need a key to get through his front door, he just needs his handprint.

Harry: In the middle of one of our recording sessions, Dallas suddenly asked us if we wanted to eat. We piled into his car and started driving while he got on the phone. 'What you want to eat?' he asked us. 'Chicken? Fish?' We thought he was on the line to some restaurant; in fact we were driving back to his house where a chef, in full kitchen whites, was on the balcony – it was a boiling hot day – preparing our food to order. It was some of the most amazing food we'd ever eaten – this was the life guys like Dallas live, and now we were living it too. It was one of those moments when we really, *really* felt like pop stars. Life was very cool.

Tom: We were doing our best to keep fit, too. We had a personal trainer in our hotel and nutritionally planned meals delivered to the studio. Alcohol aside, we were properly getting into shape, although from time to time

I couldn't help noticing that Dougie was acting weird. He would disappear for a while, then come back bouncing off the walls, talking nineteen to the dozen and being, if I'm honest, a bit annoying. He seemed distracted, too, and not entirely into what we were doing in the studio. We all knew that he was having certain issues back home with his personal life, but it seemed like there was more to it than that. Like he maybe wasn't that into what we were doing. Was that right, or was I just being paranoid and anxious? It wouldn't have been the first time, but I too was experiencing the creeping sensation that the musical path we'd set out on was not the one we ought to be taking.

We were having a great time with Dallas. No doubt. But as the recording process progressed, the shadow of a worry had started to cross my mind. Dallas Austin's method of working was the exact opposite of what we were used to. Up until this record, we had always known what we were going to record before we went into the studio. With Dallas, we were writing as we were going along, and things were a lot less structured.

Dougie: It felt very alien, and I was uncomfortable with it. When you've been in a band for a while, you get a feel for what a song's going to sound like even as early as the drum track going down. I could tell that this bunch of songs wasn't going to end up as something I was into. I had no problem trying stuff out in front of the guys. That was what we'd always done – if it sucked, it sucked, and we'd just move on. But I wasn't that into letting other people in on that process. In the end, I just raised the white flag. I disengaged, and concentrated on partying instead.

Tom: We couldn't all disengage. The heat was on to finish this album by the time our second Atlanta trip came to an end. This new album had been so drawn out in its gestation that we were painfully aware how long it had been since we'd actually released a record. If we started from scratch again, it would be another year before we had anything ready for our fans. And another year was too long. But increasingly I felt like we were sliding out of control down a path we'd started, and from which it was too late to turn away. One day, outside Dallas's studio, I had the longest phone conversation I'd ever had with Fletch – and that's saying something. Things were so unstructured that I wasn't sure we were even going to get the record finished, and in any case the uncomfortable feeling that we weren't heading in the right direction was nagging away at me even more. Two songs in particular – 'This Song' and 'Party Girl' – weren't sounding that good to my ears, and although I knew we'd gone too far to change direction, I was still worried.

Fletch tried to reassure me. He loved what he'd heard. The record label loved what *they'd* heard. Everything was going to be great.

Maybe it was. Maybe we were wrong to be worried. Maybe we should have a bit of faith in other people's opinions, and pay no attention to our own nagging doubts.

I remember hanging up and walking back into the

studio. All our eggs were in Dallas's basket now. He was an exceptionally talented producer. We were certainly having an awesome time with him.

I just hoped that the eggs didn't end up getting cracked.

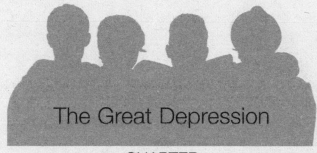

The Great Depression

CHAPTER

Tom: Sometimes, songs come when you're least expecting them. Out of nowhere. Taio Cruz is a great singer and producer who was also signed to Universal. Before our first trip to Atlanta we had got together to do some writing, which had culminated in a song called 'Nowhere Left To Run'. Back home, after we'd finished recording with Dallas, we hooked up with Taio again in a studio, thinking that we would be recording that song. But it was only a rehearsal studio – Taio was under the impression that we were meeting to do some more writing, so that's what we did. I had an idea I'd been playing around with in Atlanta on a Fender Rhodes in Dallas's studio. I knew it had potential, but the opportunity hadn't come up to develop it out there. We worked on it that day with Taio, and the result was 'Shine A Light'. It was the last song to come together for the album that became *Above The Noise*, and it would turn out to be one of our biggest singles ever.

We recorded 'Shine A Light' and 'Nowhere Left To Run'. They sounded good. Everything felt positive.

And then the world of McFly took a dive. We were entering a period of our career that we now refer to among ourselves as the Great Depression. It was going to be a bumpy ride.

Danny: After recording 'Shine A Light' and 'Nowhere Left To Run', the mixes came back for the work we'd done in Atlanta with Dallas. Over the years, we've developed an understanding for how our songs are produced. With Hugh Padgham and Jason Perry, we would spend hours working on a simple bass drum sound; our sessions were structured and we always knew what we were supposed to be doing. Dallas, amazing producer though he was, didn't work that way. Once we'd returned to London and the mastered tapes came back for us to listen to, there was no getting away from it. They sounded amazing, but something wasn't right. It was too polished. Not real enough. Our new album didn't sound like a band. We wanted to stay open-minded about things, but it didn't sound like us.

Dougie: Everything I'd been worrying about while we were out there had come true. The songs sounded too urban. Too generic. Hardly any guitars. Sparse drums. Really not our thing. Everybody at the label still seemed excited by it, but we argued our case that it needed some extra production and went grovelling back to our friend Jason Perry, to see if he would take us back.

Harry: With Jason, we headed out to a residential studio in Belgium and re-recorded those drum and guitar parts that we felt weren't big enough. There's no doubt that we improved it, but still: this was not the album any of us had set out to make.

Tom: There are times in the creative process, though, when it's easy to doubt your own opinion. Nothing ever ends up sounding *exactly* the way you first imagined it, not when it's been through the musical filter of someone who perhaps doesn't share your own sensibilities. And although none of us in the band were wild about the record we had ended up with, we seemed to be in a minority of four. Other people's opinions appeared to be completely different to ours. It was decided that 'Party Girl' should be released as the first single, even though none of us liked it very much. Even though none of us thought it really *sounded* like McFly.

Danny: There were other reasons, too, why we were under pressure to release. It had been a long time since McFly had been in the public eye. With our trip to Australia, then toing and froing from Atlanta, it had been a couple of years since we'd done much TV or even played many shows. People had started to ask us when we'd split up, or if we were thinking of doing some comeback shows.

What?

Even family and friends started asking us similar questions, and it really got to us. We were desperate to release our new record. Desperate to get back out there. And if experience had taught us one thing, it had taught us this: when you decide to get behind something, you have to properly get behind it. Forget about your doubts and put your heart and soul into it. Otherwise, what's the point? And it wasn't like we weren't full of ideas.

Our Internet following had gone through the roof. Hundreds of thousands of fans, from all over the world, had started to follow us on Twitter, and we felt that the time had come to sort out our online presence so that we could properly connect with our fans, and give them back something for all the support they'd given us over the years. The result was a subscription site where fans could access exclusive content and merchandise, free music, advance ticket sales and have proper interaction with the band. Our label was called Super Records; this would be called Super City. The launch of the McFly Super City site should have been so great. We *wanted* it to be great, not so much for us but for the fans. In reality, it was an unmitigated disaster.

Tom: We put a lot – a *lot* – of time, effort and money into the Super Site. Like, almost a million pounds of our own money. The idea was awesome. What if we could create a virtual McFly world, a cross between a website and a video game, that our fans could navigate and delve into? And if you subscribed to the site, you'd get everything we released – new albums, music videos, extra content – for free, and first. If you came to our gigs, you'd get the best seats, or be allowed into the venue an hour early. We'd do weekly webchats so that we could have the ultimate in interaction between a band and their fans. It would cost £40 a year or £6 a month – affordable for most kids out of their pocket money. It was revolutionary – nobody had ever really done anything like it.

We decided that we wanted the album artwork of *Above The Noise* to tie in with the Super City imagery, and to have an almost cinematic quality. As usual, Dougie and I went nuts with our visual references, getting together a bunch of graphic novels, film artwork and cinema posters. As the discussions evolved, we decided that to tie in with our Super Site, we'd go down a superhero route. Not cheesy superheroes, but something a bit more sophisticated and darker. Think *Watchmen* or *The Dark Knight*.

Dougie: There's a problem, though, with handing over your ideas to someone else who doesn't quite get them. The ideas themselves get diluted, or misinterpreted. You might be thinking *The Dark Knight*, they might be thinking *SuperTed*. It can be a constant battle to get other people to understand what's in your head and often, if it doesn't happen, you give up. It becomes too tiring and not much fun. And that's what happened. The album imagery that came back wasn't what we had in mind at all. The artwork was an action replay of the music.

But again, other people around us seemed to like it, and before we knew it the imagery on both the album and the site was something we never intended it to be.

Tom: And then some. The front cover of *Above The Noise* was supposed to be so cool. In the final version, I ended up carrying a cane! Everything seemed to be conspiring against us. The record wasn't what we'd wanted it to be; the imagery sucked. But hey, we still had this awesome website to launch, right? Like Danny said, you can't go out there and promote anything convincingly if you don't get yourself a hundred per cent behind it. And that's what we did. In the weeks leading up to its launch, we told *everyone* about our revolutionary new site, and focused on talking about that even more than talking about the album. And the site *did* look unique, like nothing else out there. We were genuinely excited for it as launch day approached.

Dougie: We did this massive countdown. The upcoming launch of the Super Site in November 2010, which was going to coincide with the launch of *Above The Noise*, was news – the press were talking about it, it was trending on Twitter, the fans were abuzz. Everyone involved in the site came round to Tom's house for launch day, when the site was going to go live at 10 a.m. The first ten thousand subscribers would be called Pioneers, and would get a certificate signed by all of us, so we knew that there would be a lot of activity the moment the site launched.

Danny: We'd had meeting after meeting with the people involved in creating the site, explaining to them that McFly fans were hardcore. That every time we tweeted, we would get flooded with so many responses it was impossible to keep up with them. That they were so fanatical, every time there was any online poll involving us, we'd win just on the back of our online demographic.

The band go to some remote locations in order to disengage from the everyday and get creative on their writing trips.

The *RadioACTIVE* tour in 2008. Check out the
platform that took the band between stages.
Opposite below: The guys with tour manager
Tommy Jay Smith – a total legend.

Victory on the dancefloor for Harry as he wins *Strictly Come Dancing* 2011.

Well done, Dougie! The king of the jungle wears his crown well.
Inset: With Dr Bob, whose advice is invaluable for contestants on *I'm a Celebrity, Get Me Out of Here!*

Love is in the air. Each bandmate is now in a happy, settled relationship. **Above left:** Lara has been described as the female Dougie, as they are so perfectly matched. **Above right:** Tom and Giovanna got married in May 2012. **Below left:** Harry and Izzy got engaged shortly after Tom and Giovanna's wedding. **Below right:** Danny with his model girlfriend Georgia.

Tom and Giovanna's wedding – the perfect day. No prizes for guessing who the wedding band were . . .

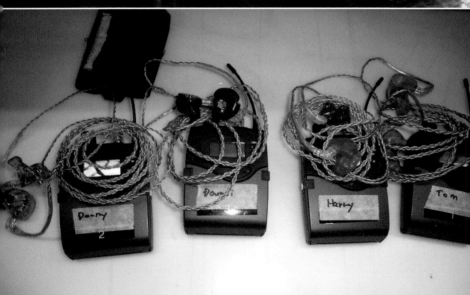

That thanks to our fans online, we got our songs played in *space*.

That when this site went live, there would be a *lot* of activity, and the servers *had* to be able to cope.

Tom: Even though the site had been two years in the making, we still found ourselves staying up till 4 a.m. the night before it went live, uploading old song demos and other content we thought the fans would enjoy. When the day arrived, my house was filled with screens and wires and cameras as we waited for it all to go live. The holding page for the site was a clock counting down, and I think we scarcely breathed as the seconds ticked away, waiting for everything to go nuts.

5, 4, 3, 2, 1 . . . lift-off . . .

Nothing happened.

Everyone refreshed the screen on their laptops.

Still nothing happened.

And *still* nothing happened.

And then, Twitter went nuts. Hundreds of thousands of McFly fans from Brazil to Birmingham to Barcelona started tweeting that they couldn't access the site. It had crashed from the amount of traffic, and we were presiding over an epic, *epic* fail.

The McFly Super Site took in the region of ten million hits in its first hour. That meant a *lot* of unsatisfied fans. To make things worse, some people had managed to get through to the subscription page, had paid their money, and now couldn't access the content they'd been expecting. It looked like we were ripping them off.

It was bedlam in my house. People were shouting at each other, phones were ringing, tempers were bubbling over. And four McFly boys were sitting in the middle of it, wondering how everything could have gone so wrong.

Harry: As that awful day wore on, it became clear that there were fundamental issues with the site, and that parts of it would have to be rewritten. And that meant taking the site down completely. On day one.

And remember, this wasn't just the launch of our Super Site. It was the launch of our album too, the first day our fans could hear all this new music that, for better or worse, we'd worked on so long and so hard. At the end of the day, once everyone had sheepishly left Tom's house full of apologies and we were alone, we put out a live webchat to our fans, saying the only thing we could say: sorry.

Tom: The fans were amazing. They could tell how bummed out we were, and the messages of support came thick and fast. It was good to know they were still behind us, just like they'd always been. But sometimes, even that kind of support isn't enough to pull you back from the brink.

Dougie: Around this time, boy bands were coming back into fashion. We'd always, we thought, stood out from the crowd. Always sounded a little bit different – a real band who played their own instruments and wrote their own songs. And we'd achieved so much with

Radio:ACTIVE. Songs like 'One For The Radio' had made it on to Kerrang! Radio and XFM. Guys, realizing that we were a proper guitar band, had started getting into us. But with 'Party Girl' we'd released something bland, a record that any other boy band could have produced. Aside from the cock-ups on the Super Site and the album artwork, we'd done all this work on the new record and had ended up sounding like everybody else. We'd stripped McFly of everything that made us good in the first place, set ourselves on a path of more generic R & B, and it felt like we'd squandered some of the traction that we'd had.

Tom: Those were dark days, especially for me and Dougie. And they were about to get darker.

When I look back on my life, and especially on my time in the band, I can see a cycle. It repeats, not quite as regularly as clockwork, but regularly enough for it to be more than just the usual ups and downs people go through. I'll have periods of great excitement, when I feel completely inspired. Anything creative seems possible. If I wanted to, I could write film scripts, or books, or musicals. *Anything*. Remember I told you that when I was a kid and I went to see *Oliver!* I came away *knowing* that I would end up being in that show? You remember the burst of optimism and creativity I had before *Motion In The Ocean*? These are times when the world feels as if it's my oyster, and episodes like that can be amazingly productive. They can be confusing for me, too, because even though I might be rubbish at something, being in McFly has always meant that people take me seriously when I give it a go. All in all, though, times like that are the periods in my life that I remember as being golden.

But for each high, there's a low. Periods of such despair and listlessness that you don't ever see a way of getting out of it. Everything's bad. Nothing's ever going to be all right again. There's not even a reason to get out of bed in the morning. You don't want to talk to anybody, and when you do you end up pissing them off. You can't remember what it's like to be happy. As for writing music, or doing anything creative: forget it. I'd gone through a depression like this around the time of *Wonderland*, when I was short with my best friends and didn't even know if I wanted to continue with the band any more. Giovanna refers to it as my 'period'. She knows when I'm going through one of these rough times because I start looking for job openings at Disney. Not that I'd fit in there very well, because I'm really not a lot of fun to be around.

Being in a band makes this condition more intense. When things are good, they're amazing – you're filming a Hollywood movie, winning a BRIT, being screamed at by thousands of fans. When things aren't going so well – when you're not getting the credibility you want, or people are taking the piss out of you, or your album hasn't turned out the way you hoped – they can be terrible. Disheartening. We'd just come through a dis-heartening time in our career, and it was sending me into the deepest episode of depression I'd experienced since *Wonderland*.

We'd tried to experiment. We'd tried to do something

new. And we'd ended up on a path which led us to a place we didn't want to go. We'd become everything we hated. Now we had to do the usual round of interviews and touring centred around something I didn't feel all that passionate about. It sent me off on one. Big time. Secretly, I *wanted* our singles to fail. That, in the twisted logic of my depressed mind, would prove that I'd been right. And to make matters more confusing, I felt I'd been at the helm of our unfortunate new direction. It was all my fault that *Above The Noise* turned out the way it did. I felt responsible, and suddenly I didn't want to be in charge of any decision-making in the band. I wanted no say in which songs were released as singles. I wanted no input into our upcoming *Above The Noise* tour. I felt utterly, completely wretched.

Christmas 2010 approached. The old worries re-appeared in my brain. I wasn't enjoying my life. I didn't know what the future was for McFly, but in my head it didn't look good. Dougie moved into my house. He was having his own problems, not only in his personal life, but in *all* aspects of his life. He was keeping the extent of his problems a secret from everyone, but I'm sure that the depressed, late-night drinking sessions we shared didn't help. We found ourselves staying up all night, wallowing in our own self-loathing, bitching about how badly our careers were going and how we hated everything McFly had suddenly become. It never struck us to talk positively about the future, or discuss what we could do to get ourselves out of this hole of our own making. One night, halfway through the album campaign for *Above The Noise*, when 'Shine A Light' had just been released and we were at my house, both deep in our cups, Dougie said, 'Mate, fuck it. Let's just do one more album and then call it quits. One more for the fans, and that'll be it. Over.'

I stared at Dougie. Then I stood up and walked out of the room, up the stairs and into the toilet. And there I sat down and cried. Dougie's drunken suggestion seemed to have cut to the chase. McFly was almost done.

My depression peaked at Christmas. Or should I say that it troughed? I didn't want to get out of bed. I had no enthusiasm for anything. My mood was as black as it had ever been. And while I knew I didn't want to feel like this, there seemed to me no possibility of picking myself up again. This was me, for the future. For ever.

It didn't make any sense. How could I be so high and then so low? How was it that I couldn't control the way I felt, or keep myself on an even keel like Danny and Harry seemed able to do? I realized that I needed to speak to someone. To get help.

I didn't talk to anyone else about it. I wouldn't have known what to say. I just went to see my doctor, and tried my best to explain what was going on in my head. He had no hesitation in referring me to a doctor at the Priory. I told him about what was happening, and how these cycles had been repeating for years. And it was only then that I heard the word bipolar being used.

I don't want to be flippant about issues of mental health. It's too serious for that. In the months that were to follow, I'd be seen by two doctors. One of them gave me a diagnosis of bipolar, the other didn't. Whatever the truth, all I know is that when the symptoms of bipolar disorder were read out to me, it was like a light going on in my head. The manic episodes, when everything seems possible. The depressions, when nothing seems worthwhile. That was my life in a nutshell.

The doctor asked me if I had trouble sleeping, and so I explained to him about the alien at the window. I told him about my night terrors and how, almost every night for as long as I could remember, I had been rigid with fear – too scared even to tap Giovanna on the shoulder and wake her up when it all got too much. And in a weird way, the more I spoke about these strange fears that had haunted me all my life, the more relieved I felt. The doctors I spoke to didn't look at me as if I was crazy. They just started talking about what I could do to fix things.

One of my doctors gave me a set of hypnotherapy tapes to listen to when I went to bed. They took some getting used to: listening to music while I slept had obviously always been a no-no – how would I ever hear the aliens coming in? I was also prescribed medication to help me with my moods. I was even warier of this. The truth is, I'd have done almost anything to rid myself of the depressions, but the one thing I *wouldn't* have done was rid myself of the ups – those wonderful, manic, creative periods when everything seemed possible. What if this medication stopped those episodes from happening? What if, by suppressing my moods, I suppressed everything that made me me?

I didn't tell the guys about my diagnosis. I didn't tell anyone except Giovanna. Some things you just want to keep to yourself. It would have been the wrong news at the wrong time in any case, because one of our number was about to go through the darkest period any of us had yet encountered. None of us realized it at the time, but it was by no means certain that he'd come out of it the other end.

Dougie's Secret

CHAPTER

Dougie: The truth, I've found, is always better than lies. But how can you be honest with other people, when you're not even being honest with yourself?

We're a band that tells each other pretty much everything. There are some things, though, that you can't even tell your closest friends. Perhaps you're too ashamed to come clean in front of them. Perhaps you're worried they'll make you stop doing what you're doing. Perhaps you just don't know what to say. For several years I had a secret like that. And like everybody else who has the same secret, I didn't think it was a problem. Quite the opposite: I thought it was one of the best bits of my life. I was wrong.

When I was seventeen, I started getting into alcohol in quite a big way. Red wine was my thing – it felt a bit more sophisticated, somehow. Danny and I would go down to the supermarket and pretend that we knew what we were talking about as we chose our wine. I suppose that, by pretending I was being rather debonair, I could ignore the fact that I was becoming slowly dependent on alcohol.

Red wine wasn't my only vice. More and more, we'd come back to the house after a show and, after a few beers, I'd hit the vodka until everything started spinning. Only then would I go to bed. I'd wake up hungover, and at first it was a miracle that I could get through the day without puking. Gradually, though, my system became more and more tolerant to these hangovers. I grew used to spending the first half of every day feeling like shit, and found I had a talent for powering through it. Once I realized I could do that, I started *really* digging the sauce.

By the time I was eighteen, my innate confidence had grown thanks to all the things I'd experienced with McFly. That confidence manifested itself in different ways, not least that I had sufficient cojones to ask people about other substances that might be available. I was super-paranoid about anybody finding out, of course. With me being in the public eye, the press would have had a field day. But worse than that, I knew how disappointed my bandmates would be if they found out.

My eighteenth, nineteenth and twentieth birthdays passed. Make no mistake, I was having a great time; at least I thought I was. Only a small group of people knew what I was doing. I was careful. I never went out clubbing late at night at venues where I was likely to get papped. I kept myself to myself. That way, I could carry on without anybody getting suspicious.

Little by little, however, something started to happen.

I told myself I was loving this way of life, but I wasn't being honest. I had started to feel – and this is the only way I can describe it – uncomfortable in my own skin. I was no longer Mr Confident. I was a nervous wreck. It dawned on me that I wasn't really enjoying what I was doing, but I didn't seem to be able to stop, and I hated myself for doing it. I'd make snap decisions: that was it for the drugs I was using. Never again. I'd carry on drinking, of course, and sometimes I would manage to go for as long as a month without touching anything else. The psychology of the addict, however, always got the better of me. Surely a month of good behaviour deserved a little reward . . . It was backwards logic, but it dragged me down. I'd treat myself to a blow out, but that blow out would always carry on to the following day, and the day after that, and the day after that . . . And each time I hit rock bottom, the rock was a little lower.

Mornings were the worst. The downers. That feeling of being uncomfortable in my own skin became more intense. I'd need a little drink just to keep it at bay. To get me going. And as time passed, that little drink became insufficient. I needed something else the moment my eyes opened, just to face the day. I'd find myself lying in bed, dog-tired but eyes wide open because I was afraid that if I closed them I wouldn't wake up again. I felt like I wanted to peel back my own skin and crawl out of my body, like that was the only way I'd get rid of this horrible feeling. But of course that was not possible, and the only other thing that would ease the feeling, for a little while, was more drugs. It was a downward spiral, and it was getting worse.

I hated myself, but I couldn't stop. I started to get sloppy. It's not very hard to cover things up, but Harry twigged that something was going on. He took me to one side and confronted me with his suspicions. I fessed up. Sort of. 'Yeah, I've been doing a little bit of this and that. You know, now and then. No big deal . . .'

But Harry's not stupid, and I think I could tell even at the time that he didn't believe me. He knew that I didn't do restraint. But I swore him to secrecy and he was as good as his word. My secret was safe.

Harry: I knew that I was the only person Dougie could confide in. Tom would have found it difficult to take; Danny might have got angry. It seemed to me that Dougie was going through a rebellious streak. It would pass, but in the meantime it was much more important that he had someone he felt he could talk with, than for me to try to force him into a recovery he wasn't yet prepared to enter.

That's not to say I didn't get worried. We would get drunk together a lot – more so than the others – but Dougie's drinking was always more urgent. It wasn't about having a good time; it was only about getting as drunk as possible. For most people it was just a pastime. For Dougie, it had become a necessity. The dilemma was intense. Was I being a good friend keeping it quiet? Would I be a bad friend if I spilt the beans? Rightly or wrongly, I decided that it was more important that I had Dougie's confidence. That way, if something went badly wrong, he would come straight to me. Wouldn't he?

Dougie: I don't doubt that if Harry had stepped in at the wrong moment it would have spurred me on even more.

But even so, left to my own devices, the downhill trajectory of my addictions continued.

There's paranoia, and then there's paranoia. I became convinced that someone was spying on me. If I looked out of my window at night and saw a light, I thought it was a camera. I would spend hours pacing the length of my flat, checking all the windows, then running to the bottom of the garden and checking over my fence in case anybody had eyes-on. It was hell. I could get through the day, but only if I knew there was a party at the end of it – even if it was just going to the pub where I could get off my face.

Getting smashed became a daily occurrence, even when we were working. If we had a show, I'd sleep on the tour bus right up until soundcheck, and my breakfast would be everyone else's dinner. More than once I remember lying on the dressing-room floor thinking to myself that there was no way I could even stand up, let alone play an instrument in front of tens of thousands of people. The guilt was unbearable: the guys in the band worked so hard to put on a good show, so many people had spent so much money to see us, and the night before I'd got myself into such a state that I didn't even feel I could set foot on stage. I constantly felt that I was letting those fans down, walking out like that to play. Guilt led to hate. I loved everybody in the world except one person, who I despised: me.

Harry: But he hid it so well. Frighteningly well. Give the man an Oscar.

Dougie: I was nearly twenty-one when I found myself in a new relationship. Her name was Frankie Sandford. I was so off my face around this period that I don't really remember how we got together. In time our relationship would become more widely documented than most, and I don't want to add to that, other than to say that we were very different people and entirely unsuited. We both had a lot of issues, and it was never going to work out. Even the people closest to me had no idea that I was playing around with anything more than alcohol. The stuff I was taking made me feel so mellow and sleepy that all it would take was a few drinks on top for me to pass out. And when I was passed out, I couldn't feel like shit. Or hate myself.

Even those people who *did* know about my drug use didn't know the extent of it. I lied to them about how much I was using, and the more I did so, the more I believed the lie I was telling. The truth was that I drank and did drugs the same way some people smoke cigarettes. There was no enjoyment involved with it any more. It was simply what I did.

Frankie and I broke up in the autumn of 2010. You know that feeling of freedom you get when a relationship ends? It was dangerous for me. Now that I didn't have to hide anything from anyone I could abuse my body in whatever way I saw fit. I'd have a few shots as soon as I woke up, just to take the edge off the previous night's excesses. And although I would tell myself *every single day* that I wasn't going to touch anything other than alcohol, I'd get to a certain point of inebriation when my willpower would crumble.

Months passed. I didn't sleep in my own bed once. I simply collapsed on the sofa, or on the floor, or round the houses of random people. I forgot what it was like to feel sober.

Harry: In November 2010, I cut drinking out of my life completely. My new-found sobriety became a massive part of my life, something I was, and am, immensely proud of. But as Dougie was about to find out, some people find cleaning up their act harder than others.

Dougie: It was February 2011. I was sitting on my kitchen floor. It was the lowest I'd ever been. I didn't feel I could talk to anyone. Nobody would understand what I was going through. Why would they? Why *should* they? I was in a mess of my own making, and there was no way out. I'd tried and failed so many times to kick my various habits. I didn't understand why I couldn't go to the pub and just have one or two drinks like Danny and Tom seemed able to do. Even Harry, my drinking buddy, had made the decision to cut out the booze entirely. What was different about *me*? Why was *I* so much worse than everybody else?

How could I make it stop?

And it was as I was sitting on the kitchen floor that the answer came to me. It was so stunningly obvious I couldn't understand why I hadn't thought of it before.

My life had turned into a relentless hell, so the only solution was to end it.

I continued to sit there. And as I sat, I tried to work out the best way to kill myself. I knew I was no good with blood – I faint at the sight of it – so I'd never be able to bring myself to slit my wrists. I had no idea how to go about hanging myself, and I didn't have enough prescription medicines or anything else to overdose with. (Plus I'd heard horror stories about people who'd tried to OD and woken up not dead but paralysed.) Then I remembered: I'd seen something on TV about attaching a hosepipe to the exhaust of your car and slipping the other end through a partially open window. The carbon monoxide would send you to sleep, permanently. I had a hosepipe and I had a car. Which meant I had an escape route.

I don't remember feeling bummed out about my decision, or nervous, or guilty. All I remember is an overwhelming sense of relief that I wouldn't have to wake up the following morning feeling like this. Suddenly I was in control of one aspect of my life. I might not be able to stop myself from taking drugs any more, but at least I could do something to stop the hell I was going through. The idea made me feel more contented than I'd been for years. It made me feel happy.

It was 5 a.m. and quiet outside when I stumbled into the garden and found the hosepipe. I carried it to my car – an Audi Q7 – out in the street, and slid one end of the hose into the exhaust pipe. I wound the hose round to the side of the car and fed it through a tiny gap in the top of the driver's window. Then I sat behind the wheel and turned on the ignition.

To this day I don't know why I'm still here. I could smell the exhaust fumes and inhaled them deeply. But the Q7 is a large car with quite a big exhaust. Maybe more fumes were escaping than were diverted down the hosepipe. Maybe I screwed it up in some other way. I sat there for twenty minutes, waiting to fall asleep. But I didn't.

I was sobering up now. I turned off the ignition and stumbled out of the car, feeling even more self-loathing than before. I couldn't give up my addictions. Now I couldn't even kill myself. I'd tried and failed – like I had with everything else in my life.

That was my nadir. My lowest point. When I realized what I had just tried to do, and understood that the thought of doing it hadn't even stirred an ounce of regret in my addled brain, I knew, in some corner of my mind, that I'd hit the bottom. And if I couldn't end my life, I needed to find some other form of help.

We have a band doctor who has looked after our health since day one. I went to see him, and I told him everything. I held back from confessing my suicide attempt, though, because I was scared that he might section me. He referred me to a counsellor.

I turned up at the counsellor's place at one o'clock in the afternoon, absolutely steaming. I'd been drinking whisky, and I remember walking around the clinic and bumping into the walls. I was expecting the counsellor to put me on some kind of antidepressant, but he took one look at me and his mind was made up: he was sending me into rehab. No messing around. I was to be admitted in two days' time.

How do you tell your best friends you've been lying to them for the past four years? How do you find the words? The following day – Valentine's Day 2011 – we had interviews booked in at our management's office in London. I was going to have to explain to them why I was about to drop off the radar, for how long I didn't know.

I told Harry first. He knew something of what I'd been going through, and although he was surprised that it had got this far, it wasn't a total bolt from the blue.

Harry: He was dry-heaving as he told me, clearly terrified of the ordeal that was round the corner. I tried to comfort him. To reassure him. But behind the mask I couldn't believe how serious it had got. This was no attention-seeking cry for help. This was real.

Dougie: Tom, when I told him, was almost shocked into silence. He'd known that all was not well, but he'd had no idea of the extent of my problems. Once he'd got his head round it, he was full of questions. He remembered times I'd been acting weird. Had *that* all been to do with *this*?

Yeah. And some.

When I told Danny, I started dry-heaving again. He clearly didn't know what to say. I held back from mentioning my abortive suicide attempt to anybody, but as I sat in front of my three best friends and admitted that I had a massive – *massive* – problem, I felt a weight lifting from me. Looking back, I can see that I had taken the first step to recovery. But there was a long way to go.

Harry: It being Valentine's Day, I'd booked a table in London for dinner with Izzy. In the car on the way we spoke about how worried we were. It dawned on us that Dougie would be on his own that night.

Valentine's Day.

The night before he went into rehab.

It was a recipe for disaster.

We decided that we could forego our own romantic evening, cancelled our reservation and re-routed to Dougie's.

I called Dougie on the way. 'What you doing tonight, dude?'

He sounded pretty quiet. 'Nothing.'

I tried to sound casual. 'Well, me and Izzy are coming up your way, so maybe we'll come and hang out with you?'

'OK. Cool.' Typical Dougie, he didn't seem to twig that we might have had other plans.

As soon as we arrived at Dougie's flat, I took him to one side. 'Mate, it's your last night before you go into rehab. I'm going to be with you, but maybe it's best you don't drink tonight, hey?'

Too late. There was a quarter-full bottle of Jack Daniel's on the side.

The three of us sat down to a romantic takeaway. The evening took its course. At around 1 a.m., I called Tom, since he lived next door. I explained that we were leaving and that perhaps he should check in on Dougie once we'd gone. Then I took Dougie to one side again. 'Listen, Doug – you've had a drink, but nothing else tonight, OK?'

The smile returned. A twinkle in his eye. 'Too late, dude,' he whispered. 'Too late.'

Dougie: Harry's memories of that night are much better than mine. All I know is that Tom *did* come round, and he spent some time trying to persuade me that everything would be OK in rehab, showing me pictures on his laptop of the institution I was heading for in the morning. By all accounts the very mention of it turned me into a shaking, trembling mess. Personally, I don't remember a single second of that conversation.

Morning came. Things seemed a little brighter. Tom drove me to the Priory in Southgate. I was still drunk from the night before, and the booze in my veins helped me relax. Rehab was going to be fine, I repeated to myself. A breeze. We even managed to joke about it a little. And when I checked in, it was nothing like what I was expecting. In my mind I had an image of a Victorian sanatorium, with communal showers and grim-faced orderlies. Tom, who'd been to the Priory just a month or two before me, had tried to explain that it wasn't like that, but I hadn't been able to get rid of the expectation that it would be a bit like prison. In reality, it was more like a Holiday Inn. I had my own, not very luxurious, room; and although there were people checking in on me every hour, there was nothing to stop me walking out of the place if I wanted to. Maybe it *was* going to be OK . . .

But then the time came for Tom to leave. For me to be alone without my bandmates to support me. And it was only once he had driven away from my new home that the reality sank in: there wasn't going to be any drink at the end of this day.

That one thought was enough to sober me up, and to make panic rise in my gut.

All of a sudden I was surrounded by doctors doing tests on me, therapists asking me questions. I was trembling again. I was throwing up. It was, beyond question, the most scared I'd ever been.

It got worse. On my first night, the dude next door to me flooded his room. I heard all this commotion through the wall, and opened my door to see what was going on. My neighbour was right there, standing on the threshold, a wild look in his eyes. 'All right, mate?' he said in a mad voice. 'Good to meet you . . .' I closed the door again. Another guy looked like Jesus and was always walking – he only ever *stopped* walking when he went to sleep. I was one of the youngest there – the majority of the other patients were in their thirties or older.

My panic increased. What the hell was I doing here? I shouldn't *be* here, surrounded by these mentalists. I wasn't like them. I wasn't crazy.

Was I?

I soon found out that there were two distinct groups of people at the Priory: those on the Addiction Treatment Program (ATP), and those on the general ward. The general ward was for people suffering acute depression or other mental health issues. The ATP was full of people in exactly the same boat as me, and although the ATP was my group, my room was closer to the general ward.

I was prescribed Librium. It's like a very strong Valium, that is used to treat anxiety and acute alcohol withdrawal symptoms. I'd have got off my face if there had been any booze about, but there wasn't, and the Librium at least made me sufficiently laid-back not to suffer too much from the cold turkey. It helps you detox, and reduces the likelihood of you running away from rehab just to get another fix of whatever substance you're craving. Not that I didn't try: I packed my bag on three or four occasions, but there was always somebody on hand at the last minute to persuade me to do the right thing.

Mobile phones were banned – you were supposed to surrender them on arrival – but I managed to keep hold of mine. Every night during that first week I would call Harry or Tom, bawling my eyes out. The Librium might have been masking some of the withdrawal symptoms, but that feeling of being uncomfortable in my own skin had returned, and now I had nothing to make it go away.

Harry: Dougie was inconsolable. It was almost impossible to make sense of what he was talking about, let alone think of anything we could say to make him feel better. Eventually we pieced a few things together. He was in his room on his own. He didn't know what was going on. They were making him take pills he didn't want to take, and asking questions he didn't know how to answer. He clearly needed company, but visitors were only allowed on Sundays and this was still the beginning of his first week.

I got on the phone to the Priory and somehow blagged my way in to see him. The Librium had calmed him down, but he was clearly on edge, not the Dougie we all knew. It felt terrible having to leave him there, in that spartan room, half spaced-out, half on the brink of panic.

The following Sunday, Tom, Danny and I went to visit together, along with a good mate of Dougie's – a sweet guy who displayed an amazing talent for saying the wrong thing.

Dougie: I don't think it had really sunk in yet that my only chance of recovery was *never* to drink again. When my mate asked me how long it would be before I could go out and have a beer with him, the penny dropped. 'Never,' I said.

His face went a bit white. '*What?* You can never come out for a beer ever again?'

I shook my head. And then I started to dry-heave again.

I don't blame him for not understanding. He wasn't the only one. All my friends drank, but they could control it and didn't understand the core problem with an addiction: that one drink is too many, and a hundred is never enough.

I only knew one other person who'd been to rehab: Matt Willis from Busted. He was a huge help. I called him daily and told him what I was feeling, about the storm in my head and how hard I was finding this detox. Just to talk to someone who'd been through it was a relief; just to know that someone else had experienced the same as me and come out the other end gave me the little bit of courage I needed to see it out.

Gradually, something changed in my head. I'd wanted to be clean for years now, and this was my only chance. If I failed, I knew I'd never come back here. And so I owed it to myself to succeed. And I owed it to the band.

I was on the Librium for a hazy, tear-fuelled week before they took me off it. By then I had detoxed and something remarkable had happened. I suddenly felt better than I had felt for years. Full of energy. I'd gone from wanting to jump out of the window because I was depressed and wanting to fill my body with damaging substances, to wanting to jump through the window because I was so happy. As I got to know other people on the ATP, it dawned on me that I wasn't the only person in the world who'd had these problems. I wasn't alone. I was surrounded by all these great people who'd been up to the same as me, who'd had the same routines and the same secrets.

The original plan had been to stay there for a week's detox, but now that I'd seen a glimmer of light at the end of the tunnel, I decided to stay for the full twenty-eight days. I was three weeks in before the press found out I was there. They made their own story. Because I hadn't ever been spotted falling drunk out of clubs, I hadn't built up a reputation as a lasher. They decided I was recovering from a broken heart. That was categorically not true, but I didn't see any point in correcting them.

By the time I was halfway through my month-long

stint in rehab, I entered a phase of recovery. I started to believe that I actually could get better. That I actually could stay abstinent, at least for a while. Once a day, we would all sit down in a circle and discuss what was on our minds. I loved that by the end. It was a chance to relieve myself of all the nagging little worries that were eating me up. I could say to a group of people that I found myself looking at the alcohol content of my after-shave and wanting to drink it. Instead of feeling like a freak, I'd learn that the others had had exactly the same thought. Not only that, but some of them had seen that there was alcohol in mouthwash and had been necking it every morning.

We were due to go on tour immediately my month of rehab came to an end. Harry picked me up and drove me home. Back at my flat, I enlisted Tom's help to go through all my stuff and discard anything associated with my former life. Before I got sober, I'd thought I was quite nifty at hiding the evidence of my addictions. Now, I realized how obvious my hiding places really were. It was tough throwing it out, as was getting rid of all the booze in the place. But I knew it was the only way I could stay clean. The only way I could stop my life from going back to the way it had been.

As I write this, the past eighteen months feel like the longest since I was fourteen. Why? Because I can remember it all. My time of sobriety has been the best of my life. I can remember our tours properly; I can go on stage feeling enthusiastic; I don't wake up in a mess; I'm experiencing life the way it's supposed to be lived.

But I always have to remember this: I'm not cured.

I'm in recovery, and I will be for as long as I stay clean, which I intend to be for the rest of my life. I still talk to other people in recovery on a daily basis, because it helps to have contact with those who are dealing with the same experiences. I go to meetings of AA – not as often as I should because of our touring schedule, but often enough to keep me on the straight and narrow. I have a counsellor, and a sponsor who has been through the same trouble with addiction as me and is now nearly a decade clean. Staying in recovery is an active, every-day thing for me now. Each morning when I get up I do my meditation, read my recovery books, take my 'personal inventory' – a checklist of what has happened in the past twenty-four hours and whether I could have dealt with events better. I need to know that I'm being a good person, because if I start acting like an idiot that could be the first step taking me back to where I was before. If I allow the self-loathing that I used to experi-ence to creep back into my mind, I know I'll end up back at square one.

Sobriety isn't always easy. I go through patches when I know I'm more likely to relapse, but I take things one day at a time. I know that if I set myself the modest task of reaching the end of the day clean, I'm more likely to succeed than if I stop to imagine the rest of my life with-out a beer or any of the other substances that have plagued me in the past.

And while my ego would prefer it if nobody knew about my troubles, and would be perfectly happy if I was just the quiet one in McFly again, I know that being honest and open about what I've been through gives me the best chance of continued recovery. Because the truth, I've found, is always better than lies. And you can't be honest with other people, unless you're being honest with yourself.

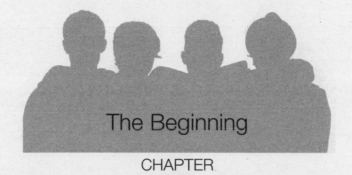

The Beginning

CHAPTER

13

Tom: Dougie had been through hell, but made it back. Life hit an upward turn for me, too. I'd been worried that the medication I was taking would rob me of my periods of creativity, but that didn't seem to be happening. My ups were unaffected, but life had become a bit smoother. Easier to cope with.

I didn't talk to the guys about my diagnosis at first. Not until I'd settled into my medication. But if Dougie could be honest with us all, so could I. Danny and Dougie aren't really the types for deep, meaningful conversations, but I knew Harry would be a good person to talk to. We had a few DMCs when I told him everything that had been going on. And the more I talked, the more relieved I felt. This wasn't an excuse for my occasionally weird behaviour in the past, but it was at least an explanation.

Harry: And it explained so much. I remember saying to Dougie that Tom hadn't been a dick for ages, and when Tom told us about his diagnosis, it felt like everything clicked into place. Tom's mood swings over the years had been intense, but now he was suddenly back to how he'd been when we were first in the band house together

337

all those years ago. And now that we knew what he'd been struggling with, it took away the bad taste his past behaviour had sometimes left in the mouth. It all made sense.

Tom: All of a sudden I found myself feeling positive about the future. And it sounds daft to say it, but my laugh had returned. I hadn't laughed like that for years. It sounded like it used to in the band house back in the day. It was almost as though we'd come full circle.

And finally, I found I had banished the alien at the window. I had rid myself of that crippling fear I'd experienced every single night of my life. I still sleep with the TV on, but at least I can now bring myself to move my arms out from under the covers, and take a more rational view of the world.

And a more rational view of McFly.

We'd made a big mistake with our last album: we had doubted ourselves. Now that sanity had returned to the band, we weren't going to make that mistake again. We were going to do things *our* way, and we were going to throw everything we had at it. As luck would have it, three of us were about to be given the opportunity to take our public exposure to another level.

Danny: For years, we'd always been asked to take part in reality shows. *Big Brother* this, *Celebrity* that; you name it, we'd been asked to do it. Our answer had always been the same: thanks, but no thanks. When Fletch came to me to say that the producers of a show called *Popstar to Operastar* had been in touch, he explained that he'd originally sent them packing. But they were persistent, and it had got him thinking . . .

Dougie: Danny as an opera star? It was just about the funniest idea we'd ever heard, but it wasn't as silly as it sounded. Well, not quite. He and Tom were in the habit of putting on fake opera voices when they warmed their voices up before a show, and more than once we'd found ourselves looking at Danny and saying: 'You know, that's actually pretty good!'

Danny: When Fletch asked me if I'd do it, I simply burst out laughing. But then *I* started thinking, too. I'd never had a challenge like that before, and it did feel like something I could get my teeth into. Besides, we were all a bit worried that with all the delays to *Above The Noise* – this was just after our second trip to Atlanta – we hadn't been in the public eye much, so maybe it would do the band some good. I decided to give it a go.

To this day I wish I'd let myself go a bit more on that show. Not worried so much about being cool. I was *so* nervous before each performance. Backstage before a McFly gig I'm happy as Larry; before one of these shows I'd be sniffing lavender oil to calm my nerves, headphones fixed to my ears to take my mind off the horrors to come. There's nothing scarier than live TV. You'd think I'd be used to it by now, but it still freaks me out: my head gets filled with what-ifs – what if I do it wrong, what if I forget my lines – and before I know it I'm panicking and all the what-ifs start to come true. I'm bad enough with lyrics at the best of times, but these ones were in Italian! How the hell was I supposed to remember them? In the end I had to write them all out phonetically in a notebook and learn them from that.

The training and filming for the show took place immediately after our second trip to Atlanta, and for that period I felt more like I worked at ITV than was in a band. The singing teachers were all brilliant, but strict, and they pushed me hard. I'd never sung scales in my life before – I could hold it together for the simple ones, but when the exercises became more complicated, I was rubbish. I got better, though, as I started to learn about the correct placement for my throat, and all the little tips and techniques that make an opera singer sound so great. I still use some of those techniques now when I perform.

We didn't just have singing teachers, but also dialect instructors and acting coaches. I don't think I've ever done anything more cringeful (at least, not that I'm pre- pared to own up to) than try to act out the lyrics to an opera song in a small room with just me, my teacher and a TV camera for company. Makes me shudder just to remember it. There was no chickening out, though: if I didn't put my heart into it, I wasn't getting out of that room.

I got on well enough with the other contestants, but it would be a push to say I made any lifelong friends there. There's a tendency for 'celebrities' in the UK to assume that the tiny details of their lives are interesting to everybody, and that it's a foregone conclusion that others know everything about them. I find it hard enough to remember what I did last week, let alone what some soap actor did last year. I only vaguely recognized the other contestants, and I certainly didn't know much about them. I felt a bit like a fish out of water in that kind of environment, and kept myself to myself. The guys I got on with the best were, weirdly, my fellow contestant Jimmy Osmond, and one of the judges: Meat Loaf. Me and Meat hit it off straight away. After one of the shows he came up to me, a vodka in his hand, and said, in his dramatic way: 'Danny! There's seven people in this world that I like, and they're all actors. You're number eight!'

Cheers, Meat!

I didn't over-think *Popstar to Operastar*. I wasn't all that competitive. I just went out there and did it, and my motivation was simple: to raise the profile of McFly. Of course, if I were to do it again now, I'd take it a bit more seriously. I'd want to win, because in the months to come, once Dougie had got himself clean and the Great Depression was a thing of the past, it became clear that the McFly boys *could* go on these shows and come out on top.

Harry: Not that we were exactly chomping at the bit to appear on any more reality shows. When the offer came in for me to do *Strictly Come Dancing* while we were on our 2011 arena tour, I was in two minds. I'd already done a one-off *Strictly* charity special for Children in Need the previous November. I'd only agreed to do that because Fletch targeted me on the tour bus back from a show when I'd had a few beers (this was a couple of weeks before I stopped drinking, so those few beers were the catalyst for everything that was to come for me), and the producers had rejected our frankly brilliant idea of me and Dougie learning a dance together. *Strictly* had always struck me as being the classiest of all those kind of shows, but in truth I wasn't sure that I really wanted to put myself out there on prime-time TV every week. When Fletch called me to say that I'd been asked to do the main show, I said no. I was happy with my life the way it was. Happy just being Harry from McFly. I didn't really want to be any more famous. I didn't want to lose what anonymity I had. And after the stress and the nerves of just four days of *Strictly* for Children in Need – it had been *very* hard work – I wasn't sure I could put up with it week in, week out. But at the same time, my heart had sunk a little. I think I knew deep down that I'd end up being persuaded to do it.

Tom: I definitely thought he should do it. Sure, I thought it would be good for the band, but knowing Harry as I do I knew he'd be brilliant at it. He'd kicked arse in the Children in Need special, and have we mentioned that he's quite competitive?

Danny: I kept my opinion to myself, but deep down I was thinking that most people who appear on reality shows are dicks. Harry *isn't* a dick, which meant he couldn't fail to make a good impression.

Dougie: I was less enthusiastic. Reality shows weren't cool, surely? They were wrong for our image. What if it cheapened us? What if it got edited in such a way as to make Harry look like an arsehole? What if it made it look like our careers were over, or we were just trying to cash in? And anyway, *Popstar to Operastar* aside, we always did everything as a unit. Why would we want to go off and do stuff on our own?

Harry: Tom and Dougie were like the devil and the angel on my shoulders. I could see where they were both coming from, and as the deadline for my decision approached, I didn't feel any closer to an answer. Izzy was firmly in the 'do it' camp, and in the end, I came to the conclusion that I should give it a go. It would be great for the band, I figured, and it would be great for me as a life experience.

Dougie: And it turned out to be like waiting for a bus – two reality shows came along at once. I knew I'd never be able to do something like *Strictly Come Dancing* – I can hardly stand up and talk at the same time, let alone do the tango on live TV. The only one I'd *ever* be able to do would be *I'm A Celebrity…Get Me Out Of Here!* because of my interest in wildlife. Ordinarily I'd have said no way – what if I said something stupid and made a total prat of myself? – but once Harry had agreed to appear on *Strictly*, I crumbled. In for a penny, in for a pound – a pound of ostrich anus in my case. I agreed to do the show.

I was not long out of rehab and living with Tom and Giovanna because I wasn't quite sure I could handle going back to live by myself again. Quite how I was going to deal with living in the Australian jungle for three weeks with a bunch of people I'd never met, I didn't know. It was, after all, a very public way for me to continue my recovery.

Once Harry and I had both agreed to do our respective shows, we were standing outside Tom's house one day having a cigarette. 'Imagine if we both won,' I said. 'How cool would that be?'

And of course, we both laughed. I mean, what were the chances of that?

Dougie: It doesn't matter who you are. The way guys meet girls always seems to be the same: you go out, you drink to lose your inhibitions, and you hope that will give you the confidence to pull. But now I was clean, and I wasn't really going out much. I was living with Tom and Gi, learning how to be sober, and so hardly meeting any girls. All the other guys were in strong relationships: Tom and Gi, Harry and Izzy – and even Danny was a changed man.

Danny: It's true. Remember Miss England? After meeting her in South Africa, I saw her on and off for the next few months. She lived out of town, and it wasn't a serious thing. Much later, in 2008, she asked me if I wanted to go along to see the Miss London contest. I agreed. And it was then that I first saw Georgia.

Georgia had also been Miss England, in 2007. The moment I saw her, my eyes almost fell out of my head.

Who is *that*? She looked amazing, like an angel in this sea of girls. As the night went on, I couldn't take my eyes off her, and she looked better by the minute.

I half-expected her to be your typical high-maintenance model; she half-expected me to be your typical dickhead pop star. But then she heard me speak. 'You northern?' she asked.

'Yeah!'

'Me, too!'

The ice was broken. We chatted all night and instantly hit it off. I invited her for lunch the next day, but she turned me down because she already had a boyfriend. It took me precisely a year after that to persuade her to go out with me. I haven't looked back since. Georgia's amazing for me. Always there, and she keeps me sane. She's beautiful inside and out, and when you meet someone like that, you've got to hang on to them. She's the one. And I've grown up since meeting her. The old Danny, the kid in the sweetie shop every time pretty girls were around, is gone. I don't want anybody else but her.

Dougie: So I was the only single one. I was talking this alarming predicament over with Harry one day, when I suddenly remembered him mentioning that he knew a really sweet, funny girl called Lara. What was the deal with her?

Harry: She was a friend of the family, and the more I thought about it, the more it seemed to me that she and Dougie would be perfect for each other. She was a really talented painter, and pretty much Dougie in a girl's body. Why hadn't I thought of it before? My brother lived in a shared house with Lara's sister, so I put the feelers out. Did she have a boyfriend? Word came back that she did. Bummer.

Dougie: It called for a plan, so I cooked one up. I was in the process of decorating my flat, trying to make it a bit more personal, ready for me to move back into. A lot of the people I hang out with are artists, and I had this one massive blank wall on which I was going to ask someone to make a painting. Lara was a painter. Her stuff is awesome. I could ask her! If I commissioned her to do a painting for me, we could at least get talking . . .

Me and Lara met up at the Ivy Club in London to discuss the painting. I knew before I even walked in the room that she was something special (I had stalked her on Facebook and grilled Harry for any info), but as soon as I laid eyes on her I became even more infatuated. She looked amazing: awesome clothes and headband, and grinning from ear to ear. She looked like a much fitter, real-life version of Esmeralda from *The Hunchback of Notre Dame*, and she was very, very funny. I kept testing the water, seeing how far I could take my jokes. Lara would always push them one step further. We met at twelve o clock; we didn't finish talking until about seven. The only way I can describe meeting Lara is as if you had spent your entire life walking around with one leg, then one day you meet someone and all of a sudden you have two legs and life becomes amazing. Now you can run and jump and everyday life becomes easy and wonderful, all because you have met this one person.

I left the Ivy Club buzzing, and after that first meeting we found ourselves constantly emailing each other – pages and pages of jokes and pictures, links to sites we liked and videos we found funny. The emailing thing went on for a couple of weeks, but all I really wanted to do was see her again. With Harry's help I composed an email asking her if she wanted to hang out. She declined because she had a boyfriend. 'That's not what I meant,' I lied. 'Strictly platonic . . .'

So, just as 'platonic fuck-ups', we hung out. We were best mates from the word go. It was a new experience for me. I was enjoying the company of someone else without booze or drugs. I was on top of the world. We hung out about four times. One of the places we went to was Viktor Wynd's Little Shop of Horrors, a curiosity/taxidermy shop in town that also sells vintage porn, penis-shaped pepper shakers and monkey heads attached to fish tails so they look like mermaids. Of all the things in that shop she could have picked out, Lara fell in love with a little plastic Fisher-Price egg. That's exactly the sort of thing that made me fall so hard for her. But the more we hung out, the more I got hung up on her. And the more I got hung up on her, the guiltier I felt.

I wasn't that far into my recovery, and one of the things I had been advised to do was to always look at my part to play in any drama and keep my side of the street clean. To keep myself in check and not upset or harm others around me. To be as spiritual as possible.

My situation was getting too much. I REALLY liked Lara.

I asked her to meet up again and, knowing it would be our last time, I tried to make it a bit special. I took her to a freak burlesque show. As the night came to an end, I somehow found the courage to tell her I couldn't see her any more. It killed me to say those words. I explained that I had fallen for her and us hanging out wasn't a good idea or fair any more. Lara agreed, and the next day I picked up the painting I had commissioned. That day was an über-bum-out. How the hell could I never see this girl again?

We were supposed not to really speak again after that last time, but I only managed about twenty-four hours before texting her. And I gradually began to realize something. If Lara really was the one, should I just let her slip through my fingers? If she was the one, was it really so bad to let her know it wasn't just a crush and that I had actually fallen madly in love with her?

So I wrote her a letter. It said all the things I found it hard to say in person. I told her I was totally in love with her and that she was the most amazing person I had ever met. And I sent it in a box full of the Fisher-Price eggs she had fallen in love with in the taxidermy shop. Our equivalent of roses, I guess. And my plan, once I'd sent it, was to drop off the radar. Easily done, because the next day Danny, Tom and I had work to do.

Danny: Harry's training for *Strictly* started at the end of August 2011. Dougie wasn't due in the jungle till November. While Harry was out of action, the rest of us took the opportunity to start thinking about what to do with the band. Tom had hardly picked up a guitar or sat down at a keyboard since *Above The Noise*, not least because of the difficulties we'd had with that record. We had no idea what was coming next, musically speaking, and it was almost a blessing in disguise: when the three of us finally did sit down together, we found we had all these ideas just waiting to get out.

Tom: We decided to get away from the distractions of London. We hired a house on the coast in Holyhead, North Wales, so remote that you could only get to it when the tide went out. We packed all Danny's recording gear into the back of the car and headed off for ten days of seclusion.

Dougie: The day after I sent my letter to Lara, we arrived at this old house in the middle of nowhere, with beautiful views and total quiet. After the difficulties of the past year it was exactly what we needed, and it was a place where we could feel inspired. It was also a place where I could stay occupied, and not brood too much on the effect the letter might be having on Lara.

I shouldn't have worried. There was only one place in the house that had any mobile phone reception. A few days into the writing trip I was passing that point when my phone jingled with two text messages: one telling me Lara had split up with her boyfriend, the next telling me she felt the same way.

What an amazing moment! My life had changed the day I came out of rehab. Now it was changing again. It felt like things couldn't get any better. I'd got the girl of my dreams. I felt like I was fifteen again, with my life spread out in front of me. The whole world felt awesome, as though I'd been asleep for the past nine years, and now I was awake. It improved every aspect of my life, and it meant I could focus on our music, and look at it through fresh eyes.

Tom: Sometimes it's daunting, being faced with a blank canvas. Sometimes it's inspiring. We knew the mistakes we'd made with our last album. We knew that from here on we were going to trust our own instincts. Danny would be producing the next record – his skills had really developed, and it would mean our songs would get even closer to how we wanted them to sound, because it was one of us behind the desk.

Danny: We converted the living-room area into a studio and started experimenting. It didn't take long for us to realize that the stuff we were coming up with was some of our most exciting music ever. We were writing lyrics inspired by the sea and our surroundings, and for the first time in years it felt like we were doing what we were truly *meant* to be doing. It felt right, in our hearts and in our heads. The polar opposite of *Above The Noise*. The music we wrote in that short trip away gave me goosebumps, and like I always say: goosebumps don't lie.

Dougie: It felt awesome. Everything was coming together. Songs were pouring out of us and with tunes we'd written with working titles like 'Hyperion' and 'Break Me' (a song all about Lara that gives me tingles every time I hear it), a sound for the future was developing. With nobody else about to put a dampener on things, we were able to follow our own muse. We didn't think about what sort of person would like each song. We didn't think about whether they were radio-friendly. We just did what we wanted, and it dawned on us that we would much rather do that and not be the biggest band in the world, than swap greater success for less musical satisfaction.

We couldn't stay in the house for long: Harry was still back in London, making the nation swoon with his dance moves, and I had the small matter of a trip to the Australian jungle to get out of the way.

Shit.

I felt entirely comfortable going on TV with the band. Our chemistry was there, well honed after years of doing it. Now I had to do a day's advance publicity for *I'm A Celebrity* by myself. This was way out of my comfort zone, and I hated it. I went back to Tom and Gi's place determined that I was going to pull out of the show. It wasn't for me, full stop. And besides, I was with Lara now. It had taken such a long time to get with her, and we had tumbled headlong into a full-on relationship. Why would I want to take time out from that? Of course, they talked me round.

Tom: When the time came for Dougie to go, he was visibly scared. Physically shaking as we sat and waited for Tommy to pick him up to go to the airport. Even in those last few minutes he was thinking of pulling out. After everything he'd been through, putting himself on the front line like this was a very big deal.

Dougie: I wasn't nervous about living in the jungle. I wasn't nervous about dining on witchetty grubs or bathing with bugs. I wasn't nervous of mosquitoes, snakes or cockroaches. I was just scared of making a tit of myself, of saying something stupid on live TV that would cause a storm and harm the band. We crack a lot of jokes when we're by ourselves – just us pushing the boundaries – that we wouldn't want anyone else to hear. What if I slipped into tour-bus mode in front of millions of people?

They send you out to Australia by yourself, which means you can't get to know anyone beforehand, or share your nerves with your fellow contestants. Consequently, I was absolutely bricking myself. I tried to keep my spirits up by watching nothing but Disney movies on the flight over. The moment you arrive in Australia, you're chaperoned to individual hotels and your phone's taken off you. The chaperones won't tell you anything about what's happening or what to expect, because they don't *know* what's happening themselves. You don't even know what *day* you're going into the jungle. You simply get an hour's notice and you have to be ready to go. And your best bet is to get used to that kind of uncertainty, because you never know what's going on or what's about to happen for all the time you're in the jungle.

The only people I recognized when I walked into the

camp for the first time were Antony Cotton and Mark Wright. It was a bit embarrassing – I didn't have a clue who anybody else was. I assumed Stefanie Powers was some old-school Hollywood actress, and I reckoned Fatima Whitbread was probably a wrestler. It worked both ways – only a couple of them knew who *I* was, but I was totally expecting that. We all introduced ourselves and tried our best not to be too awkward as we made small talk in front of the cameras. I don't really think I succeeded, but all my fellow contestants seemed pretty cool, so that was a small weight off my mind. Now all I had to do was tough it through the next three weeks without making a twat of myself.

There's no camera trickery or artistic licence in *I'm A Celebrity*. You really are dumped in the middle of the jungle and left to fend for yourself. You have to fetch water from the creek and boil it before drinking it. You have to collect your own wood – quite a mission even in the early morning when the heat and humidity are both still high – and you're hungry. The food is strictly, and meanly, rationed. A lot of people might think it's all done for TV, but believe me: you're hungry most of the time, and you *really* want to win those stars in the trials because they truly are the only way to get more food. Think about it: if people weren't genuinely hungry, why the hell would they stick their head into a box full of spiders? If one of the contestants comes back to camp and says, 'Sorry, guys, I only got two stars,' everyone's very sympathetic on the outside. Inside, you can bet your bottom dollar that they're cursing, because the chicken leg and handful of veg for which those stars can be redeemed simply isn't enough to keep hunger at bay when it's shared among you all.

So you're hungry, and you're hot. Even so, I loved it in the jungle. For the first week, I didn't really *do* anything. All the others seemed to be getting the tasks, and I was getting along well with everyone. The only thing that really bummed me out was boredom and the occasional hunger blues. None of us had a watch, so we had to estimate the time by the position of the sun, but I guess it was around four or five o'clock that the hunger hit the worst. All we ever talked about in camp was how starving we were. 'Dude, have you ever tried . . . spaghetti bolognese with Worcestershire Sauce?' 'Have you ever tried . . . Ben and Jerry's Caramel Chew Chew?' 'You know what I'm going to eat when I get out? A Milky Way. I haven't had a Milky Way for frickin' years . . .' And we'd all roll around in paroxysms of hunger-induced agony. I must have smoked about forty cigarettes a day just to keep the hunger and the boredom at bay. My fingers had turned orange by the end of my stay.

You don't get to see on TV how much wildlife passes through the camp. Different creatures come out at varying times of the day. When the sun starts to set, the midges and greenfly rise; as it gets cooler, they disappear and you'll find little bullet-like insects on your skin. Other insects will fill the air towards nightfall – moths, and then bigger bullet-like insects that go kamikaze for any source of light and which you can hear whizzing through the air and feel crash-landing on your head. When it rains, the tree frogs start their chorus – if you walk down to the creek you'll see them in their thousands, and the water where you wash is filled with their tadpoles. Blue yabbies – a kind of freshwater lobster – fight each other underwater, and there are wild turkeys wandering about in the bush. Seeing those turkeys was the only time I've ever looked at an animal and thought to myself: will somebody *please* kill that thing so I can eat it?! I tried to persuade Fatima Whitbread, who was always making things, to fashion a spear so she could use her javelin skills to nail one, but we were told we weren't allowed to do that. There were even occasional pink-tongued skinks – incredibly rare lizards that I didn't even know existed until my trip to the jungle. I found one hiding among the rocks. When I went to check if it was a male or a female, it pissed on my head. We lizard fanciers live for moments like that. One night, I was settling down into my hammock when a baby bandicoot shot past. Seconds later its mother followed, and the baby jumped into her pouch.

As it grew dark, I heard swearing from Mark Wright's hammock: 'Dougie! *Dougie! There's a snake!*'

'Relax,' I told him. 'It's not a snake, it's a bandicoot.'

Mark wasn't having it, so I climbed out of my hammock and padded over in his direction. Sure enough, on the ground beneath him was a carpet python constricting the baby bandicoot and trying to eat it. Carpet pythons are similar to royal pythons, which I'd had as pets, so I wasn't too freaked out by it, but there were properly dangerous creatures in that jungle. I knew it wasn't unheard of to find funnel-web spiders or highly poisonous snakes in the vicinity. For that reason, one of the guys behind the scenes is Doctor Bob. Everyone had told me that meeting Doctor Bob was one of the coolest things about doing the show. They were right. He's like a cross between Crocodile Dundee and David Attenborough – a handy guy to have around in a place like that. When I left the jungle, Doctor Bob gave me a preserved funnel-web. Unfortunately I left it in the champagne cooler of the limo that took me back to my hotel – probably not the most welcome surprise for whoever used it next. All in all, I found the jungle wildlife a million times more interesting than the wildlife back home in England – only to be expected, I suppose, from a country whose spiders grow to the size of your hand, and can kill you.

Tom: A week after Dougie entered the jungle, I went out to be there too – not in the bush, of course, but in an ultra-posh hotel a couple of hours' drive away. Everyone's friends and family stay together, and because the show goes out live in the UK at 7 p.m., they all have to bundle into a minibus to get to the set at about four in the morning.

The vibe in the hotel among all the contestants' friends and families was that Mark was *definitely* going to win. I kept quiet, apart from the occasional: 'Don't be too sure . . .'

Dougie: I'd like to tell you that life behind the scenes in *I'm A Celebrity* was a hotbed of gossip and strife. Sorry to disappoint. I hit it off with everyone. I guess I was closest to Mark – it was good to have someone my own age out there who was relatively chilled – but I never found myself having much of a problem with anyone, and all in all, despite my initial nerves, it was an entirely positive experience. You even find that you actively *want* to go and try the nasty 'food' they give you, for the simple reason that it's something to do. A single trial might only last ten minutes on TV, but it would take a good two-hour chunk out of your day. When you leave the camp you get bundled into a blacked-out people carrier manned by grim-faced army dudes who won't even speak a word to you, no matter how hard you try to engage them in conversation.

And the trials themselves? They weren't so bad for me as they might have been for other people. Back when I was at school I used to have crickets jumping out of my pencil case because I used them to feed my lizards, so a coffin full of crickets wasn't exactly 1984. I'd have preferred roaches – they don't like the light, so all they want to do is hide (as Fatima Whitbread found to her cost when one scurried up her nostril), whereas crickets are always moving, jumping about, getting everywhere. But I was used to them. During the trial where I had to put my head into perspex boxes of assorted creepy crawlies, the only creatures that really concerned me were the snakes, not because I don't like them (I like them a lot), but because it would have been uncomfortable if they'd started biting my head.

It's not false modesty to say that I completely expected Mark to win. It seemed that he was picked to do far more tasks than me, and I had the impression that he was getting a lot more airtime. Not that it really worried me. I hadn't been sure that I'd be up to the experience of living in the jungle and having my every move scrutinized, especially after the year I'd had. In truth I was just relieved to have pulled it off, and when it came to the final day, with just me and Mark left, I was thinking more about the blow-out meal we were going to be given than about who was going to win. When it was announced I'd been crowned King of the Jungle, I was so shocked my first thought was: 'I am actually now going to spew on live TV.' Thankfully I managed to keep my spew to myself, as my shock turned to delight. It was an awesome moment for me. Having been so low, now I felt on top of the world.

Before I'd gone into the jungle, I'd been adamant: when it was over, I didn't want to do any interviews or publicity. It's amazing how short periods of your life can change you. I'd had such a great time that I actively wanted to talk to everybody about it. All of a sudden, being out there on my own didn't bother me. I was feeling the kind of confidence I'd never felt before.

And the kind of appetite too. I've never seen anybody eat as much as I did when I got out of the jungle. The following day I had three breakfasts – a stack of pancakes with syrup and ice cream, a huge omelette, and a fry-up. I ate every last scrap and was in agony from overeating, but that agony never felt so good. Kinky, huh?

Tom: And when we made it back to the hotel, there were crowds of Australian McFly fans waiting and cheering.

The producers said they'd never had that kind of response for a winner before.

Dougie: It was awesome to see all the fans there. It was awesome to see Tom and Gi. But most of all, it was awesome to see Lara. Embracing her as I walked out of the jungle was, in my head, the most romantic moment of my life.

Lara had been properly thrown in at the deep end. We'd only started going out three weeks before I left for the jungle, but already the tabloid press were interested in her. Add this to the fact that she was going out with a contestant in a big reality show, and you can see how she might be suddenly thrown into the limelight. Some people deal with it well; others don't. Some people change; others stay the same. Lara took it all in her stride.

Tom: In the early days with Lara, Dougie had arranged an amazing night out: a show, an expensive restaurant, a comedy club – an impressive and public display of affection. But I'd met Lara, and I knew he was barking up the wrong tree. She wasn't that type at all. It soon became clear that she wasn't seeing Dougie because he was famous, or because he was going to lavish her with opulence. She was with him for him alone, and it was good for us all to see that our friend was finally in a relationship that was more supportive than gossiped about; that allowed him to be accepted for who he was and a partner who mirrored his generosity.

Fresh from his success in the jungle, it was good to see him happy at last.

❖

Tom: As a reward for one of the tasks in *I'm A Celebrity*, we were allowed to send in a pack containing, among other things, a photograph. All the other friends and family members put a lot of thought into what photo they should send into the jungle. The contestants' wives? Husbands? Kids? Well, Dougie didn't have any of those, but I had a much better idea anyway. Several thousand miles away, his bandmate was burning up the floor in a reality show of his own. Obviously Doug would be missing him desperately, so I thought it would be an excellent idea to send him a picture of Harry dressed in his *Strictly Come Dancing* outfit. What more could a lad want when he's pining for a few home comforts?

Dougie: I was *so* pissed off . . .

Harry: Cheers, poo breath!

Strictly Come Dancing had always seemed to me like the reality TV show that made the most sense, because at least you got to learn a new skill. Not that I'm dissing what Dougie did. Well, maybe I am. A bit. ☺ But I was reluctant to do it. I was used to being the drummer at the back, not the show-off at the front. That was Danny's job. My life was great the way it was, and I was quite happy for it to keep plodding along. Imagine if I did well on the show – everyone would be talking about it the whole time, and I'd lose the little bit of anonymity I still had. Imagine if I did badly – it would be embarrassing. If I'm honest, I was scared, too: scared of taking on this big challenge and finding out that I wasn't up to the task.

As soon as I'd made the decision, however, I told myself this: you're not going to complain, you're going to work your arse off, and you're going to throw *everything* at it. I know how obsessive and competitive I am, so I knew it would take over my life. I was right about that.

I'd made my decision in the middle of July 2011. I spent a solid two months training in the gym, getting myself into the best shape I could for the challenge ahead. I spoke to Kara Tointon, who had won it the year before, and got a few tips. She told me to make sure my cardiovascular fitness was very good, because the training I was going to undergo would be physically gruelling. I wasn't allowed to take any dancing lessons in advance – we were warned that we'd be disqualified if we did – so I set myself a regime of swimming, running and pushing weights six or seven times a week. My obsession had started.

I didn't know at first who else would be on the show. I hoped we'd have some decent contestants so it wouldn't look too tacky – I guess Dougie's words about reality shows not being cool were still ringing in my ears. I needn't have worried. They called it *Strictly*'s golden year. The first time I met my fellow contestants was when we all shot an advert together for the show. It was then that my love affair with Robbie Savage started. Being a football fan, I knew who he was, and at first I didn't think much about meeting him. Within five minutes he was ribbing me something rotten, pulling up

my Children in Need dance on YouTube and announc-
ing to anyone who'd listen that I was a dirty cheat.
I'd never experienced ruthless football dressing-room
banter like his. Hilarious. He and I ended up being the
naughty ones at the back of the class. I met Chelsee
Healey as I was sitting in the make-up chair and didn't
have a clue who she was. She turned out to be absolutely lovely, and we got on well from the first day. I'd
worked with Lulu before, when we'd played 'Shout'
with her, but I'd also make some new friends during my
time on the show. Russell Grant – one of the campest
men I've ever met, but a really sweet, lovely guy. Nancy
Dell'Olio – who I realized was the polar opposite to me
when she admitted that she'd never dream of not wearing high heels even when she was by herself at home,
but who I struck up a real rapport with anyway. I'd
stick up for Nancy in front of anyone – she's a really
wonderful person. Anita Dobson – Brian May's wife –
was adorable. Bottom line was that pretty much everyone on the show was cool. Jason Donovan? Total
legend. Funny, sweet and one of the people from the
show who I'd like to stay in touch with in the future.
But Robbie and Chelsee were the two that I found
myself spending most of my time with.

In the past, I'd always been the loud, confident one.
Not on *Strictly*. I went into the whole thing with the
attitude that I should keep my head down and not open
my mouth too much. Perhaps it was because I was one
of the youngest people there; perhaps I was out of my
comfort zone doing something on my own without the
band; perhaps I've just changed a bit over the years. I

certainly wanted to make as good an impression as possible, without the bravado and banter that some people in the public eye often bring to the table. On our first full day, I simply sat back and observed. We were divided into 'pros' and 'celebs', and you could see the pros checking out the celebs the moment we were all in a room together. It was a relief to watch the celebs dancing and realize that none of them would make the Bolshoi. At least I had the advantage of being able to count in time.

Even though I was lying low, the celebs and the pros could instantly tell how competitive I was. They were telling me I'd win even before I'd danced a single step. I tried to pretend that I didn't care, but from day one I was thinking to myself: How *can* I win this thing? It soon became clear that there was only one way to do it: to treat it like a sport and work bloody hard to be the very best I could be. And that was why Aliona Vilani was the perfect partner for me. Not that you'd think that to look at my face when it was announced during the first episode that we were a pair. I was so convinced I was going to get Flavia Cacace, who eventually went with Russell, that my face dropped slightly with disappointment. But as we walked off stage together, Aliona seemed pretty chilled.

Izzy got on well with Aliona, and was totally cool about me having to spend so much time with her. A lot of her friends wondered how she could cope with it, but there didn't seem to be a single moment when she appeared jealous or was anything other than totally supportive. Without Izzy, I'm not sure I'd have made it through to the end.

Everyone else had three weeks' rehearsal before the first live show. Aliona and I were only allowed two, because I'd already practised for the Children in Need edition. It didn't seem quite fair to me – I'd spent four days on the paso doble, and I wouldn't be allowed to dance that again anyway. I tried to persuade Aliona to meet up with me during that first week so that we could start our rehearsals without anybody knowing, but then I got another warning: if we were caught practising before time, we'd be disqualified. I didn't realize how seriously they took it.

So I had to wait a week before we made our way to our first rehearsal in a leisure centre in glamorous Luton. The cha-cha. Within ten minutes of practising I realized this would be harder than I had ever imagined. I felt stupid, like I had two left feet in front of the cameras in the room. Thankfully, though, Aliona and I instantly got on, even though she would spend half our rehearsal time in hysterics at my feeble attempts.

I was numb with anxiety before my first live dance, despite (or maybe because of) the guys being in the audience to cheer me on. I was treading a fine line between bottling it and going for it. I did the latter. The judges made some nice comments; as soon as we went off air my phone didn't stop ringing with friends calling me up to tell me how great it was.

But then I watched it back on TV.

What an anticlimax. I thought it was awful. An embarrassment. And I knew I could do better.

Most of the contestants took Sundays off. Not us. We were rehearsing again the very next day. I soon realized that Aliona wasn't the type of teacher to let me get away with anything, which was exactly what I wanted. Each week, the training got more and more gruelling as her expectations became higher and higher. I was trying to learn techniques that most people spend years mastering, and whenever I told her I simply couldn't do a certain move, it fell on deaf ears. And no matter how exhausted I felt every Sunday, dragging myself into the rehearsal studio after our live performance the night before, she wouldn't hesitate to put me through my paces – literally.

Some weeks I picked the dances up quicker than others, and really enjoyed our rehearsal time. Other weeks were more of a challenge. When we danced the foxtrot in the second week, I felt fairly confident before hand. But it was a slow dance, and once I'd started, the nerves kicked in. In drumming, when you're nervous you tend to speed up. Same with dance. I could feel myself trembling, and I knew Aliona could feel it too. I hated every second, and the moment we ran off stage after speaking to Tess Daly, I couldn't apologize enough to my dance partner. Aliona laughed it off, and even though I felt I'd messed up, I was hopeful that I'd get through the first couple of weeks solely on the back of the McFly fan base voting for me, if they took an interest.

Week three was the jive, dancing to 'Greased Lightnin''. I loved that – I'd auditioned for the school production of *Grease* when I was a kid, but had only made it into the chorus, while my best friend Ben had landed the part of Danny Zuko. Seemed only right that I should invite him into the audience that night. 'Come down, mate – let me show you how it's *really* done . . .' It's a show-off number, so I figured I'd dance it better if I had someone to show off to. I just had to imagine the boys on their writing trip, shouting encouragement at the TV hundreds of miles away.

If the jive was a high point for me, the following week's waltz was a low. Everything about it was foreign – proper ballroom dancing of the type I'd never even contemplated before – and the moves Aliona taught me were incredibly hard. Halfway through our week of practice I was on the point of breaking down, terrified that I was going to make a fool of myself in front of millions of people. You've probably noticed by now that the McFly boys aren't averse to crying. It was a miracle I didn't bawl my eyes out that week with frustration and anxiety. It wasn't until the camera rehearsals on the Friday that I managed to get through it to the end, and there's no doubt that when I was performing it on the Saturday I was the most scared I've ever been. The song – 'Come Away With Me' by Norah Jones – is very slow, which means that any mistake you make shows up even more. Watching the performance back, I can see my legs wobbling with fear. People say I didn't look nervous; believe me, I was bricking myself.

But I got through it, and the judges were kind. It gave me a boost – I felt that if I could do the waltz, I could do anything. What's more, I found myself loving the ballroom dances, which I can safely say I never thought would happen. It's an amazing feeling when you know you've got your head (and your feet) round something so difficult. That's not to say I wasn't petrified every week, but my confidence had increased a little now that I'd put myself well out of my comfort zone and come through it OK. I was characteristically critical of each performance when I watched it back, but that was a good thing: it spurred me on to do better next time.

In the ninth week, the judges gave us a nine and three tens for the quickstep, and we won the swing-a-thon. But it was neither of these things that made week nine perhaps the most memorable for me. My parents were in the audience that night. The following morning I was lying in bed when my dad called. He was full of con-gratulations and telling me how much he'd enjoyed the evening when suddenly he started to cry. I hadn't seen or heard him cry since I was eight years old, the day I left for boarding school at OBH, and I thought he was joking with me. He was so proud that he completely broke down, before handing the phone over to my mum. That was a very special moment for me.

As the series progressed, I grew to realize that every-thing I'd been worried about, I shouldn't have worried about at all. The extra attention I was receiving was universally positive. People were full of enjoyment and genuine praise for the show, and I was feeling so much more confident in myself. Even my granny, who never really had a clue what McFly was all about ('Do you have any new "records" out, Harry?'), was aware of *Strictly*. ('Harry, darling, you're the talk of the town!') And while I was used to getting attention from McFly fans, now I had seventy-year-old women whispering to each other if they saw me. It had gone to a whole other level, and although I'd been scared of this, I found myself enjoying it because everyone was so enthusiastic and kind.

The obligatory McFly tears came during the final. I sat watching the VT they'd put together: an interview with Izzy, and then with my mum and dad. I held it together, confident I'd be able to avoid turning on the waterworks. But then, up on the screen, came my friend James. I was so tired, so emotional and I knew how nervous James would be doing that interview. It was all too much.

Was I nervous for the final? Nervous for a final to be held in the stunning Blackpool Ballroom, the home of ballroom dancing, in front of a TV audience of millions and millions? Nervous isn't the word. My mouth was dry and I could barely bring myself to speak to anyone. The dress rehearsal went badly – we messed up a lift at the end of the American smooth, and I kept forgetting the quickstep. An hour or two before the show I was more highly strung than I'd ever been in my life. I couldn't get my head straight. Couldn't focus. I was supposed to be all organized beforehand, to have had a haircut and a shave, but I somehow couldn't even get myself in gear to do that. Suddenly the half an hour call came and I hadn't even started to get ready. Total panic, like some horrible dream where I knew I was about to go on stage but didn't know my lines. There was no time to do anything – I almost didn't get any fake tan on, people, which in the world of *Strictly Come Dancing* is a bit like not having any clothes to wear. I was nearly pulling my hair out backstage when suddenly I heard a voice. It was Izzy. I practically broke down in front of her. I couldn't go through with this. I couldn't do it. Like she always does, she gave me some calm words of reassurance, but I was still a mess . . .

Show time. The contestants came on to the stage in chariots. Ultimate cheese, and I could see my bandmates in the audience absolutely wetting themselves. I can't even begin to describe how terrified I was before going on to do the first dance of the evening. Twenty seconds into the quickstep, however, something changed in my head. It was like a wave of relaxation had passed over me. I suddenly realized – for the very first time – that I *knew* what I was doing, that I could dance *and* enjoy the performance at the same time. A smile crept on to my face, and for the first time in the whole series it was absolutely genuine. Watching it back, I was finally proud of myself. I'd done all right.

With my nerves out of the way, the rest of the final was an incredible experience. I didn't only want to get down to the last two contestants that night because I wanted to win. The truth was that I was looking forward to the dancing. I knew I could do it, and I wanted to perform for the audience.

Bruce Forsyth's announcement that I was the winner was all a blur. Tom, Danny, Dougie and my brother had stormed the stage and were jumping all over me. Bruce wasn't quite sure who they were – he started whacking them with his cards and yelling at them to get off the stage . . .

And then my dad was there, gliding on to the stage on live TV, hugging me . . .

And then Izzy . . .

And people were cheering, and the music was thundering . . .

And then it was over.

I was backstage with Dougie, and we sloped off to get away from all the commotion and have a quiet chat, just as we had done six months before outside Tom's house. 'Imagine if we both won,' Dougie had said back then. 'How cool would that be?'

And now, outside the Blackpool Ballroom, both of us winners, we grinned at each other. 'We did it, mate,' I said. 'We *did* it!'

We grinned at each other some more and went back inside to find Tom and Danny. There are moments when being in a band is more than just being a bunch of mates. Moments you absolutely have to share. This was one of those times.

Tom: So. We're reaching the end of the book. But it doesn't feel like we're reaching the end of the story. Quite the opposite.

With *I'm A Celebrity* and *Strictly* out of the way, it was time to look to the future. And the future seemed bright. Dougie and Harry's reality shows felt like they'd refreshed things for the band. After the ups and downs of the previous couple of years, we were back on the map.

And our lives are full. More than full. In 2011, I took Giovanna back to the assembly room at Sylvia's where we had first met. She didn't know I'd filled it with flowers and candles. She didn't know I was about to propose. We tied the knot in May 2012. And no prizes for guessing who my three best men were. Because you've got to ask your best mates, haven't you?

Getting married was an incredibly important day in my life, but it felt like it was a significant day for all of us. We've grown up together – not just us four guys, but Giovanna too, who has been there from the beginning and has become a close friend of the whole band. (When Dougie was staying with us, it dawned on me that Gi might actually get on better with him than she does with me!) Giovanna has been a part of every event that has happened throughout our career, and has had a hell of a lot to put up with. It felt good that for one day at least, it was undeniably, without question, *all* about her.

Harry: The night before Tom's wedding, the four of us stayed at his place. As a surprise, we'd asked Richard Rashman to dig out the old footage of Tom's original audition with Busted, and of the Busted/McFly tour all those years ago. It was a special moment. A time to reminisce before the biggest day of Tom's life, and for those few hours, as we sat around eating pizza and watching old footage, it was almost like we were back in the band house again. Almost, but not quite: watching those films was a reminder of how different we were back then, and how much we've grown up. Sometimes, when people grow up, they grow apart. But not us.

Danny: Let's not forget that we had a good laugh at Tom's Busted audition, while Tom watched it from behind a pillow. Fair to say that he came across as a confident little fella? A little cocky? Changing his expression every time he knows the camera's on him, like David Brent with bleached hair? I think so . . . ☺

Tom: The wedding itself was perfect. I know there will never be a day that even comes close for the rest of my life. Giovanna was more beautiful than she'd ever been, and you probably know us well enough now to guess that there were tears a-plenty – especially from me. The guys played their roles perfectly. Danny helped me with my speech, Dougie was my ring-bearer and Harry organized a stag do to remember and a best-men's speech – delivered by all three of them – that was everything it should have been. Dougie had all the slightly shocking lines, because somehow he can get away with saying things that the rest of us can't.

Dougie: Shocking? It seemed only polite to thank Debbie for squeezing Tom out all those years ago. With a chin that big, it can't have been easy. Off-colour jokes aside, everything about that day was amazing. Two of your best friends, so obviously in love, saying what they want to say, the way they want to say it, in front of the people they want around them.

Danny: And then, of course, there was Tom's speech.

Words can't do it justice. As he delivered it, you could see all the guys in the room thinking: That's it – no point getting married now because I'll never be able to top this. Tom had put together a medley of McFly songs, and I'd helped him make some backing tracks, but as a surprise for everyone there, he had changed the words to thank the people he wanted to thank.

Tom: The hardest part for me to sing was the section when I thanked the guys in the band. I'd practised it twice at home, and never managed to get through it without crying . . .

Harry: And then, just when you thought it couldn't get cleverer, funnier or more moving, the side doors of the venue opened and, with perfect choreography, a choir of kids from Sylvia Young's filed in to join him in a new version of 'All About You', the song that so many people have taken to their own heart, but which was always about Giovanna. They sang amazing harmonies and perfect new words suited to the occasion.

Dougie: It was honestly just about the greatest thing any of us had ever seen. By the end, all a hundred and fifty guests were in tears. There was a moment of shocked, stunned silence at the brilliance of it. And then, a standing ovation, the most genuine you've ever seen in your life.

Tom: And when the speeches were over, it was time for some music. Our first dance was 'Easy' by the

Commodores – the song Gi and I had danced to on the kitchen tiles of my parents' house all those years ago. And no prizes for guessing who the wedding band were. We learned some cover songs – The Beatles, Stevie Wonder – that everyone could dance to. A fitting end to one of the best days of our lives.

Harry: And there must have been something in the air.

I'd known for a while that I wanted to propose to Izzy, but it didn't seem quite right doing it before Tom's wedding. Instead, I decided to whisk her away on a surprise holiday to St Lucia afterwards. By chance, this was where Tom and Gi were heading off on honeymoon. We were booked on the same flight. Big relief: I had pictures in my head of my suitcase being opened at customs and the ring being discovered in front of Izzy. If that had happened, I'd have had to propose there and then, but now I was able to get Tom to carry the merchandise over the border for me. Once we went through customs in St Lucia, we slipped off to the gents together, where he handed back the ring. Then we went our separate ways.

Izzy and I were staying at a beautiful resort, where I arranged a candlelit dinner on the beach for the first night. I think she must have twigged at that point that something was up, so the moment we were alone I got down on one knee and asked her to marry me. And when she said yes, it felt like everything had slotted into place. I reminded her of the time when I was nineteen and she was twenty-one. She'd been in two minds about whether to go out with me, and I'd told her on the phone that one day I would marry her. I'd never forgotten that promise. Is it cheesy to say she's made me the happiest man in the world? Maybe. But it's true.

I'd put together a proposal playlist for that night. A couple of songs in, we were treated to Danny singing us 'Walk In The Sun'. It seemed appropriate, somehow . . .

So life now is everything it should be, and not just for me and Tom. To see Danny with his long-term girlfriend Georgia is to look at somebody who has been searching for something for years, and has finally found it. And to see Dougie and Lara, sitting quietly at the back of the tour bus while the craziness of McFly erupts all around them, is to see two people who don't much care for fame and adulation, but just for each other.

Dougie: That brings a tear to my eye, and a boner to my pants. (Another line from the best man's speech, coincidentally.)

Tom: Somebody once said that you should be regular and orderly in your life, then you can be violent and original in your work. Life in McFly is never going to be all that regular or orderly, but there's no doubt that as life has settled down for us, as demons have been exorcized and our personal lives have become more complete, our ambitions for our music have become greater than before. You have to start off every album believing it's going to be the best that you've ever done. Otherwise there's no point. But there's something different about what we're doing now. Because imagine this. You have an idea for a painting, so you describe it to an artist. He or she does the very best they can to render your painting, but it'll never be exactly how you imagined it. The only way to make that painting just how you want it is to do it yourself. It's the same with music.

Somebody also once said that Danny knows a lot about a little, while I know a little about a lot. I think that's true. I'm pretty average at lots of things without really excelling at any of them, whereas Danny is amazing in very specific areas, like his guitar playing, his singing and his music production. I know as much about producing an album as I do about flying the Millennium Falcon, but I do know this: with Danny producing our new material, and with us as a band following our own muse without being influenced by anybody else, the music we make in the future is going to be the best we've *ever* made.

Danny: Producing the next McFly album is a massive responsibility. But my heart beats faster with excitement every time I think about it. It feels like we're embarking on the next stage of our musical career. A stage where it's all about the music. None of us are in any doubt that our best stuff is still to come. On our *Keep Calm And Play Louder* tour, we debuted some of the new material – something we'd hardly ever done before. The response was amazing, and it was a reminder that at the end of the day the only people whose opinions matter are us, and our fans. There's no bigger thrill than hearing lyrics chanted back at you for a song that hasn't been released yet, but pieced together from YouTube videos as a tour progresses. No bigger thrill than feeling that connection with an audience.

Dougie: It's a reminder that while we might not have the most fans in the world, there's no doubt that we have the best. And we know that as long as we're true to our fans, and true to ourselves, the McFly story is in no danger of coming to the end.

In fact, ten years in, it feels like it's only just beginning.

Dougie: In the months since this book was first published, a lot of things have happened.

Tom: Thanks to my wedding speech going viral, I'm no longer Tom from McFly but Tom from YouTube.

Harry: I got married, and managed to deliver a speech that was, if anything, just a shade better than Tom's.☺

Danny: And I managed to win a 200-metre race. Admittedly against a dude who'd had a heart transplant, but hey, a win's a win!

Dougie: I'm not saying Danny's competitive or anything, but you're unlikely to spend more than ten minutes in his company before he tells you in minute detail about the time he was playing a charity soccer match for Soccer Aid and he . . .

Danny: . . . crossed the ball to Alan Shearer who nudged it in for the winning goal. No biggie.

My success on the running track was almost as cool as my moment of glory on the footy pitch. We were taking part in an event to highlight the importance of donor transplants. Our fellow racer was, in fact, the world's fastest heart-transplant survivor over a 200-metre distance. I was absolutely convinced this guy would nail us, so I made it my aim just to beat Harry (I was pretty sure I'd be able to take Tom and Dougie – no offence, dudes.) I'd done a bit of running when I was at school, so I knew I could leg it when I had to, but I'd forgotten all my running technique. So I just booted it round the pitch and was astonished to look back over my shoulder and see that none of the others was even close to me. Maybe it was a bit insensitive of me to celebrate quite so hard when I'd finished – the dude was on his second heart, after all – but I *was* pretty pleased with my time. The slowest woman in the 2012 Olympics was 23 seconds. I managed 24. Get in!

Dougie: But far more important than any of this: I grew a beard. And not a demure little covering of face fungus either. A big, full-on cross between Jesus and Tom Hanks in *Castaway*. It did, admittedly, get to the point where I could detect slightly unpleasant smells on my 'tache, but that was nothing a few squirts of shampoo couldn't sort out. Trouble was, I used a volumising brand, which meant I ended up having a head that almost doubled in size. Takes a bit of getting used to, but I'd recommend it to anyone, if only so you can experience the awesome sensation of shaving it off. It's like hacking away bits of your face, with the added bonus that you can give yourself the world's creepiest goatee – the kind of thing that you can only bear to wear for a few minutes, before shaving it off in case anybody else sees you . . .

Danny: Running round the track. Growing beards. As you can tell, it's high-pressure work being in a band. While I was busy lapping up glory for my sporting prowess, and Dougie was concentrating hard on the important business of experimenting with his facial hair, Tom was otherwise occupied with becoming a global heartthrob, crushing the hopes of single women in the four corners of the earth. And Harry, of course, was getting married. For some reason, it attracted a little bit of interest. Even we were quite surprised by the number of fans who had congregated outside the church on his and Izzy's wedding day.

Dougie: (Rumours that he blew half the wedding budget hiring in extras from Rent-a-crowd remain unconfirmed.)

Harry: In fact, the fans were there – quite rightly – to see Izzy, who had grown up in the neighbourhood and whose family were well known. At most weddings, it's the organist who announces the arrival of the bride. At ours, it was the screams from outside.

Tom: What a day. And what a reception. I'd been

massively nervous about my own wedding speech, but I knew Harry would be fine delivering his. He's that kind of guy: confident when it comes to standing up and delivering jokes. The direct opposite of me.

Harry: It helped knowing I was standing up in front of my home crowd. Didn't stop me being nervous, though. I sat down about a month before the wedding and started writing my speech without really thinking too hard, until I had three A4 pages. When I read it back to myself, it seemed pretty funny to me. But as the big day arrived, I started getting the collywobbles. Three A4 pages seemed pretty long to me – and was it *really* that funny? Was I just going to make a bit of a fool of myself? I was starting to get an idea of why Tom had been so nervous. Cut to the day itself, and I found myself sitting and listening to Izzy's dad giving his speech. It was brilliant. People were laughing. How was I going to follow that? Maybe I should be singing a song like Tom did. (On second thoughts, maybe not.)

I was anxious right up until the moment I delivered my first attempted gag. Everyone laughed. Relief. I wasn't going to be a YouTube sensation, but it went down well. Just one small part of a very special day for the two of us. Izzy and I had arranged a choreographed first dance, *Strictly*-style. We danced to 'Can't Help Falling in Love' by Michael Bublé, which was the song I'd danced the American Smooth to in the *Strictly* final. Izzy had always loved that dance, so we worked hard on it together – lifts and everything, which got as wild a response from the guests as anything I'd ever done on TV.

Tom: All in all, an awesome day, lots of fun, and topped off, of course, by a McFly set.

At my wedding, it was just us – we were the only band, so there was nothing to compare us to when we were a bit the worse for wear and not that tight. Harry, though, had hired the most insanely incredible covers band. Amazing singers, fantastic drummer and guitarists, and they played all the great tunes. So when us four dribblers crawled on to the stage to completely ruin a bunch of our songs, we were properly shown up. Frankly, it was a relief when the silent disco came around, so we weren't the only people making fools of ourselves . . .

Harry: But all in all, it was a beautiful day for me to get married to a beautiful girl.

Dougie: That brings a tear to my eye, and a . . .

Harry: And with two of the McFly boys safely married, we thought that maybe wedding talk was off the agenda for a while. We were wrong about that.

Tom: I'd never intended to make the video of my own wedding speech available to anyone except my family and close friends. Trouble is that if I ever put anything on my personal Facebook, sooner or later it leaks out. I make a rule of never posting anything there that I wouldn't want to unleash on the world at large. So I figured I might as well stick it up on YouTube and be done with it.

To be honest, I didn't think people would be that interested. I mean, there must be thousands of wedding speeches on YouTube, right? Normally, when I put a YouTube video up, I'll get maybe 100,000 views. But this was just something personal, so I didn't expect to get more than half that. I couldn't really have been more wrong. The first night I posted it, I saw that it had 100,000 views. Not bad. But that was my lot, surely.

Surely not.

The following morning the number of views had gone up to 400,000. And by the end of that day, a million people had watched me singing and blubbing my way through my wedding speech.

For the next week, the views increased by a million a day and for a little while life became impossibly crazy. It was featured on the TV news. I even had to do an interview with CNN in America because it was going viral stateside. I'd been so nervous about giving that speech, and not at all certain that it would work, but it felt great to have it so well received by so many people around the world.

Danny: It was a bit of a game-changer for us as a band, too. A couple of months previously, we'd released a new single – 'Love is Easy'. We were very proud of it, and it went down a storm with the fans. But it struggled to get much radio airplay. Now that we had a world-famous romeo in the band, however, everyone was playing it. Fickle, but that's the music business for you.

Tom: And, of course, there was controversy along the way. Harry had got married before Christmas, and photos of the day were going to be published in a magazine. I had no idea when they were going to appear, so it turned out I'd inadvertently posted my wedding speech on the same day. The press jumped on it, of course, saying that I was trying to steal Harry and Izzy's thunder and detecting a rift in the band that simply wasn't there. They couldn't have been more wrong – I was just being a bit of a space cadet.

Harry: To make matters worse, the four of us were due to make a TV appearance, but I had to pull out at the last minute because I had norovirus. That was just fuel to the fire. Everyone thought I was throwing my toys out of my pram. Truth was, I was puking my guts out. All in all, I felt a bit sorry for Tom – his speech was so good, and here he was getting rinsed for putting it out there. Still, 9 million views and counting can't be argued with. We were all just really happy for Tom and Giovanna. And happy, of course, that a few more people got to know who McFly were, and listen to our music. Because as always, we had plans to move on to bigger and better things.

Dougie: In September 2012, we played our first shows in America (not counting the promos we did back in the *Just My Luck* era). Four gigs in all – two in New York at the Gramercy Theater in Manhattan, and two in LA at the Roxy. It was gratifying that the shows sold out instantly, and it felt good that we could finally perform for our fans in the States who'd had to wait so long to see us play live. The feedback was great, and we hope those shows will be stepping stones to more McFly appearances in America.

Tom: And, in fact, a good deal of our time of late has been spent on the other side of the Atlantic. You know what they say about policemen – how you can tell you're getting old when they start getting younger? Same goes for pop stars. There's something a little weird about hooking up with one of the biggest bands in the world, and finding out that the first gig they ever went to was a McFly show.

We could tell One Direction were going to be big the first time we met them. We'd gone down to see them perform on the *X Factor*, and they reminded us a bit of ourselves when we started out. In fact, in a weird way, they almost looked older and more experienced than us, but maybe that's just because we're such an immature-looking band.

Dougie: Tom has a baby face, whereas they have stubble and loads of tattoos.

Tom: They were certainly full of enthusiasm. But more than that, it was immediately obvious that they had something special. You could tell they were going to be massive. The rest, of course, is history – but a history in which we would have a small part to play.

I'd been asked to write a song for Miley Cyrus. A good song – I was pleased it with it – but she ended up not using it. It sometimes happens that a song gets knocked around all over the place. At one point Demi Lovato was going to use it, but didn't. Then the Jonas Brothers were going to use it . . . but didn't. We were even thinking of using it ourselves. This song had been doing the rounds in the music industry, so it wasn't a great surprise that it came under One Direction's radar. The song was called 'I Want', and it made it onto the boys' first record, *Up All Night*.

When the time came for One Direction to record their second album, they asked if we wanted to write something else for them, so of course we said yes. The result was 'I Would'. We collaborated on another song too, called 'Irresistible', which came out of a writing session we had with the guys, and which has been a massive hit on YouTube – 23 million views and counting. Hanging out with Harry, Niall, Zayn, Liam and Louis has been a blast, and has also given us an insight into a level of fame and success that we've never experienced. Trying to get time with them is almost impossible – we've found ourselves being flown out to Ireland in order to catch an hour and a half in a hotel room to record one of their vocals.

Danny: We've found ourselves having to record a vocal harmony without the two guys in the same room together, since their schedules won't allow it. More like fitting a jigsaw puzzle together than recording a song.

Tom: But although it's not the ideal way of creating a track, it's part and parcel of working with one of the world's biggest bands – and a thrill for us to be partially involved with them.

As always, though, our biggest focus is McFly. The new album has been a while in the making, but that's not for want of material, enthusiasm or hard work. It's because we want it to be right – for us, and for the fans. We went away on some early writing trips knowing only that we didn't know what we wanted to do. What sound we were aiming for. As we write this, we've become more focussed, narrowed down our references and established a sound in our head that has made us excited about making music all over again.

So many bands fall into the trap of trying to sound like someone else, just in order to get radio play. We did it ourselves. Trust us: it's bad news. It means you've lost sight of what made you a good band in the first place, which is almost always that you don't sound like *anyone* else. Our new songs are, for my money, classic McFly – fun, summery, happy-making pop – but with a contemporary edge that makes us feel we've gone back to doing what we do best, but still managed to move forward at the same time. The eureka moment for us was when we recorded 'Love is Easy'. It was almost as if we'd breathed a sigh of relief. We suddenly realised that this was what we should be doing, and the reaction we had from our fans only confirmed that.

There have been a lot of songs on the way that have acted as stepping stones to where we are now – songs that we love, but which have been left behind because they don't fit with the sound we're aiming for. But that's the creative process. Sometimes you just have to kill your darlings. And happily, the songs are still flooding out of us at a tremendous rate. Now that everything is good in our lives, the effect on our music has been nothing but beneficial.

When the new music comes, we know it's going to be awesome. Awesome for us, of course, but awesome for the fans too. Which is the way it should be, because without the fans, McFly would be nothing at all.

Doing a Runner

EPILOGUE

A tour bus pulls up outside the stage door of the venue.

Which venue? It's easy to forget where you are when you're on tour. The guys could always ask Tommy – Tommy knows everything – but it doesn't really matter. All that matters is that it's a show day. When you're in a band, it's all about the show. Those ninety minutes on stage are what you live for.

A crowd of fans has congregated around the stage door. The guys can see them through the tinted windows of the upper deck. They can certainly hear them, and the screams only get louder as their security guy escorts them, one by one, into the venue. Each of the fans clearly has their favourite. *Tom! Danny! Dougie! Harry!* The guys wave as they hear their names, before disappearing into the bowels of the venue.

Once inside, Tom looks around vaguely. 'I remember this place,' he says. Hardly surprising. There aren't many venues around the country whose stage they haven't graced. They follow the signs pinned to the wall directing them to their dressing room. They never quite know what to expect. Sometimes it's a poky little cupboard that can barely hold them all. Sometimes it's a giant warren of rooms big enough for the band and their entourage: the backing vocalists and keyboard player who have travelled separately; the sound guys and guitar and drum techs who've been there for hours, setting up the stage and making sure everything's ready; the physio; the management; and of course Tommy, who quite literally keeps the show on the road.

They step into an enormous dressing room. Three sofas. Two fridges. But not luxurious. There are no flowers and drapes or any Mariah Carey-esque back-stage finery. Just the bare essentials for a hard-working band. A small rider of soft drinks, fruit and health bars – their days of pre-gig beers and secret stashes are at an end – and a dressing table filled with every hair product under the sun. Their stage gear is hanging on a costume rack, with clean boxer shorts in a container next to it. 'Important to have clean boxers after a gig,' Danny tells nobody in particular, with a grin.

In an adjoining room there's a Gretsch drum kit, a key-board, two guitars and a bass. If they need to warm up before the show, the instruments are waiting for them. But now it's time to soundcheck. They follow the signs to the stage, and enter from the wings, past the jumble of flight cases – big, sturdy black boxes, maybe twenty or thirty of them. It takes a lot of equipment for the band to get the sound they want, and their crew have the business of rigging it down pat. In the past, the guys have flown in by helicopter and taken straight to the stage without sound-checking – that's how good the crew are. But tonight there's no need to wing it.

The keyboard player and BVs are already on stage. Harry gets up on the drum riser, to the accompaniment of jazz chords from the keyboard. Tom, Danny and Dougie strap their guitars around their necks. Dougie starts to play. The bass line to 'I Wish' by Stevie Wonder echoes round the hall, before morphing into the theme from *Star Wars*. Harry joins in – four to the floor and a backbeat that cracks through the venue like a firework. A guitar riff cuts through it all: Tom has started the screaming intro to 'Red'. The guys join in, and now Danny's voice is soaring above it all. It's loud. Very loud. But tight. If anyone's in any doubt that this is a band who know what they're doing, that uncertainty is soon dispelled.

The song comes to an end. There's a bit of noodling on stage. Snippets of familiar tunes emanate from the PA: 'I Heard It Through The Grapevine', 'Beat It', 'Day Tripper', 'I Want To Hold Your Hand'. Danny asks for one of the lights to be altered – it's shining onto the neck of his guitar and he can't see the frets. Tom jumps down into the auditorium to listen to the sound from the audience's point of view. And when the guys and the sound crew are happy with the levels, they put down their instruments and return backstage.

They follow the backstage signs to the catering area, where the band and their road crew eat the food that's been prepared for them. Tommy walks in. Unflappable, as always. 'We're doing a runner tonight, fellas,' he announces. The guys nod. Doing a runner – getting onto the tour bus immediately they've finished playing, leaving the venue before the fans can hinder the vehicle's exit. It means they can be in the hotel ten minutes after they leave the stage, showering off the sweat.

When they've finished eating, Harry wants to chill on the tour bus. It's difficult to sneak outside because there's already a queue of fans snaking around the venue, their eyes on every possible exit. He puts on a hoodie and manages to slink out without being recognized. It's not that he wants to avoid the fans. It's just that it's difficult when there's hundreds of them waiting, like there are tonight, queuing round the venue for several hours before the doors open.

Ninety minutes till show time. Dougie walks into the dressing room, humming a Jennifer Lopez tune. Tom's chatting to Izzy – an accomplished violinist – discussing songs to play at his wedding. It can't be anything that'll make Tom cry. He cries too easily anyway. At the drop of a hat, some would say.

Sixty minutes till show time. From one side of the dressing room you can hear Harry next door, giving himself a workout on the drums. Complex, funky rhythms, solid and in the pocket. From the other side, the muffled sound of the support band, already ripping it up on stage. Tom lies on the physio's bed, needles sticking into his knee. They've flown their physio, Ryan, over from Australia specifically for this tour – their own little treat to themselves. But to listen to Tom's howls as the needles puncture his skin, you wouldn't *think* it was a treat.

Thirty minutes till show time. The guys change into their stage gear and the air is suddenly thick with the smell of hair wax. Tommy enters, hands round the band's in-ears and helps the guys get them fitted. Tom sticks his iPod onto the portable speaker. 'Helter

Skelter' by The Beatles blasts out at full volume, and he starts jumping up and down to it, air drumming, air guitaring, getting into the mood. On stage he's manic when he plays. Back here, he's not far off. Danny sips from a mug of honey, lemon and ginger. Ninety minutes on stage can take its toll on your throat, but there's no way he's going to hold back when he's in front of the microphone. Dougie sits quietly in the corner, fiddling with his phone before giving his hair a final check in the mirror. If he's going to get nervous before a show it'll happen in the last few minutes before they go on stage. So maybe his quietness means something. Richard Rashman and Fletch are sitting nearby. 'You look very sexy, Dougie,' Rashman jokes, and Dougie flashes a smile.

Two minutes to show time, and the audience can sense it. Their screams become more frequent. Louder. The security guy flashes his torch in the wings. He's looking for any fans who might have managed to sneak backstage. They can be persistent. But there's no one.

Behind the protection of the curtain, back-up and keys take their place on the stage. Dougie and Danny arrive in the wings, Dougie swigging from a tin of Red Bull, Danny clutching his water and punching knuckles with everyone he passes – a pre-gig ritual.

The lights drop. The screams are enough to make your eardrums tremble. If the band weren't wearing in-ears, they'd have no hope of hearing what they're playing tonight. Or any night.

The air is thick with dry ice. The whole building feels like it's vibrating.

Suddenly the curtains rise. The band take the stage.

The crowd goes berserk. The band give it everything they've got. And for ninety minutes, neither of them stop the noise.

Keep Calm And Play Louder? One out of two ain't bad.

❖

The final notes of 'Shine A Light' die away. Tom, Danny, Dougie and Harry leave the stage. They're soaked with sweat. They're also hyper. Grins on their faces. Eyes bright. No time to loiter. Like Tommy said, they're doing a runner. Security leads them through the empty corridors backstage while the audience is still shouting for their band. There's no hanging around. If the tour bus doesn't leave quickly, it won't leave at all. It's hard for a vehicle to move when it's surrounded. The guys hurry through the stage door and into the waiting bus. They grab sandwiches from the fridge, then hurry upstairs to where Giovanna, Izzy, Georgia and Lara are waiting.

When it slips quietly away, the audience are still inside the venue. Some of them will be hoping for a glimpse of the guys. Tonight they'll be disappointed. McFly have left the building.

Picture Acknowledgements

All images have been supplied courtesy of the authors unless otherwise stated. Every effort has been made to contact the copyright holders. We apologize for any omissions in this respect and will be pleased to make the appropriate acknowledgments in any future edition.

Section One
Page 2 (inset) © Dean Sherwood

Section Two
Pages 4 and 5: © Arthur Edwards/*Sun*/NI Syndication
Page 7 (above): © Brian Rasic/Rex Features
Page 8 (below): © Matt Baron/BEI/Rex Features

Section Four
Pages 2 and 3 (above and middle) © Dean Sherwood
Page 3 (below) © www.TomLeishman.com
Page 4 (main picture and inset) © BBC Photo Library
Page 5 (main picture and inset) © Rex Features
Page 6 (above right) © Alex Lake
Page 7 (above and below) © Alex Lake